Introduction to Compiling Techniques

A First Course using ANSI C, LEX and YACC

Second Edition

T0204431

THE McGRAW HILL
INTERNATIONAL SERIES IN SOFTWARE ENGINEERING

Consulting Editor

Professor D. Ince
The Open University

Titles in this Series

Further titles in this Series are listed at the back of the book

Introduction to Compiling Techniques

A First Course using
ANSI C, LEX and YACC

Second Edition

J. P. Bennett

Senior Software Analyst, GPT Limited, Poole

THE McGRAW-HILL COMPANIES

London · New York · St Louis · San Francisco · Auckland · Bogotá · Caracas
Lisbon · Madrid · Mexico · Milan · Montreal · New Delhi · Panama
Paris · San Juan · São Paulo · Singapore · Sydney · Tokyo · Toronto

Published by
McGRAW-HILL Publishing Company
Shoppenhangers Road
Maidenhead, Berkshire, SL6 2QL, England
Telephone 01628 23432
Fax 01628 770224

British Library Cataloguing in Publication Data
Bennett, J. P. (Jeremy Peter)
  Introduction to compiling techniques: a first course using
  ANSI C, LEX and YACC. – 2nd ed. – (The McGraw-Hill
  international series in software engineering)
  1. Compiling (Electronic computers)
  I. Title
  005.4'53

  ISBN 007709221X

Library of Congress Cataloging-in-Publication Data
Bennett, J. P. (Jeremy Peter)
  Introduction to compiling techniques: a first course using
  ANSI C, LEX and YACC / J. P. Bennett. – 2nd ed.
      p.   cm. – (The McGraw-Hill international series in software
  engineering)
  Includes bibliographical references and index.
  ISBN 0–07–709221–X (pbk. : alk. paper)
  1. Compiling (Electronic computers)   I. Title.   II. Series.
  QA76.76.C65B46   1996
  005.4'53—dc20   96–31278
                                                            CIP

McGraw-Hill

A Division of The McGraw·Hill Companies

1234 BL 9876

Typeset by Paston Press Limited, Loddon, Norfolk
and printed and bound in Great Britain by Biddles Ltd, Guildford

Printed on permanent paper in compliance with ISO Standard 9706

Dedication

for Jenny

Contents

Preface to first edition

There are now several excellent comprehensive texts on compiling on the market. The problem with all these books is that they are very large and detailed. The present work is at a lower level and gives an introduction to compilers and their construction.

This book is aimed at two audiences. The first is the second- or third-year honours undergraduate in computer science taking a first course in compiling techniques. The second is the working programmer, who although not having formal qualifications in computer science needs to use compiler technology in his or her work. To this end a balance is maintained between providing enough theoretical background to enable a clear understanding of the subject and giving a practical presentation that will both illustrate concepts and allow the reader to develop effective compilers.

A certain amount of knowledge is assumed on the part of the reader. Familiarity with C is essential. Throughout we have used ANSI standard C, but this is readily comprehensible to anyone more familiar with K&R C. A general familiarity with machine language is required at the level that would be taught in any introductory computing course.

At its heart compilation is based on a few very elegant algorithms. This book is short enough to allow the reader to see the elegance of the subject without being frustrated by obscure detail. The main parsing, translation, and code generation techniques in use today are presented with many diagrams and examples. Methods that are no longer of importance are either omitted or only presented to the extent that they help the understanding of modern practice.

Examples throughout are presented using the C programming language. The section on compiler generators uses the LEX scanner generator and YACC parser generator, highlighting the modern emphasis on tools. These are widely available under Unix with similar programs being available under other operating systems. This is far and away the commonest teaching and development environment today, making the practical examples directly available to a wide audience. The book culminates with the presentation of a compiler for a simple programming language, VSL. Compilation is for a simple abstract machine, VAM, which has many of the properties of modern microprocessors.

Exercises are suggested at the end of each chapter. Some of these are practical programming problems to help the student understand the workings of practical compilers. Others are essay subjects and questions suitable for exam revision. Finally there are discussion topics, which lead beyond the level of this book into more advanced areas of computation. A brief reading list at the end of each chapter provides initial assistance in further developing the ideas introduced.

I am indebted to my colleagues in the School of Mathematical Sciences at Bath University for their assistance. In particular Dr Dan Richardson provided much perceptive criticism of the manuscript. Undergraduates on his language theory course used the first draft as their textbook in the spring of 1989 and suggested many improvements which I have adopted. Mr Richard Nuttall of Torch Computers made many helpful suggestions on improving the text from the perspective of an industrial programmer. Finally I must express my gratitude to the anonymous reviewer from McGraw-Hill who gave the manuscript a very thorough analysis, making many perceptive suggestions that have greatly improved the text.

J. P. Bennett

Preface to second edition

One of the most rewarding results of the first edition of this book was the response of the wider computing community. Across the Internet over the past five and a half years I have received suggestions of corrections needed or improvements that could be made in the text. Numerous academics and students have sent in improvements to the VC compiler.

In the first edition I described the construction of SLR(1) parse tables in detail. However, only outline descriptions of canonical LR(1) and LALR(1) parser construction were included, since I felt full details were beyond the scope of an introductory text. By popular request, this edition includes a much more detailed description, including constructions of canonical LR(1) and LALR(1) parsers for the same example grammar as that used to demonstrate SLR(1). This will be particularly helpful in understanding the Bison and YACC parser generators which use LALR(1).

The example sequence of basic block optimizations given in Chapter 11 on code optimization proved particularly popular in demonstrating the power of such techniques. Although comprehensive coverage of code optimization is still beyond the scope of an introductory text such as this, I have now added a new chapter giving more detail on the advanced optimization techniques possible using global dataflow analysis. I have tried to use the same approach as that in Chapter 11, showing how each technique in turn can be applied to an example sequence of code. These are the principle alterations to the book. Beyond this there are numerous minor corrections and changes which I hope keep the book up to date.

My thanks go to those, many known only through the Internet, who have contributed suggestions: Alan Barnes, John Beaven, Paul Daly, Andrew Dunford, John Kirk, Mark Knight, Rosemary M. C. Lau, S. Lyon, Ken Macfarlane, Subhasish Mazumdar, D. L. Mountain, Steve Preddy, Atanas Radenski, Imhad Rahman, Dave Redman, Jamie Roots, Tom Rushton, R. C. Shaw and Richard Tearle. Particular mention should go to Ken Schweller, Professor of Computer Science and Psychology at Buena Vista College, Iowa, who supplied the VAX MACRO code generator, and to Jonathan R. Johnson, who as a final year student at Carlton University wrote an optimizing code generator for the VC compiler. I am grateful to both for allowing their work to be made available as part of the distribution.

I have now moved from the academic to the commercial world. My former employer, Bath University, has provided the computing facilities through which the software has been distributed for the past six years. My colleagues new and old have given me great support, particularly Icarus Sparry of Bath University Computing Service, my former student Deborah Hall of the School of Mathematical Sciences at Bath University, and Pete Martin of GPT Limited. In my new location, Southampton University library and its staff were very helpful in providing me with key background papers. Once again McGraw-Hill's reviewers remained anonymous, but made many perceptive comments, which have helped me greatly in preparing this second edition.

Finally I have to thank my wife, Jenny, for putting up with the chaos while this edition was prepared. Without her understanding support, it would never have been done!

Jeremy Bennett
January, 1996

1
What is a compiler?

A compiler is a translator from a program written in one language, the *source language*, to an equivalent program in a second language, the *target* or *object language* (Fig. 1.1). Typically the source language will be a programming language such as FORTRAN, Pascal, or C, and the target language will be machine code for the computer being used, which is hence known as the *target machine*. The compiler will usually supply error and diagnostic information about the source program being compiled.

1.1 The need for machine translation

The earliest machines were very small and simple. For example, the Manchester Mark 1 produced in 1948 had only seven opcodes and 32 words of main memory. For such a computer, entering programs as sequences of binary digits at a keyboard was not that difficult. However, it was convenient when writing down such programs not to use the sequence of binary digits, but a shorthand notation for the opcodes. Table 1.1 shows some of the early mnemonics for opcodes used with this computer.

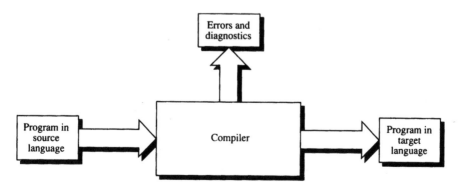

Figure 1.1 Overall structure of a compiler

Table 1.1   Assembler mnemonics for the Manchester Mark 1

Binary opcode	Mnemonic	Meaning
011	a,S	Store the contents of the accumulator at address S
100	a-s,A	Subtract the value at location S from the accumulator
111	Stop	Stop and await operator action

With more complex machines and longer programs, hand translation of mnemonics into binary for entry into the computer became tedious. In the late 1940s it was pointed out that this translation could perfectly well be done by the computer itself. Programs to do this were known as *assemblers*, and the mnemonic codes as *assembly languages*.

Because of their simplicity, being essentially a one-to-one mapping from mnemonic to machine opcode, assembly language programs are very verbose. More complex languages, known as *autocodes*, were developed to describe programs more concisely. Each autocode instruction could represent several machine code operations. Programs to translate these *high-level languages* into machine code were more complex than assemblers and became known as *compilers*.

During the 1950s high-level computer languages evolved to describe problems independently of the machine code of any particular computer. Early languages such as FORTRAN and the autocodes from which it was derived were strongly influenced by the available operations in the underlying machine code. For example, FORTRAN IV had a restriction of 3 on the number of dimensions of an array partly because its original target machine, the IBM 709, had only three registers for indexing arrays. Even C, designed in the mid-1970s, has some constructs (e.g. the increment operator + +) because of the availability of an equivalent opcode on the original target machine, a PDP-11.

Algol 60, which was actually proposed in 1958, heralded a new approach to high-level languages. It was designed with problem solving in mind, and questions of how it might ever be translated to be run on real machines ignored. For example, it allowed local variables and recursive routine calls. How were these to be translated to run on machines with a single address space and just a jump to subroutine opcode? Most modern computer languages since, such as Pascal, Ada and C+ +, have also been designed to be independent of any particular target architecture.

Compiled high-level languages are now well established. Advantages are their conciseness which improves programmer productivity, semantic restrictions (such as type checking) to reduce logical errors, and ease of debugging. Disadvantages are their speed (typically 2–10 times slower than hand-written assembler) and size, both of the compilers and the compiled code.

Compiler theory has developed to enable languages such as these to be translated without difficulty. Many tools have been developed to automate much of the process. While the first FORTRAN compiler took 18 man years of effort to construct, it is now perfectly feasible for an undergraduate to write a simple compiler for Pascal in a term.

1.1.1 APPROACHES TO MACHINE TRANSLATION

There are two ways of running a program written in a high-level language on a computer. The first is to translate the program into an equivalent program in the machine code of the computer. This is the process of compilation described in the previous section.

The second approach is to write a program that can interpret the statements of the high-level language program as they are encountered and carry out their actions. Such programs are called *interpreters*.

Compilation has the advantage that we have to analyse and translate our high-level language program only once, although this may be a time-consuming process. Thereafter we just run the equivalent machine code program produced by the compiler. A disadvantage is that if our program goes wrong we will get an error in the machine code program and must try and work back from this to find the corresponding error in the high-level language program.

Interpretation is much slower than compilation, since we must analyse each high-level language statement to determine its meaning each time we encounter it. However, if there is an error we are still dealing with the original high-level language program and can immediately pinpoint its source. This is often a great help when developing and debugging programs.

These two approaches are the extremes, and many machine translators are a bit of both. A common approach is to compile the high-level language not into the machine code of the target machine, but into a lower-level *intermediate code* which is then interpreted. This intermediate code is chosen to be easy to compile into and efficient to execute, so we end up with a system where compilation is not too time consuming, programs run reasonably fast, and if there is an error we see it in an intermediate code that is easier to relate to the source language than machine code. Compiler/interpreters like this have been written for many languages. A good example is the UCSD Pascal compiler, which generates an intermediate code, PCODE, for interpretation.

The choice of whether to compile or interpret is to a large extent influenced by the nature of the high-level language and the environment in which it is used. FORTRAN is relatively simple, designed for translation to machine code, and often used for solving big numerical problems on mainframe computers, where speed of execution is essential. It is thus invariably compiled. BASIC, on the other hand, is mainly used on personal microcomputers where clear error handling is important, and where lack of processing power and memory could make compilation very difficult. It is invariably interpreted, although modern interpreters often do an element of compilation, analysing keywords as the program is typed in. LISP is a language that often uses both interpretation and compilation. Programs are interpreted during program development to avoid time-consuming compilations each time the program is changed and to give clear error handling, and then compiled when development is complete.

Although this book is essentially concerned with the techniques involved in compilation, much of the information is of use in writing interpreters. Analysis of the source code is much the same in both cases and finding the most efficient way of interpreting a particular construct is not dissimilar to finding the best code for a compiler to generate.

1.1.2 THE WIDER USE OF COMPILERS

By far the commonest and best known use of compilation techniques is in the translation of high-level programming languages into machine code for execution on a target machine. However, these techniques have relevance throughout software engineering. Application software often makes use of a command language interface, for which compilation techniques are essential. The same techniques are required for analysing the complex configuration files required by many modern systems. Good examples are the .ini files of Microsoft Windows and resource files in X. As another example international standards for data communications are now specified using the Abstract Syntax Notation, ASN.1, a complex high-level language. Advanced compilation technology is required to create reliable and high performance communications software directly from the formal protocol specification. In other areas, source languages may be word-processing languages such as TeX, natural languages such as English or special languages to describe the layout of silicon integrated circuits. Target languages may be driver codes for laser printers such as PostScript, other natural languages or integrated circuit masks. In all these, the comprehension of computer languages and translation into other languages is important. An understanding of compiler techniques is thus a requirement, not just of the specialist, but of any software engineer.

This book concentrates on compilation from conventional procedural languages, such as Pascal or C, into conventional machine codes as typically found on a modern microprocessor. Ideas are illustrated throughout by examples using VSL, a very simple block-structured procedural language and its compilation for VAM, a byte stream machine with a reduced instruction set.

1.2   The structure of a compiler

The translation of a programming language naturally breaks down into a number of logical phases. These phases may run simultaneously, or they may run consecutively. At its simplest level we may break down a compiler into a *front end*, responsible for the analysis of the structure and meaning of the source text; and a *back end*, responsible for generating the target language.

Each of these may be further subdivided into logical blocks. The front end can be divided into *lexical analyser*, *syntax analyser*, and *semantic analyser*. The lexical analyser, sometimes also called the *scanner*, carries out the simplest level of structural analysis. It will group the individual symbols of the source program text into their logical entities. Thus the sequence of characters 'W',

'H', 'I', 'L', and 'E' would be identified as the word 'WHILE' and the sequence of characters '1', '.', and '0' would be identified as the floating point number, 1.0.

The syntax analyser, often also called the *parser*, analyses the overall structure of the whole program, grouping the simple entities identified by the scanner into the larger constructs, such as statements, loops, and routines, that make up a complete program. Just as the structure of English prose is determined by the rules of English grammar, so we have *formal grammars* to describe the structure of computer programs.

Once the structure of the program has been determined we can then analyse its meaning (or *semantics*). We can determine which variables are to hold integers, and which to hold floating point numbers, we can check that the size of all arrays is defined and so on.

At this stage we are part way through translating the source language into the target language. We have finished processing a lot of the information in the original program, and it makes sense to represent the program in a simpler way, without this information, making for simpler processing in subsequent stages. There are many such *intermediate representations*. Each has advantages and disadvantages, which are discussed in detail in Chapter 4. The back end of the compiler takes this intermediate representation and with the information provided on the structure and meaning of the source program, generates an equivalent program in the target language. Often this involves more than one phase, to ensure an efficient translation of the high-level language program.

First of all an *intermediate code optimizer* may transform the intermediate representation into a more efficient equivalent. After this comes the *code generator*, generating an equivalent program for the target machine. Finally there may be a *target code optimizer* to improve further the generated code.

Good optimizers can be very time consuming. It is not at all uncommon for the optimizer not to be used during program development and only to be brought in for the last compilation of the complete program.

This is not quite all that is involved in a compiler. It is usual to have to provide a *run-time system* to support the compiled language. Some high-level language constructs, such as input and output and interrupt handling, are inherently complex. Compiled code would be immensely large if such constructs were translated into target code each time they were encountered and so instead we provide them as subroutines and compile calls to the subroutines when necessary. These subroutines form the *run-time library*. In addition the run-time system will include some start-up code to initialize the machine before the compiled program is run, and some termination code to put the system back in a standard state at the end of a run.

The operation of a compiler with such a structure is shown in Fig. 1.2.

As we shall see in Chapter 4, there are a number of different intermediate representations. Some are better suited to intermediate code optimization, others are particularly good for code generation. Some compilers gain advantage by using both. The front end generates one intermediate representation, particularly suited to intermediate code optimization. At the end of

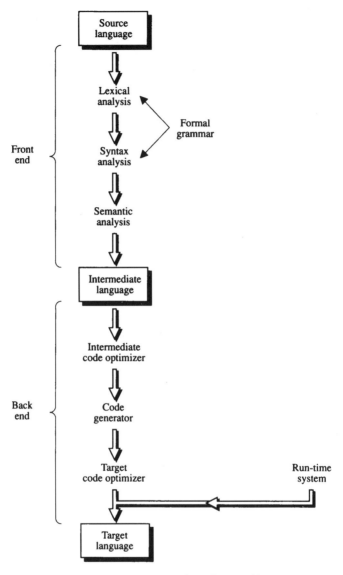

Figure 1.2 Operation of a compiler

the intermediate code optimization phase a second intermediate representation is generated, particularly suited to code generation and target code optimization.

The stages of the compiler where the intermediate representations are generated and transformed is often known as a *middle end*. A good example is the Norcroft C Compiler.

1.2.1 LANGUAGES FOR WRITING COMPILERS

Compilers are relatively large programs involving a lot of programming effort and we wish them to be as portable as possible. The front end can remain the same for a wide range of target machines. The back end differs for each target machine, but even here there is scope for reuse of code.

Which language should we choose for maximum portability? Machine code has the advantage that it is always available. This was invariably the approach used with early compilers, a typical example being the FORTRAN compiler for the IBM 709. However, it is the least portable, since our compiler will only run on one machine. Furthermore, writing a program as large as a compiler in machine code is extremely demanding.

An alternative is to implement in an existing high-level language that is already widely available. We then have the programming power of a high-level language and our compiler can be ported to any machine that supports the implementation language. This does not give us the widest portability, since we are restricted to those machines supporting the implementation language. It does not help matters that the two most widely available computer languages, FORTRAN and COBOL, are far from ideal for compiler writing. Despite these drawbacks this approach has been widely used, particularly for compilers under the Unix operating system. Under Unix the C programming language is always available and often used for implementing compilers. The approach is also common with specialist research languages, usually because the compiler writer needs the flexibility of a high-level language, rather than for reasons of portability. A typical example of this is the compiler for the Ponder higher-order functional programming language, which is written in Algol 68.

A compromise approach is to write our compiler in a 'generalized' assembly language. To port the compiler to a new machine we have to write an assembler for this language to generate our target machine code. Greater portability is achieved if the target language of our compiler is the same generalized assembly language, since we can use the assembler to translate this into the target language. Using this approach we have simplified the problem of porting a compiler to one of porting an assembler. An example of this approach is the Macro-SPITBOL compiler for the SNOBOL4 string-processing language, which is implemented in the generalized assembly language, MINIMAL. The target language for this compiler is in fact an intermediate code for interpretation, the interpreter for which is also written in MINIMAL, aiding portability.

There is one other approach to compiler writing, which gives the greatest flexibility of all, and that is to write the compiler in its own source language. For example the standard BCPL compiler is written in BCPL, and C compilers under Unix are written in C. Portability is achieved by the technique of *cross-compilation*. Let us consider porting a compiler for BCPL, written in BCPL, from an existing machine, A, to a new machine, B. We take our existing compiler, running on machine A and modify its back end to generate machine code for machine B. We then compile this on machine A using the existing compiler. This gives us a compiler for BCPL that runs on machine A and generates code for machine B. We then run this compiler on machine A, using it to compile our modified compiler for machine B. We now have a compiled version of the modified compiler in the machine code of machine B. We can then copy this across to machine B, giving us a BCPL compiler on machine B, generating code for machine B. From now on we can work on machine B alone, since we have a working BCPL compiler. This sequence of operations is shown in Fig. 1.3. We still have the problem of writing the first ever BCPL compiler, which must be done using one of the techniques described earlier. However, once we have this initial compiler running on one machine, then cross-compilation gives us a very powerful way of writing a portable compiler.

T-diagrams

When considering how compilers are implemented it is often helpful to show the programs required using *T-diagrams*. For each program in the system we draw a T, with the name of the program across the top. The left and right arms of the T show the source and target language of the program, respectively, and the bottom leg of the T shows the language in which the program itself is

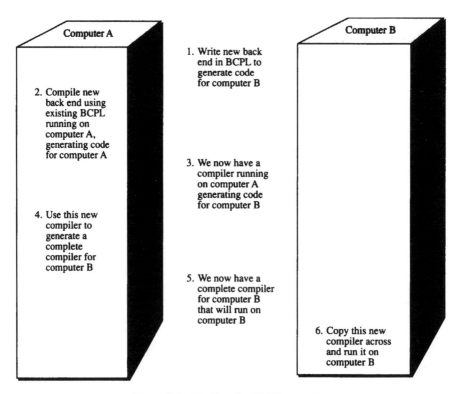

Figure 1.3 Porting the BCPL compiler

implemented. If the implementation language itself must be translated we can slot together a number of T-diagrams, showing the translations that must be carried out for the system to work. Figure 1.4 shows T-diagrams for the examples described in the previous section.

1.2.2 THE IMPORTANCE OF VARIOUS PARTS OF A COMPILER

Different languages make different demands on the compiler writer. Conventional block structured languages, such as Algol, Pascal, or C, have relatively complex formal grammars. The syntax analysers for such languages are a major part of the compiler. Once the structure is understood, then simple code generation is relatively straightforward, because modern computer architectures are orientated towards such languages. The large numbers of cases that have to be considered mean such code generators are not small, but they are not too difficult to write and execute quickly. Should a code optimizer be added then this will increase the size, and reduce the performance of the whole back end. In addition, such languages need a run-time system, but again this need not be too large. In general with this type of language we see a fairly even balance between front end and back end of the compiler.

Other types of language place different emphasis on the parts of the compiler. Functional languages and their relatives, such as LISP or ML, often have simple grammars, which can be handled by a very small front end. However, the programming concepts embodied may be difficult to generate code for and require a lot of run-time support. Complex optimizers may be essential to get any performance out of the language at all. In these languages we see a strong emphasis on the back end of the compiler.

Most compilers will lie somewhere in between. When designing a compiler, it is important to consider where most of the effort will have to be put.

1.3 A demonstration compiler

Throughout this book we will look at writing a compiler for an elementary programming language. This is VSL, the *V*ery *S*imple *L*anguage. VSL is a simple block-structured procedural language, with assignment statements, while loops, if-then-else branches and simple expressions.

The target language for the VSL compiler, is VAM, the *V*SL *A*bstract *M*achine. VAM is a byte stream code for a machine with simple arithmetic and a large number of registers. It has relatively few instructions, and draws on many of the ideas embodied in modern Reduced Instruction Set Computers. VAM is discussed in Chapter 2.

1.3.1 VSL—A SOURCE LANGUAGE FOR COMPILATION

VSL programs consist of one or more functions for execution. The first of these will be called from the system at the start of the program run. Functions may contain declarations of variables, simple loops and conditional statements, assignment to variables, and PRINT statements to output results. A VSL

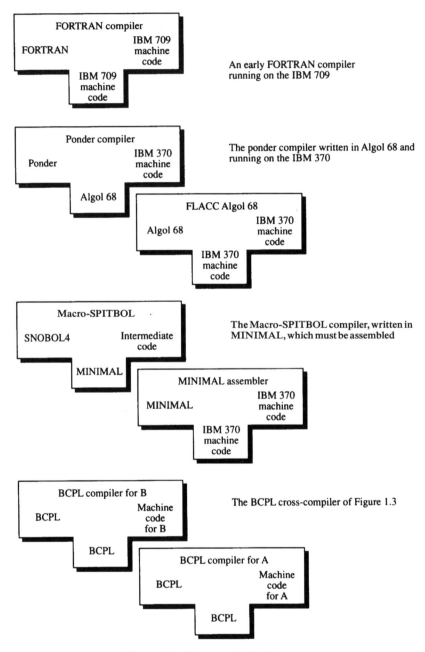

Figure 1.4   Some typical T-diagrams

program with just one function to print out the message 'Hello World' would be as follows.

```
FUNC hello()
    PRINT   "Hello World\n"
```

VSL uses unsigned integer arithmetic. Expressions can involve variables, integer constants, function calls, addition, subtraction, multiplication, division, and negation. Variables must be declared at the top of the block in which they are used.

Blocks contain a sequence of variable declarations (optional) and statements and are surrounded by section brackets ({ and }). Output of results is by the PRINT statement, which takes a list of text strings and expressions to output. The following is a simple program to print out the result of squaring 12.

```
FUNC main()
{
    VAR a, b

    a := 12
    b := a * a

    PRINT a, " squared is ", b, "\n"
}
```

Loops are provided by means of the WHILE statement and conditional statements by use of the IF statement. Each is conditional on an expression, with zero meaning false and non-zero meaning true. Functions are declared globally and may be called recursively. The following program tabulates factorials from 1 to 10.

```
FUNC main()
{
    VAR i

    i := 0

    WHILE 11 - i
    DO
    {
        PRINT "f( ", i," ) = ", f( i ), "\n"
        i := i + 1
    }
    DONE
}


FUNC f( n )
    IF n
    THEN
        RETURN n * f( n - 1 )
    ELSE
        RETURN 1
    FI
```

The complete formal specification of VSL is given in Appendix A.

Exercises

At the end of each chapter we give a number of problems for the user to solve. Some of these are practical problems involving the material of the chapter, often using the VSL compiler as an example. Others are essay titles, suitable for exam revision, or as a basis for further study. Finally one or two discussion topics are suggested, which could form the basis for small group seminars and which considerably extend the material covered in the chapter.

PRACTICAL PROBLEMS

1.1. Consider some compilers to which you have access. What approaches do they use. Illustrate their structure with T-diagrams.
1.2. The computer algebra language, REDUCE, is implemented as an interpreter in RLISP. RLISP in turn is compiled by a compiler written in Cambridge LISP. Cambridge LISP has an interpreter written in BCPL. The BCPL compiler is itself written in BCPL. Both compilers have IBM 370 machine code as their target language. Draw the T-diagrams to illustrate REDUCE running on an IBM 370.

ESSAY TITLES

1.1. Why compile?
1.2. Trace with examples the development of machine translation, from the earliest assemblers to modern compilers.
1.3. Compare and contrast compilation and interpretation of high-level languages.
1.4. Outline the structure of a compiler, explaining the functions of each part.

DISCUSSION TOPICS

1.1 Compare the speed of execution of compiled programs in various languages to which you have access. Identify the reasons for the variations you observe.
1.2 Investigate some compilers of the 1950s.

Further reading

At the end of each chapter sources of further information on the topics covered are suggested. These are useful both to help the reader clarify areas with which he or she may have had difficulty and as a source of new information when considering the discussion topics at the end of the chapter. These bibliographies are kept as short as possible in order not to swamp the reader with information.

This book is very definitely an introductory text. For further reading on any aspect *Compilers: Principles, Techniques and Tools* by Alfred V. Aho, Ravi Sethi, and Jeffrey D. Ullman and published by Addison-Wesley (1986) is to be recommended. This 800-page book covers every aspect of compiling and itself features a comprehensive bibliography. It has the advantage of being geared towards users of C, LEX, and YACC, but its size means that it is very much for dipping into and not for reading from cover to cover.

More details of early computers (and more recent ones) can be found in *Computer Structures: Principles and Examples* by Daniel P. Siewiorek, C. Gordon Bell, and Allen Newell, published by McGraw-Hill (1982). This is a collection of key papers by a wide range of authors describing the evolution of computer architecture. It includes details of the design of the Manchester Mark 1. Details of some early compilers can be found in *Programming Languages and Systems* by S. Rosen, published by McGraw-Hill (1967). This is a collection of early papers on compilers.

More specific examples include a discussion of the use of MINIMAL in 'Macro SPITBOL—A SNOBOL4 Compiler' by R. B. K. Dewar and A. P. McCann, *Software—Practice and Experience*, **7**, 95–113 (1977). A description of the BCPL compiler complete with a listing of the lexical and syntax analysers is given in *BCPL—The Language and its Compiler* by Martin Richards and Colin Whitby-Strevens, published by Cambridge University Press (1980).

2
Target languages

To translate one computer language into another we need a clear understanding of source and target languages. In this chapter we look at the features of typical target languages, and the problems involved in translating into such languages.

All programming languages provide fundamentally three types of operation: *data access, data manipulation,* and *flow of control.*

Data access in high-level languages may involve access to variables and constants of different types—integer, real, arrays, and so on. The variables may be stored in different areas in memory—static area, heap, or stack, for example. We have both to retrieve data from and to store it to these areas.

Data manipulation is by operators on the various data types. These include the standard arithmetic operators as well as more specialist operators such as string concatenation. We may have to provide conversion between the different data types. More complex data manipulation is provided by functions. Some operators, such as those to give the address of a variable, have both data access and data manipulation behaviour.

Flow of control operations vary from language to language. They may include GOTO statements, conditional statements such as IF-THEN-ELSE and SWITCH, and looping constructs such as FOR and WHILE. Overall flow of control is provided by procedures. Functions are procedures that have both data manipulation and flow of control behaviour.

If we are to understand a language effectively we need to understand how these operations interact and how they may be implemented in the target language.

2.1 Types of target machine

There are currently two principle and conflicting approaches to the design of computers. The established approach through the 1960s and 1970s was to provide processors with ever greater numbers of ever more powerful instructions. Even an 8-bit microprocessor such as the Z80, launched in 1975 had in excess of 700 instructions. The VAX-11 computer launched at the end of that decade even had two different instructions for evaluating polynomials.

Writing compilers for such computers proved more and more difficult. The code generator had to select from a bewildering array of possible instructions. Furthermore, very complex instructions did not always match exactly the semantics of data access, data manipulation, and flow of control specified by a particular high-level language. The only solution to this was to make the instructions very general in their action, and thus slow and inefficient in any specific use. Such computers are known as *Complex Instruction Set Computers* or *CISCs*.

In the early 1980s a new approach was developed in response to the problems in writing compilers for CISCs. Instead of providing large numbers of complex instructions in the processor, only a small number of very simple instructions were provided. To translate any source language construct in a compiler required several very simple instructions instead of perhaps just one or two instructions for a CISC. However, because of the small number of instructions the compiler could select precisely those needed for the job, with no redundancy. Because the processor was so simple it could be made to go very fast, and more than offset the effect of using more instructions in compiled code.

Such computers are known as *Reduced Instruction Set Computers or RISCs*. They are characterized by large numbers of registers and a small number of instructions, mainly working register to register. RISCs do pose a problem for the compiler writer. Their advantage relies on very effective optimization techniques to ensure just the right set of instructions are generated.

2.1.1 INSTRUCTION SETS

The instruction set is the interface to the computer. An instruction must specify the operation to be carried out, where the operands are to be found, and where the results are to be put. We must consider both the semantics of an instruction set and how the instructions are actually represented in store.

Instruction set semantics

We can make the operations of an instruction set arbitrarily complex. However, it is reasonable to consider that all complex instructions can be broken down to a series of simple instructions consisting of a binary operator taking two operands and yielding a result.

$$\text{result} := \text{operand}_1 \ \text{operator} \ \text{operand}_2$$

We refer to such instructions as *three-address instructions,* in that we must specify the addess of each operand and the address of the result separately. Clearly for some operations (unary arithmetic operators, for example) we may not need to specify all the addresses. This is quite common with RISC instruction sets where operands are all registers. The arrangement is not always ideal for computer instruction sets if there are a large number of possible sources for the operands and result (such as registers, memory addressed in various ways, constant data, and so on). The large number of bits needed to specify each address make for very large instructions. To avoid this, various compromises in specifying one or more of the addresses are possible.

Two-address instruction sets   In these instruction sets the address of the result is the same as that of one operand. This is a very common compromise between flexibility and instruction size and is used by VAM, the example instruction set used in this book.

One-address instruction sets   Here the address of the result and one operand are the same and fixed. Invariably this address is a register in the processor, usually known as the *accumulator*. Such an arrangement is common in very small processors, particularly small 8-bit microprocessors.

Zero-address instruction sets   In this arrangement no addresses are specified. All operands are popped from a stack in main memory and results pushed back. Such an arrangement has been used in a number of novel architectures and can lead to very compact code, but tends to lose in efficiency because of the absence of registers.

Instruction representations

There are two main approaches to instruction set representation.

Ad hoc instruction sets   In an *ad hoc* instruction set we break the instruction, which is typically an integral number of machine words long, into different fields to specify the operation to be carried out and where to find the operands and put the result. The precise number of bits in each field varies, depending on how many bits are needed to specify operands and so on. As a consequence we must add another field to specify the format of the instruction. Such instruction sets are commonly used for RISCs. They have the advantage of being compact, but can be quite complex (although fast) to decode.

Byte stream instruction sets   In this approach the instruction set is viewed as a stream of bytes coming into the computer. The first byte is the 'opcode byte' and specifies the operation to be carried out. It also specifies the format of the operands and result. Each operation can only have one format for its operands and result. The operands and result are specified in the following bytes. For example, a byte stream might have opcode byte = 134 meaning ADD REGISTERS, with the two operand registers specified as two halves of the following byte, and the second operand register also to be used for the result.

   Byte stream instruction sets are more common amongst CISC designs. They are easy to decode, but not always particularly compact or fast to decode.

2.1.2 VAM—A TARGET LANGUAGE FOR COMPILATION

VAM is the example instruction set used for our VSL compiler. It has many of the characteristics of modern RISC designs, but is a two-address byte stream instruction set.

The overall structure of the VSL Abstract Machine is as follows. It has a 32-bit processor, with 16 general-purpose 32-bit registers, a program counter, a single-bit status flag and up to 4 Gbytes of byte-addressed memory. There is a port, handled via a trap opcode, which can output a single ASCII character. VAM has a byte stream instruction set with 15 two-address opcodes. All arithmetic is unsigned and register to register, with opcodes to load and store registers using indexed indirect addressing and an opcode to load memory addresses. Register 0 is permanently zero. These opcodes all set the status flag if a result of zero was computed and unset it otherwise. These are two conditional branch instructions, to branch on whether this flag is set. The TRAP opcode outputs the low byte of R15 as an ASCII character. Finally there is a branch-and-link instruction, providing a mechanism for function call. The VAM instruction set is summarized in Section 2 of Appendix A.

The complete formal specification of VAM is given in Appendix A. A simulator for VAM, written in C, is available in machine-readable form from the publishers.

2.2 Implementation methods

Once we have decided on the precise meaning of different language constructs, we must then consider their implementation on the target machine. To some extent this is target machine dependent. For many cases there is a simple one-to-one correspondence between source and target language construct. Obvious candidates in this category are arithmetic operators. For example, addition in the source language will clearly be quite simply translated using the addition opcode of the target machine.

However, there are one or two areas that regularly cause problems in language translation. These are:

- *Data structure representation*   How are different data types represented on a target machine.
- *Implementation of different storage classes*   How do we represent variables in different storage classes—global, local, static, and so on.
- *Implementation of high-level flow of control operations*   A number of constructs, such as for loops or switch statements require attention if they are to be implemented efficiently.
- *Implementation of routine calls*   This causes by far the most trouble, not least because it also involves handling local data.

Variables of different data types are represented as locations in the computer's main memory. In most modern computers this is a simple linear address space, with addressing either at the level of a byte (invariably 8 bits) or a word (16 or 32 bits being common). On some machines program and data must be kept in separate address spaces, on others the two may be mixed in a single address space.

2.2.1 DATA STRUCTURE REPRESENTATION

Variables of simple types are represented by sufficient memory locations to hold them. Characters typically require 1 byte each, integers 2 or 4 bytes and floating-point numbers anything from 4 to 16 bytes. Booleans can in principle be represented in a single bit, although with the lack of efficient bit addressing on most machines they typically occupy a byte or word. For data types such as characters which occupy less than a word, we have to make special provision on word-addressed machines to obtain the required byte or bytes from within the word.

One-dimensional arrays

These are easily represented as a number of consecutive locations in memory, usually referred to as a *vector*. Enough space must be allowed for each element of the array of its basic type. For example, if integers require 4 bytes, then an array of 100 integers will require a vector of 400 bytes. The address of any particular element is then obtained as an offset from the address of the first element, the *base address*. If we index our integer array from zero, and its base address is A, then the byte address of the ith element is given by:

$$A + 4 \times i$$

Note the multiplication by 4 in the index, the size of each integer element of the array. On most machines multiplication is a relatively slow operation. Where one multiplicand is a constant power of 2, multiplication can be efficiently carried out using shift operations. In this example the multiplication by 4 could be replaced by a left shift 2 places.

Multidimensional arrays

These can be represented in one of two ways. The first is as a vector of locations in memory. In the case of a two-dimensional array this would mean storing rows of the vector one after the other in memory. The address of a particular element is then worked out by multiplying the row index by the number of elements in a row and adding the column index and using this as the offset from the base address. For example, if we had a two-dimensional integer array of m rows and n columns and base address A, then the byte address of the i,jth element would be:

$$A + 4 \times (n \times i + j)$$

Once again note the multiplication by 4 in the index, the size of each integer element of the array which can be implemented as a shift. However, the multiplication of n by i will in general not be possible as a shift.

The alternative way of representing a multidimensional array is as a vector of vectors. In the two-dimensional case we have a vector, with one element for each row, large enough to hold a memory address. Each element of this vector then holds the address of a vector for the corresponding row. Consider finding the i,jth element of a two-dimensional integer array with base address A on a machine where addresses take up 4 bytes. First we would find the address, B, of the ith row:

$$B = A + 4 \times i$$

The jth element in this vector is at byte address:

$$B + 4 \times j$$

This representation is faster, since no multiplication by n is necessary, although there is extra memory required for the row vector.

Both representations may be easily extended to arrays of greater than two dimensions. Figure 2.1 illustrates these methods of representing arrays.

Records

These are structs in C parlance and are similar to one-dimensional arrays, but in this case different amounts of space may be needed for the various fields of the record. Take, for example, the C struct defined by:

```
struct
{
        int     index ;
        char    type ;
        double  length ;
} ;
```

On a byte-addressed machine where integers take 4 bytes, characters 1 byte and double-precision floating-point numbers 8 bytes, this would require a total of 13 bytes. The three fields, `index`, `type`, and `length` would be at offsets 0, 4, and 5 bytes from the base address of the vector. Figure 2.2 illustrates this example.

It is perfectly reasonable to combine different representations—e.g. to have array of records, or records containing arrays.

2.2.2 IMPLEMENTATION OF DIFFERENT STORAGE CLASSES

Programming languages allow us to define variables in different storage classes. These reflect different areas of the program in which the variables may be referenced (their *scope*) and different periods of time for which the variables remain in existence (their *extent*). Some of the commoner classes are:

- *Global* Typically these exist throughout the program and can be referenced anywhere.

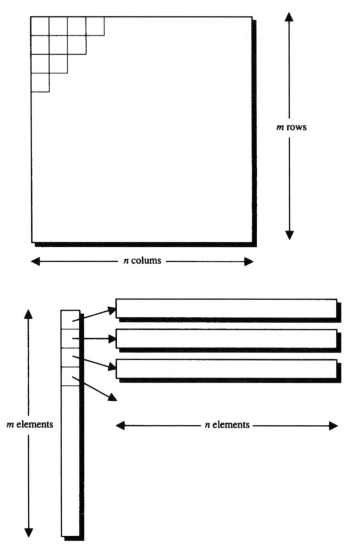

Figure 2.1 Array representations

- *Static* These also exist throughout the program, but can only be referenced in the routine in which they are declared and possibly any other routines declared within that routine.
- *Local* These are known by C programmers as *automatic* variables. They exist only for the duration of a call to the routine in which they are declared. A new variable is created each time the routine is entered (and destroyed on exit) which means there may be multiple instances of a variable in existence if

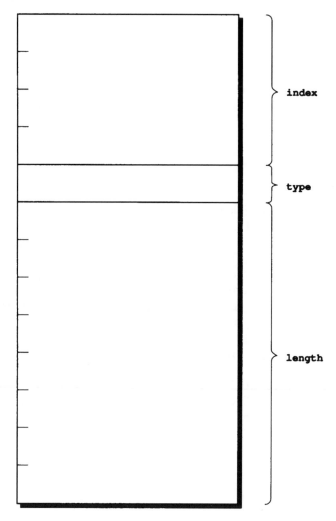

Figure 2.2 Offsets in a record structure

a routine is recursive. They may only be referenced in the routine in which they are declared and in some languages in other routines declared within that routine.

- *Dynamic* Many languages allow the programmer to request additional memory at any time. In C this is by use of the `malloc()` function. Such memory is usually represented by an address held in a variable of one of the classes above. Its extent is the rest of the lifetime of the program, unless explicitly returned to the system, and its scope the scope of any variable used to hold its address.

Global and static variables

These essentially vary only in scope, a difference to be resolved by the syntax and semantic analysers. They have a single instance which persists throughout the life of a program. They can be represented as a fixed number of memory locations either at the start of the data segment (for machines with separate program and data spaces) or at the start or end of the program code. If it is more convenient they may even be interspersed with the code of the program.

Local variables

These come into existence on entry to a routine and last until its exit. If the routine is recursive, multiple instances will exist at some times. To handle this we make use of a *stack*. The stack is a vector in memory, which is used to hold the values of all local variables. Space is used from the base address upwards, the next free location being known as the *top of stack*. The area of memory used to hold all the local variables of a routine is known as a *stack frame*. The local variables of the routine currently executing are held in the *current stack frame*, which is the stack frame nearest to the top of stack. The base address of the current stack frame is usually held in a machine register and is known as the *stack pointer* or *frame pointer*.

On entry to a routine we set up a new stack frame on the top of stack, setting the stack pointer to point to the top of stack. The first few locations on the stack frame are used for control information, typically two to four machine words. Thereafter, space is used first for any arguments to the routine, then for all local arguments in turn. The top of stack becomes the next location after the end of the stack frame. Figure 2.3 shows the stack frame that would be set up on entry to the following C routine:

```
void  f( int       i,
         double    v )
{
         char   a, b, c ;

         /* Rest of routine */

}
```

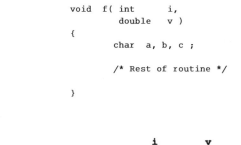

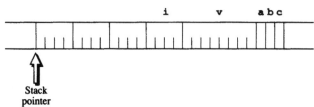

Figure 2.3   Stack frame on entry to a C procedure

Note how we allocate different amounts of space for the different datatypes. We can now find the address of i as offset 12 bytes from the stack pointer, v as offset 16, a offset 24, b offset 25, and c offset 26. We have shown 12 bytes of control information in this example. On exit from the routine we need to reset the stack pointer to its previous value. We use one word of control information (say 4 bytes) to hold a pointer back to the previous stack frame. This value is known as the *dynamic pointer* or *dynamic link* because it changes dynamically with the program as routines are called and return. The series of dynamic pointers connecting all the stack frames are known as the *dynamic chain*. If we have a language in which routine declarations can be nested such as Pascal (but not C), then a routine may also be able to refer to local variables of the routines within which it is declared. These are held on a stack frame somewhere further up the stack. If we are to have such access, then in addition to our dynamic pointer pointing to the stack frame of the routine which is called the current routine, we need a pointer to the stack frame of the routine in which the current routine was declared. This is known as the *static pointer* or *static link* and these pointers together form the *static chain*.

The other piece of control information that is needed is the point in the code to return to at the end of execution of the current routine. This is conveniently held on the stack, and is known as the *return address*.

On calling a routine we see that various operations are required as follows:

- Set up a new stack frame at top of stack.
- Copy arguments across to new stack frame.
- Save existing stack pointer in dynamic link of new frame.
- Set up static link in new frame if needed.
- Save return address in new frame.
- Set stack pointer to base of new stack frame.
- Jump to code for routine.

On return we must do the reverse:

- Retrieve return address from stack frame.
- Restore stack pointer from dynamic link.
- Save result of routine in restored stack frame.
- Jump to return address.

Note the need to retrieve the return address before we restore the stack pointer.

An example helps to clarify this. We consider a hypothetical programming language in which nested routine definitions are permitted. We consider a routine *A* in which is declared a recursive routine *B*, called from *A* as shown at the top of page 24.

Figure 2.4 shows the state of the stack at the point when *A* has called *B*, which has recursed once.

```
routine  A()
{
        int    i, j ;
        char   c ;

        routine  B( float   x )
        {
                float  y ;

                /* code of B */

                B( y ) ;

                /* more code of B */
        }

        /* code of A */

        B( 42.0 ) ;

        /* more code of A */
}
```

Dynamic data

Many languages permit the allocation of further storage during the run of a program. In the case of C this is by use of the `malloc()` function. This storage is obtained from memory not already used to hold the program code and global, static, or local variables. Such memory is known as the *heap*. There is a slight problem here, for although we know the amount of memory occupied by program code and global and static variables, we do not know how much stack space is needed for local variables. One solution is to allocate a fixed amount of space for the stack. However, we then have to deal with the problem of stack overflow if the stack grows too large for the space we allocated. If we allocate a large amount of space so that stack overflow is rare, then for the majority of

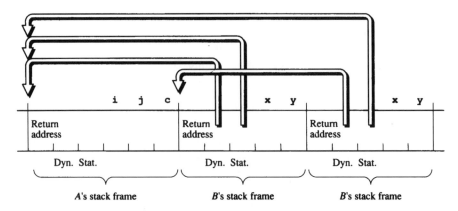

Figure 2.4   Stack frame with static chains

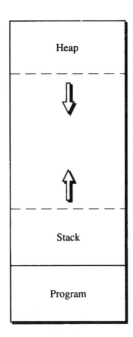

Figure 2.5 Opposing heap and stack directions

programs with small stacks we are wasting memory that could have been used for the heap. The alternative approach is to put the fixed sized parts of the system (program code and global and static variables) at one end of the memory and put stack and heap at opposite ends of the remaining memory space, growing towards each other. We then only run out of space when the top of stack and the front of the heap meet. We avoid the problem of running out of heap while there is plenty of stack space or running out of stack space while there is plenty of heap. This arrangement is illustrated in Fig. 2.5.

Dynamically allocated memory presents an additional problem. Typically such memory is represented by a memory address held in a global, static, or local variable. It is possible for that memory address then to be replaced by something else and the memory address to be lost for ever. For example, the C code:

```
a = malloc( 6 ) ;   /* Allocate 6 bytes of memory */
a = b ;             /* The 6 bytes allocated are lost */
```

Such memory is known as *garbage* and it would be useful to be able to reuse it. This becomes particularly important if by constant use of dynamic data we run out of heap space. Reclamation of unreferenced areas of memory could free up heap space for reuse.

There are three main solutions to this problem.

- *Explicit freeing*   It is left to the programmer explicitly to declare memory as
  no longer needed. This is the approach used in C with the `free()` function
  call. This has the advantage that it is easy to implement. However, it is far
  from flexible and relies on the programmer not making mistakes.
- *Reference counts*   When we allocate a piece of memory from the heap we
  allocate a small extra piece of memory to hold a count of how many people
  are referencing this piece of memory. For example, if we were asked for 6
  bytes we might allocate 10, using the first 4 bytes for the count and returning
  the address of the 5th byte to be used (Fig. 2.6a). Note that we can obtain the
  count as negative offsets from the address of the piece of memory returned.
  Initially the count will be 1. Every time this address is assigned to a new
  variable we increment the count (Fig. 2.6b). Every time we reassign a variable
  holding the address we decrement the count (Fig. 2.6c). When the count
  reaches zero we know that the piece of memory is no longer referenced by
  anyone and we can reuse it.

  The advantage of this system is that memory is available for reuse as soon
  as it becomes free. The disadvantages are the overheads in both memory (we
  always allocate 4 bytes more than we need) and time (in updating the
  reference counts). It is most useful in systems where we typically allocate
  very large amounts of memory and assign them to variables relatively rarely.
- *Garbage collection*   The alternative approach is to do nothing until the heap
  runs out and then look at the heap to recover unreferenced portions of
  memory. A number of strategies have evolved to do this but their detailed
  description is beyond the scope of this book.

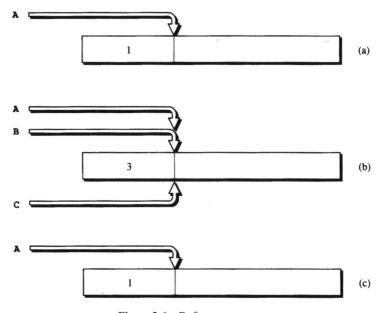

Figure 2.6   Reference counts

This approach combines flexibility with time and space efficiency. The main disadvantage is the need to stop periodically to carry out garbage collection. This may not matter within the context of batch processing, but in process control it can be a problem. It is no use if your automatic welding robot stops still for 20 seconds every so often while its control program garbage collects. *Concurrent* or *on-the-fly* garbage collectors have been devised to overcome this problem, but they invariably are not very time efficient.

In practice dynamic storage recovery is a problem in relatively few languages, LISP being the most notable. The majority of conventional block-structured languages such as C do not bother to implement such a system.

Exercises

PRACTICAL PROBLEMS

2.1. Write some VAM code, and show how the bytes might appear in memory.
2.2. Suggest VAM code sequences for function call and return in VSL.
2.3. Design code sequences for function call and return if VSL permitted nested function definitions and needed a static chain.

ESSAY TITLES

2.1. What are the two principle types of target computer available today? What are their key differences from the compiler writer's point of view?
2.2. How is access to arrays and records impemented in a compiler?
2.3. What are the problems with implementing dynamic memory allocation in a compiled language?

DISCUSSION TOPICS

2.1. Investigate some methods of garbage collecting.
2.2. Investigate coroutines, and their relation to conventional routines. How might they be implemented?

Further reading

Numerous authors have considered the question of instruction sets and a discussion will be found in any good computer architecture text. A good review of the debate over RISC and CISC may be found in 'Instruction Sets and Beyond: Computers, Complexity and Controversy' by Robert P. Colwell *et al., IEEE Computer,* **18**, 8–19 (1985). A more detailed analysis of computer instruction set evolution from the perspective used in this chapter may be found in 'A Survey of Computer Architecture' by J. P. Bennett, Bath University Computer Science Technical Report 88-08 (1988), published and available from The School of Mathematical Sciences, University of Bath, UK.

Many books on algorithms discuss garbage collection. A good paper describing a LISP system and its garbage collector is 'A Portable LISP

Compiler' by M. L. Griss and A. C. Hearn, *Software—Practice and Experience,* **11**, 541–605 (1981).

A good paper describing a particular implementation of coroutines is 'A Coroutine Mechanism for BCPL' by J. K. Moody and M. Richards, *Software—Practice and Experience,* **10**, 765–771 (1980).

3
Formal grammars

As we saw in Chapter 1, the first operation performed by a compiler is analysis of the structure of the source language program. Lexical analysis is the simpler level of analysis, grouping characters into basic entities. Syntax analysis takes these simple entities and groups them together into the structures that form the complete source language program. *Formal grammars* are used to define the syntax of programs in the source language for both the lexical and syntax analysers.

Lexical and syntax analysis are divisions of a compiler's operation essentially for reasons of efficiency. Both use formal grammars to guide their operation in the same way. For conciseness we shall refer mainly to syntax analysis parsing in this chapter. Except where explicitly stated this can be taken to refer to lexical analysis as well.

Syntax analysis checks that the program is syntactically valid and then determines its underlying structure, prior to semantic analysis and translation. For example in the following C program:

```
main()
{
        int  i ;

        for( i = 0 ; i < 10 ; i++ )
                printf( "%d squared is %d\n", i, i * i ) ;

}
```

the compiler would determine that there is an integer variable, i, declared, that there is a for loop, which initializes i to zero, continues while i is less than 10, increments i each time round the loop, and so on.

Semantic analysis draws closely on the structural analysis performed during syntax analysis, and it is important that the output from the syntax analyser should be in an appropriate form. This constraint can influence the way a formal grammar is used to define the syntax of the source language.

3.1 Defining the structure of a language

The syntax of a language is specified in a top-down fashion. We define how each component of the language is constructed from simpler components, eventually from individual characters. To do this we use *productions* often also called *grammar rules*.

The general form of a production used in the definition of a programming language is:

$$A \rightarrow B_1 B_2 B_3 \ldots B_n$$

This defines entity A as being made up of the string of simpler entities B_1, B_2, B_3, ..., B_n. These may be actual characters appearing in the program, or they may themselves be the subject of a definition elsewhere. It means that anywhere in the definition of a program that we see A we may replace that by the string $B_1 B_2 B_3 \ldots B_n$. Eventually we will have a string containing nothing that can be expanded further. Such a string is called a *sentence*. In the context of programming languages, syntactically correct programs are sentences derived using the formal grammar defining the syntax of the programming language.

When defining the syntax of real programming languages it is normal to use multi-character names, rather than just single letters, A, B_1, etc., to make it clear what we are defining. A typical example of a production would be the following definition of the assignment statement in VSL:

$$assignment\_statement \rightarrow variable := expression$$

In other words an assignment statement is a variable, followed by the symbol ':=', followed by an expression. We use italics for the entity being defined (*assignment_statement*) or those defined in productions elsewhere (*variable* and *expression*) and bold text for entities that are to appear literally in the program (:= in this example). A common variant notation for productions is the following because it does not use different typefaces, and so is suitable for entry into a computer:

```
assignment_statement ::= variable ':=' expression
```

::= is used instead of $\rightarrow$ and literal entities are enclosed in single quotes.

The syntax of a language is defined by a collection of productions such as these. At the top we must have a single entity from which all syntactically correct programs derive:

$$S \rightarrow A_1 A_2 A_3 \ldots A_n$$

S is known as the *sentence symbol* and a sentence must be derivable from S by successive replacement using productions of the grammar.

In VSL the sentence symbol is *program* defined by the production:

$$program \rightarrow function\_list$$

All syntactically correct VSL programs can be derived from *program* by successive replacement operations using the various productions of the VSL grammar.

We may have more than one production giving alternative definitions of a symbol:

$$A \rightarrow B_1 B_2 B_3 \dots B_n$$

$$A \rightarrow C_1 C_2 C_3 \dots C_m$$

Such alternatives may be written:

$$A \rightarrow B_1 B_2 B_3 \dots B_n \mid C_1 C_2 C_3 \dots C_m$$

Productions may be self-referential or *recursive*:

$$A \rightarrow A\mathbf{x} \mid \mathbf{y}$$

It is sometimes convenient to specify that a symbol can be replaced by nothing at all. To indicate this we use the null symbol, ε:

$$A \rightarrow B \mid \varepsilon$$

The VSL grammar contains examples of all these productions:

1. *if_statement*   → **IF** *expression* **THEN** *statement* **FI** |
   IF *expression* **THEN** *statement* **ELSE** *statement* **FI**
2. *variable_list*   → *variable* | *variable_list* **,** *variable*
3. *parameter_list* → *variable_list* | ε

Production (1) shows two alternatives in the definition of a symbol, production (2) illustrates recursion, and production (3) makes use of the null symbol ε.

This way of specifying programming languages is known as *Backus–Naur form* or more commonly *BNF* after its inventors. The complete BNF specification of VSL is given in Appendix A.

3.1.1 PARSE TREES

Parsing is the action of deriving a sentence from the sentence symbol of a grammar by repeated application of productions. The derivation can be clearly seen as a tree showing how each symbol is derived from other symbols. For example, take the grammar:

$$S \rightarrow AB$$

$$A \rightarrow A\mathbf{x} \mid \mathbf{y}$$

$$B \rightarrow \mathbf{z}$$

with sentence symbol S. Figure 3.1 shows the parse tree for the sentence **yxxz** using this grammar. The parse tree shows where each production has been used.

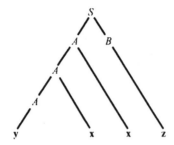

Figure 3.1   Parse tree for the sentence **yxxz**

For comparison Fig. 3.2 shows the parse tree for the VSL program:

```
FUNC f( n )
    IF n
    THEN
        RETURN n * f( n - 1 )
    ELSE
        RETURN 1
    FI
```

using the VSL grammar in Appendix A (Sec. A.1).

We are now in a position to define precisely what we mean by the term *formal grammar*.

3.1.2   DEFINITION OF A FORMAL GRAMMAR

The productions of a grammar make use of symbols. These are both the symbols that appear in sentences of the grammar, and symbols that appear on the left side of productions defining groupings of symbols, but which do not themselves appear in sentences of the grammar. This is the *alphabet* of the grammar. For example, in the grammar:

$$S \rightarrow AB$$

$$A \rightarrow A\mathbf{x} \,|\, \mathbf{y}$$

$$B \rightarrow \mathbf{z}$$

the alphabet is $\{S, A, B, \mathbf{x}, \mathbf{y}, \mathbf{z}\}$. One of the symbols in the alphabet is distinguished as the *sentence symbol*, in this case S. All sentences must be derivable from the sentence symbol by repeated replacement operations using the productions of the grammar, in which a symbol appearing on the left of a production is replaced by the string of symbols (possibly null) appearing on the right side.

This alphabet is divided into two disjoint sets. The *terminal alphabet* comprises those symbols, known as *terminal symbols*, that appear in sentences of the grammar. The remaining symbols, the *non-terminal symbols*, form the *non-terminal alphabet*. In the example above the terminal alphabet is $\{\mathbf{x}, \mathbf{y}, \mathbf{z}\}$

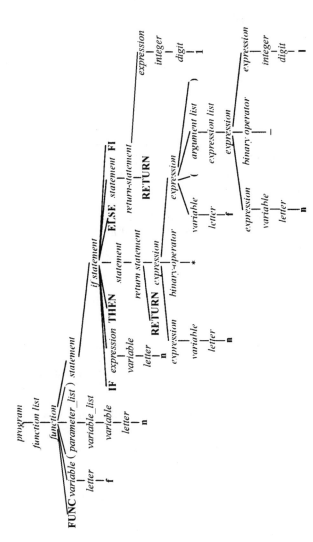

Figure 3.2   Parse tree for a VSL program

and the non-terminal alphabet is $\{S,\ A,\ B\}$. Notationally we use $\mathbb{V}$ for the alphabet, with $\mathbb{T}$ for the terminal alphabet and $\mathbb{N}$ for the non-terminal alphabet. In addition we generally use S for the sentence symbol, italic upper-case letters ($A,\ B$, etc.) for non-terminal symbols, and bold lower-case letters ($\mathbf{x},\ \mathbf{y}$, etc) for terminal symbols. Italic lower-case letters with a bar ($\bar{u},\ \bar{v}$, etc.) are used for arbitrary strings (possibly null) of terminal and non-terminal symbols.

We can describe the alphabets set theoretically as follows:

$$\mathbb{V} \quad = \mathbb{T} \cup \mathbb{N}$$
$$\mathbb{T} \cap \mathbb{N} = \varnothing$$

To define a language we need a set of productions. In general terms these take the form:

$$\bar{u} \rightarrow \bar{v}$$

In a BNF grammar $\bar{u}$ is a single non-terminal and $\bar{v}$ is an arbitrary string of terminal and non-terminal symbols. When parsing we can replace $\bar{u}$ by $\bar{v}$ wherever it occurs. We shall refer to this set of productions symbolically as $\mathbb{P}$.

We now formally define a grammar:

A grammar, G, is a 4-tuple $\{S,\ \mathbb{P},\ \mathbb{N},\ \mathbb{T}\}$, where S is the sentence symbol, $S \in \mathbb{N}$, $\mathbb{P}$ is a set of productions, $\mathbb{N}$ is the set of non-terminal symbols, and $\mathbb{T}$ is the set of terminal symbols.

We define a sentence formally as

A sentence is a string of symbols in $\mathbb{T}$ derived from S using one or more applications of productions in $\mathbb{P}$.

Using this definition of a sentence, we define a language.

The language, $L(G)$ defined by a grammar, G, is the set of sentences derivable using G.

When talking about formal grammars it is useful to refer to various different concepts with a degree of precision. We now give some useful definitions and notation that will help in talking about grammars.

3.1.3 THE NOTATION OF FORMAL GRAMMARS

A sentence is a string of terminal symbols derived from S by application of one or more productions in $\mathbb{P}$. A string of symbols derived from S but possibly including non-terminal symbols as well is called a *sentential form*.

A production $\bar{u} \rightarrow \bar{v}$ is used by replacing an occurrence of $\bar{u}$ by $\bar{v}$. We may write this more formally. If we apply a production $p \in \mathbb{P}$ to a string of symbols $\bar{w}$ in $\mathbb{V}$ to yield a new string of symbols, $\bar{z}$ in $\mathbb{V}$, we say that $\bar{z}$ is derived from $\bar{w}$ using p, written as:

$$\bar{w} \overset{p}{\Rightarrow} \bar{z}$$

We also use:

$\bar{w} \Rightarrow \bar{z}$ $\bar{z}$ is derived from $\bar{w}$ (production unspecified)

$\bar{w} \overset{*}{\Rightarrow} \bar{z}$ $\bar{z}$ is derived from $\bar{w}$ using zero or more productions

$\bar{w} \overset{+}{\Rightarrow} \bar{z}$ $\bar{z}$ is derived from $\bar{w}$ using one or more productions

A sentence is a string of terminal symbols derived from S. We often work with strings of terminal symbols derived from non-terminals other than S. Such a string is known as a *phrase* of the grammar.

3.1.4 TYPES OF GRAMMAR

We can classify grammars into different types, according to the form of productions allowed. This is useful, because if we impose restrictions on productions, we obtain grammars that are much easier to parse. The most widely used classification is by Chomsky. He suggested four types of grammar.

Type 0 grammars

These are the most general and are also known as *free grammars*. Productions are of the form $\bar{u} \rightarrow \bar{v}$, where both $\bar{u}$ and $\bar{v}$ are arbitrary strings of symbols in $\mathbb{V}$, with $\bar{u}$ non-null.

Type 1 grammars

These are also known as *context-sensitive grammars*. Productions are of the form $\bar{u}X\bar{w} \rightarrow \bar{u}\bar{v}\bar{w}$, where $\bar{u}$, $\bar{v}$, and $\bar{w}$ are arbitrary strings of symbols in $\mathbb{V}$, with $\bar{v}$ non-null and X is a single non-terminal. In other words X may be replaced by $\bar{v}$, but only when it is found surrounded by $\bar{u}$ and $\bar{w}$.

Type 2 grammars

These are also known as *context-free grammars*. Productions are of the form $X \rightarrow \bar{v}$, where $\bar{v}$ is an arbitrary string of symbols in $\mathbb{V}$ and X is a single non-terminal. In other words X may be replaced by $\bar{v}$ wherever it is found. The grammars used by syntax analysers in compilers are invariably type 2 grammars. BNF is a particular notation for type 2 grammars. All languages derived from type 2 grammars can be parsed, but there are some subsets, commonly used for programming language definition, that can be parsed particularly efficiently.

Type 3 grammars

These are also known as *finite grammars* or *regular grammars*. Productions have the form $X \rightarrow \mathbf{a}$ or $X \rightarrow \mathbf{a}Y$, where X and Y are non-terminals and $\mathbf{a}$ is a terminal. Although not general enough to describe the syntax of a complete programming language, these grammars are widely used in the lexical analysers of compilers to describe the basic entities that make up the programming language. Languages defined by type 3 grammars can be parsed very efficiently. In particular they can always be recognized by a finite state machine.

3.2 Properties of grammars

A number of properties of grammars need to be well understood. The compiler writer using the grammar to define a programming language needs to understand what effect these properties may have.

3.2.1 EQUIVALENT GRAMMARS

Two grammars G and G' are said to be *equivalent* if the languages they generate $L(G)$ and $L(G')$ are the same.

However, it should be noted that two grammars, although equivalent, may not necessarily have the same parse trees for each sentence. For example, the following grammars are equivalent:

$$G \qquad\qquad G'$$

$$A \rightarrow Ax \,|\, y \qquad A \rightarrow yB$$
$$B \rightarrow xB \,|\, \varepsilon$$

Yet the parse trees are markedly different as can be seen from Fig. 3.3, which shows parse trees for the sentence **yxx**.

It is important to bear this in mind when writing compilers, for the parse tree often reflects the semantic structure of the language and is used by the subsequent semantic analysis and translation phases. It may be convenient to rewrite the grammar of a language to make it easier to parse; however, such rewriting may change the parse tree to such an extent that the semantic information is lost. In such cases the compiler writer must use a different parsing technique instead of transforming the grammar.

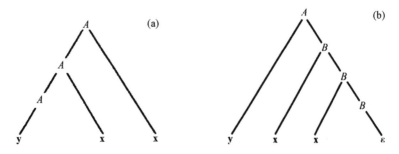

Figure 3.3 Parse trees for **yxx** using: (a) grammar G; (b) grammar G'

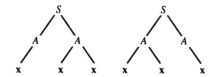

Figure 3.4   Two possible parse trees for **xxx**

3.2.2   AMBIGUOUS GRAMMARS

If a grammar permits more than one parse tree for some sentences, then it is said
to be *ambiguous*. For example, parsing the sentence **xxx** using the following
grammar:

$$S \rightarrow AA$$

$$A \rightarrow \mathbf{x} \,|\, \mathbf{xx}$$

could result in either of the two parse trees shown in Fig. 3.4.

If we are using the parse tree to convey information to the semantic analyser,
then such sentences could have two different meanings, according to which
parse tree we use. Such grammars are a problem to the compiler writer, who is
seeking to make a consistent translation into the target language.

Ambiguous grammars can be (and are) used with suitable disambiguating
rules. A common area of ambiguity is the grammar describing arithmetic
expressions. For example, in VSL part of the grammar for expressions is as
follows:

> *expression*   → *expression binary_operator expression* | *integer*
>
> *binary_operator* → + | − | * | /

This grammar is ambiguous as can be seen from the two different parse trees for
the expression 10 − 20 − 30 in Fig. 3.5. In fact, if we are going subsequently to
translate from the tree with a left-to-right depth first walk, then the tree we want
is Fig. 3.5(a), so that the left-most expression is translated first, in accordance
with conventional arithmetic precedence for expressions.

Suitable disambiguating rules for this grammar would specify that * and /
have higher precedence than + and − and that operators of equal precedence
associate to the left. Such rules ensure that when the grammar permits more
than one parse of a sentence, only one parse tree is deemed valid.

Alternatively, we may rewrite the VSL grammar for expressions to make it
unambiguous:

> *expression*   → *expression term_operator term* | *term*
> *term_operator*   → + | −
> *term*   → *term factor_operator factor* | *factor*
> *factor_operator* → * | /

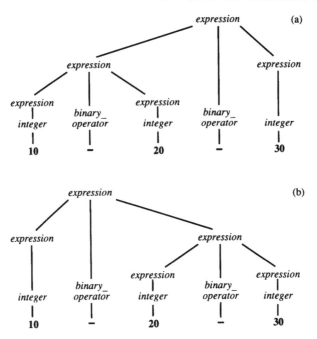

Figure 3.5 Two possible parsings of 10 − 20 − 30 using an ambiguous grammar

factor   → *unary_operator expression* | **(** *expression* **)** | *integer* |
                  variable | *variable* **(** *argument_list* **)**
unary_operator → **−**

3.2.3 RECURSION

Productions are often defined in terms of themselves. For example, a list of variables in VSL is specified by the production:

$$variable\_list \rightarrow variable \mid variable\_list , variable$$

Such productions are said to be *recursive*. It is quite common for one of the alternatives on the right-hand side of such a production to contain the recursion at its left-most end. This is the case in the previous example. Such productions are called *left recursive* and have the general form:

$$A \rightarrow \bar{u} \mid A\bar{v}$$

where *A* is a non-terminal and $\bar{u}$ and $\bar{v}$ are arbitrary strings of terminals and non-terminals.

Correspondingly we have *right recursive* productions, where the recursion occurs at the right end of the right-hand side of a production. The general form of a right recursive production is thus:

$$A \rightarrow \bar{u} \mid \bar{v}A$$

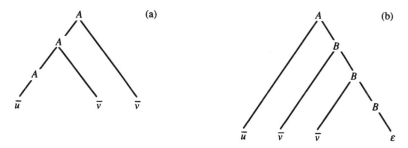

Figure 3.6   Parse tree for $\bar{u}\bar{v}\bar{v}$ using: (a) a left recursive grammar; (b) a grammar with left recursion removed

Left recursion in particular can cause problems with some parsing methods, as will be seen in Chapter 6. There is a standard transformation to give an equivalent grammar, which is right recursive instead. The left recursive production:

$$A \rightarrow \bar{u} \mid A\bar{v}$$

can be replaced by the two productions

$$A \rightarrow \bar{u}B$$

$$B \rightarrow \bar{v}B \mid \varepsilon$$

Figure 3.6 shows the parse tree for $\bar{u}\bar{v}\bar{v}$ using the two alternatives. Although the grammars are equivalent, they give different parse trees. Once again this may cause problems with subsequent semantic processing and it may be better to use a different parsing technique rather than transforming the grammar.

3.2.4   LEFT-MOST AND RIGHT-MOST DERIVATIONS

We parse a sentence of a language by successive operations in which we replace the left side of a production by its right side. There may be a choice of order in which we do these replacements. For example, in parsing the sentence **yz** using the following grammar:

$$S \rightarrow AB$$

$$A \rightarrow A\mathbf{x} \mid \mathbf{y}$$

$$B \rightarrow \mathbf{z}$$

we must use three productions, namely:

$$S \rightarrow AB \quad \text{giving the sentential form } AB$$

$$A \rightarrow \mathbf{y} \quad \text{giving the sentential form } \mathbf{y}B$$

$$B \rightarrow \mathbf{z} \quad \text{giving the sentence } \mathbf{yz}$$

Note how we expanded first A then B in the last two productions. We could instead have used the productions in the order:

$S \rightarrow AB$ giving the sentential form AB

$B \rightarrow \mathbf{z}$ giving the sentential form $A\mathbf{z}$

$A \rightarrow \mathbf{y}$ giving the sentence $\mathbf{yz}$

It is often convenient to specify a particular order in which to construct the parse tree, particularly if we are performing semantic analysis as it is built. We describe a parse in which we always expand the left-most non-terminal first as a *left-most derivation* and a parse in which we always expand the right-most non-terminal first as a *right-most derivation*. We also speak of a sentential form derived by left-most derivation as a *left sentential form* and by right-most derivation as a *right sentential form*. We may use the notation:

$$\bar{w} \overset{lm}{\Rightarrow} \bar{z}$$

$$\bar{w} \overset{rm}{\Rightarrow} \bar{z}$$

to mean $\bar{z}$ is derived from $\bar{w}$ using left-most and right-most derivations, respectively.

The first example above was a left-most derivation and the second a right-most derivation. Figure 3.7 shows how the parse trees build up during these derivations of the sentence $\mathbf{yz}$.

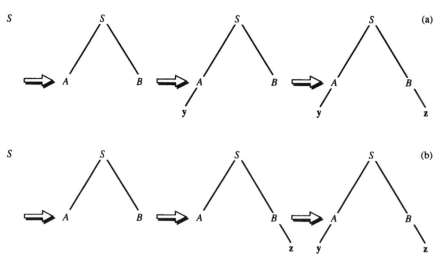

Figure 3.7 (a) Left-most and (b) right-most parses of **yz**

3.2.5 LEFT FACTORING

We often encounter productions with identical first parts to alternative right-hand sides for example:

$$X \rightarrow \bar{u}\bar{w} \mid \bar{v}\bar{z}$$

We can rewrite this as two rules, where we do not have two alternatives that start with the same string:

$$A \rightarrow \bar{v}B$$

$$B \rightarrow \bar{w} \mid \bar{z}$$

This is known as *left factoring* and leads to an equivalent grammar. Left factoring can be very helpful in syntax analysis, as will be seen in Chapter 6.

3.3 Syntax-directed translation

Parsing and parse trees are used to drive the semantic analysis and translation of the source language in a compiler. Commonly this is a separate phase of the compiler. An alternative approach is to augment our conventional grammar productions with information to control the semantic analysis and translation. Such grammars are called *attribute grammars*.

3.3.1 ATTRIBUTE GRAMMARS

We augment our grammar by associating *attributes* with each grammar symbol to describe its properties. For example, variables may have an attribute 'type' to describe the type of the variable; integer constants may have an attribute 'value' to describe the value of the constant. With each production in our grammar, we then give *semantic rules* (also known as *semantic actions*) which describe how to compute the attribute values associated with each grammar symbol in the production. An example may help to clarify this. We may augment the definition of a digit in VSL with a 'value' attribute to hold the value of the digit parsed as follows:

$$digit \rightarrow \mathbf{0} \; \{digit.value = 0\}$$
$$\mid \mathbf{1} \; \{digit.value = 1\}$$
$$\ldots$$
$$\mid \mathbf{9} \; \{digit.value = 9\}$$

We put the semantic rules in braces, { }, following each production, using a C type syntax. In these semantic rules we use the notation $X.a$ to mean the attribute a associated with grammar symbol X.

We can think of this value attribute being passed up the parse tree to be used by other productions. For example, we might augment the definition of an integer as follows:

$$integer_1 \rightarrow digit \qquad \{integer_1.value = digit.value\}$$
$$\mid integer_2 \; digit \quad \{integer_1.value = integer_2.value \times 10 + digit.value\}$$

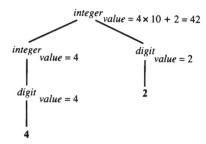

Figure 3.8   A decorated parse tree

Note how we use subscripts to clarify which symbol attribute we are referring to. *integer*₁ and *integer*₂ are the same non-terminal symbol, but we use subscripts to distinguish the particular instances.

Decorated parse trees

We may conveniently draw our parse tree with the values of attributes added. Such a tree is known as a *decorated parse tree* or *annotated parse tree*. We obtain such a tree by walking over the parse tree, evaluating semantic rules as we go. Figure 3.8 shows a decorated tree for the previous example grammar for integers.

Synthesized attributes

These examples show the value of attributes of items on the left-hand side of productions being derived from the value of attributes on the right-hand side of productions. We can think of the values being passed up the parse tree. Such attributes are called *synthesized attributes*.

In formal terms for each production, synthesized attributes associated with the non-terminal on the left-hand side of the production are generated as functions of the synthesized attributes of the terminals and non-terminals on the right-hand side. For the general production:

$$X \rightarrow Y_1 Y_2 \ldots Y_n$$

we can write the semantic rule for each synthesized attribute, *a*, as:

$$X.a = f(Y_1.a, Y_2.a, \ldots, Y_n.a)$$

Inherited attributes

It is also useful to be able to pass semantic information down the parse tree. In this case we describe how values of attributes on the right-hand side of productions are derived from values of attributes on the left-hand side and/or other attributes on the right-hand side. Such attributes are called *inherited attributes*.

For our general production

$$X \rightarrow Y_1 Y_2 \ldots Y_n$$

we can write the semantic rule for each inherited attribute, a, as:

$$Y_k . a = f(X . a, \ Y_1 . a, Y_2 . a, \ldots, \ Y_{k-1} . a, \ Y_{k+1} . a, \ldots, \ Y_n . a)$$

The following grammar illustrates how we might use an inherited attribute to maintain a list of variables for checking declarations:

$P \rightarrow DS \qquad\qquad \{S.dl = D.dl\}$

$D_1 \rightarrow \mathbf{var}\ V\ ;\ D_2 \qquad \{D_1.dl = addlist(V.name, D_2.dl)\}$
$\quad | \ \ \varepsilon \qquad\qquad\quad \{D_1.dl = nil\}$

$S_1 \rightarrow V := E\ ;\ S_2 \quad \{check(V.name, S_1.dl)\ ;\ S_2.dl = S_1.dl\}$
$\quad | \ \ \varepsilon$

$V \rightarrow \mathbf{x} \qquad\qquad\quad \{V.name = \text{'}x\text{'}\}$
$\quad | \ \ \mathbf{y} \qquad\qquad\quad \{V.name = \text{'}y\text{'}\}$
$\quad | \ \ \mathbf{z} \qquad\qquad\quad \{V.name = \text{'}z\text{'}\}$

Each time a new variable is declared its name is added to the list of variables declared so far, the synthesized attribute *dl*. This list of variables is then passed as the inherited attribute (also *dl*) to each statement for use in checking declarations. Figure 3.9 shows a decorated parse tree using this grammar.

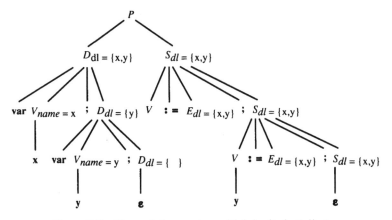

Figure 3.9 Decorated parse tree with inherited attributes

3.3.2 EVALUATING SEMANTIC RULES

The basic approach in evaluating semantic rules to yield a decorated parse tree is to walk over the parse tree, evaluating the semantic rules at each node as we go. The order in which we walk over the parse tree is important, since some attributes depend on others. In the previous example the inherited attribute *S.dl* depends on the synthesized attribute *D.dl* in the production for *P*. In this case it is important that we evaluate the semantic rules in the subtree for *D.dl* before the tree for *S.dl*.

The algorithm for deciding the order of evaluation of attributes is beyond the scope of this book. However, there are two special types of attribute grammar, for which the evaluation order is easy to determine.

S-attributed grammars

An attribute grammar that uses only synthesized attributes is known as an *S-attributed grammar*. The attributes may be correctly evaluated by a bottom-up walk over the parse tree from the leaves to the root, evaluating the semantic rules at each mode. With most parsing methods such a walk may be done as the parse tree is being built, removing the need for separate semantic anaysis and translation phases in the compiler.

L-attributed grammars

L-attributed grammars are a class of attribute grammars in which all inherited attributes in a production are functions only of symbols to their left in the production. In other words, for the general production:

$$X \rightarrow Y_1 Y_2 \dots Y_n$$

the inherited attributes of Y_k depend only on the attributes of X and $Y_1, Y_2, \dots, Y_{k-1}$.

L-attributed grammars can always be evaluated by a left-to-right depth first traversal of the parse tree. They are also in general powerful enough to describe the semantics of programming languages. However, not all parsing methods permit all L-attributed grammars to be evaluated during parsing as the tree is built. This is a problem the programmer must bear in mind when designing a compiler.

Exercises

PRACTICAL PROBLEMS

3.1. The following is a simple grammar for binary arithmetic expressions involving variables and assignment.

$$prog \rightarrow dlist\ slist$$
$$dlist \rightarrow \varepsilon \mid decl\ ;\ dlist$$

$$decl \rightarrow \textbf{VAR} \; var$$
$$var \; \rightarrow \textbf{a} \,|\, \textbf{b} \,|\, \textbf{c}$$
$$slist \; \rightarrow stmt \,|\, slist \; ; stmt$$
$$stmt \rightarrow var := expr \,|\, \textbf{PRINT} \; var$$
$$expr \rightarrow term \,|\, expr + term \,|\, expr - term$$
$$term \rightarrow int \,|\, var$$
$$int \; \rightarrow digit \,|\, int \; digit$$
$$digit \rightarrow \textbf{0} \,|\, \textbf{1}$$

Construct the parse tree for the following sentence using the above grammar

```
VAR a ; VAR b ; a := 10 ; b := 11 - a - 1 ; PRINT b
```

3.2. Which productions in the grammar of question 3.1 show left recursion. Illustrate left-most and right-most derivation of the parse tree for the sentence in question 3.1.

3.3. Rewrite the grammar of question 3.1 to remove left recursion. Show the parse tree for the sentence in question 3.1 using your rewritten grammar.

3.4. Annotate the grammar of question 3.1 to build a list of declarations, check variables are declared before use, evaluate the expressions, and print the value of any variables. Show the annotated parse tree for the sentence in question 3.1.

ESSAY TITLES

3.1. Why do compiler writers need formal grammars?

3.2. How may left recursion be eliminated from a formal grammar? What possible drawbacks may there be to such elimination for the compiler writer?

3.3. What is a formal grammar? What is meant by the terms sentence, sentential form, and phrase within the context of formal grammars? Define the four types of Chomsky grammar.

DISCUSSION TOPICS

3.1. Identify the various ideas described in this chapter in the formal grammar of VSL given in the Appendix.

3.2. Investigate the annotation of parse trees for arbitrary attributed grammars.

Further reading

Every textbook on compilers discusses formal grammars. The current work is probably unusual in the brevity of its coverage. An alternative text that has always proved helpful, even though it is now rather dated, is *Compiler Construction for Digital Computers* by David Gries, published by John Wiley (1971).

Relatively few textbooks cover attribute grammars well, although there are numerous research papers on the subject. A good starting point is Chapter 5 of Aho, Sethi and Ullman (see the further reading section in Chapter 1), which gives a comprehensive bibliography.

4
Intermediate representations

We saw in Chapter 1 the need for separate front and back ends to aid compiler portability. If this breakdown is to be effective we must have a clean interface between the two parts. In the first part of this chapter we shall look at some common intermediate representations. We shall illustrate their relevance by giving examples of semantic rules for their generation from the grammar of VSL.

In the second part of this chapter we shall look at abstract machines used as target languages to be subsequently interpreted. One or two of these are of particular interest, since they are used both as a target language to be interpreted, and as an intermediate for subsequent generation of machine code, so serving a dual purpose.

4.1 Types of intermediate representations

There are two fundamental classes of representation used as interface between front end and back end. The first class are tree representations, closely related to the parse tree for the language. The second class are the three-address codes—general-purpose assembly languages.

4.1.1 PARSE TREE BASED REPRESENTATIONS

The most obvious way to represent the information gained from lexical and syntax analysis is as a tree along the lines of the parse tree. In C this is suitably handled using a simple struct for each node:

```
struct node
{
        int         nodetype ;
        struct node *field1 ;
        struct node *field2 ;
        struct node *field3 ;
        struct node *field4 ;
        struct node *field5 ;
} ;
```

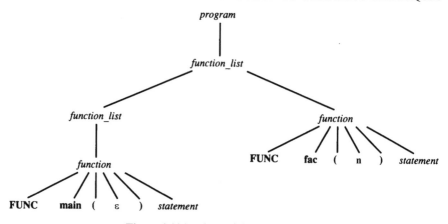

Figure 4.1(a)   A partial VSL parse tree

The `nodetype` field contains a small integer to identify the non-terminal concerned, presumably set up with a series of `#define` statements:

```
#define  NT_PROGRAM        1
#define  NT_FUNCTION_LIST  2
#define  NT_FUNCTION       3
```

The `struct` has room for up to five further fields to point to subtrees where appropriate. Unused fields may have null pointers if appropriate.

Figure 4.1(a) shows a parse tree for part of VSL and Fig 4.1(b) the corresponding tree that would be built up using such a C struct. The productions involved are:

> *program*   → *function_list*
> *function_list* → *function* | *function_list function*
> *function*   → **FUNC** *variable* **(** *parameter_list* **)** *statement*

The tree we use as our intermediate representation is not so detailed as the parse tree. Since a *program* and a *function_list* are the same thing, we merge the two and just have a *function_list* node. We do not need to show subtrees to terminal symbols (such as **FUNC**) which we know must be there if the program is syntactically correct (which the syntax analyser will already have verified). There are some productions where different alternatives require different numbers of fields in the struct. For example, *function_list* may require just one field for the first alternative:

$$function\_list \rightarrow function$$

whereas it needs two fields for the second alternative:

$$function\_list \rightarrow function\_list\ function$$

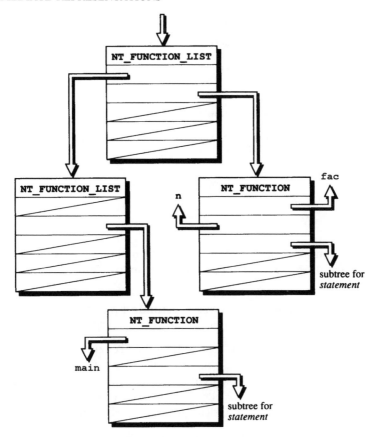

Figure 4.1(b)   C representation of a parse tree

We solve this problem by putting null pointers in unused fields of the struct. In this particular case we always use field1 to point to the *function_list* subtree and field2 to point to the *function* subtree. If there is no *function_list* subtree then we put a null pointer in field1.

For convenience in building such trees we need a simple C routine to malloc() space for nodes and fill in the fields. A typical implementation of such a routine would be

```
struct node *mknode( int          type,
                struct node *f1,
                struct node *f2,
                struct node *f3,
                struct node *f4,
                struct node *f5 )
{
        struct node *t = (struct node *)malloc(
                        sizeof( struct node )) ;
```

```
if( t == NULL )
{
        /* Can't use printf if malloc's failed! */

        fputs( "mknode: out of store\n", stderr ) ;
        exit( 255 ) ;
}

/* Set up fields */

t->nodetype = type ;
t->field1   = f1 ;
t->field2   = f2 ;
t->field3   = f3 ;
t->field4   = f4 ;
t->field5   = f5 ;

return t ;
}
```

This routine may then conveniently be used to build up the tree during syntax analysis, possibly by semantic rules such as the following:

function_list$_1$ → *function_list*$_2$ *function*
  {*function_list*$_1$.*tree* = mknode (NT_FUNCTION_LIST ,
  function_list$_2$.*tree* , *function.tree* , NULL , NULL , NULL) ;}

The synthesized attribute *tree* is used to hold the tree representation created.

For the majority of parse trees this sort of intermediate representation is fine. However, there are minor problems at the leaves of the tree. A number of non-terminals have productions that could be replaced by a number of different terminals. For example, a digit is defined by the production:

$$digit → 0 \,|\, 1 \,|\, \cdots \,|\, 8 \,|\, 9$$

In such cases we need a node that can hold subsidiary information about characters that form terminal symbols. A simple way is to extend our definition of a node to include a field for character information:

```
struct node
{
        int          nodetype ;
        struct node *field1 ;
        struct node *field2 ;
        struct node *field3 ;
        struct node *field4 ;
        struct node *field5 ;
        char         terminal ;
} ;
```

This is not particularly efficient. In practice we do not hold individual characters at the leaves of the tree. We would probably not build subtrees for the characters of a variable name, or the individual characters of a piece of text, or the individual digits of an integer. We would rely on the lexical analyser to group these together for us into character strings or integer values as appropriate, and permit string and integer fields in our struct as follows:

```
struct node
{
        int             nodetype ;
        struct node *field1 ;
        struct node *field2 ;
        struct node *field3 ;
        struct node *field4 ;
        struct node *field5 ;
        char            *name ;      /* variables and text */
        int             value ;      /* integer constants */
} ;
```

The definition of mknode could then be extended to include the setting of the last two fields. The semantic rule for an integer might then become something like:

integer → *rec_integer*
{ *integer.tree* = mknode (NT_INTEGER , NULL , NULL ,
NULL , NULL , NULL , NULL , *rec_integer.value*) } ;
rec_integer → original recursive definition of an integer

The node for the integer 561 is shown in Fig. 4.2.

This structure is rather wasteful of space, since we only use the name or value field if the pointer fields (field1 to field5) are unused. The nodetype field always tells us which is in use. A more efficient data structure is to use a C union:

```
struct node
{
        int             nodetype ;
        union
        {
                int             value ;      /* integers */
                char            *name ;      /* variable names */
                struct node *ptr ;           /* subtrees */
        }               field1 ;
        struct node *field2 ;
        struct node *field3 ;
        struct node *field4 ;
        struct node *field5 ;
} ;
```

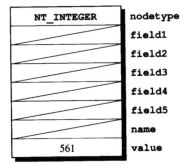

Figure 4.2   Node for the integer 561

The different parts of the union are discriminated by the nodetype field. For example, if the tree were held in a variable called tree and the nodetype field were NT_INTEGER then we could access the value of the integer as:

```
tree->field1.value ;
```

With this sort of structure it is convenient for mknode() to set all fields as pointers and to have different routines, mkvalnode() and mktextnode() to create nodes with integer fields or text fields. For example, mkvalnode() would look something like:

```
struct node *mkvalnode( int   type,
                        int   v )
{
        struct node *t = (struct node *)malloc(
                                sizeof( struct node )) ;

        if( t == NULL )
        {
                /* Can't use printf if malloc's failed! */

                fputs( "mkvalnode: out of store\n", stderr ) ;
                exit( 255 ) ;
        }

        /* Set up fields */

        t->nodetype   = type ;
        t->field1.value = v ;

        return  t ;
}
```

Directed acyclic graphs

In a tree there is only one path from the root to each leaf of the tree. In compiler terms this means that there is only one route from the sentence symbol to each terminal. When using trees as intermediate representations it is often the case that some subtrees are duplicated. For example, the parse tree for the VSL expression:

```
a * b + a * b
```

is shown in Fig. 4.3(a). A logical optimization is to share common parts of the tree, as in Fig. 4.3(b). We now have a data structure in which there is more than one path from the root to each leaf. Such a data structure is known as a *directed acyclic graph* or *DAG*.

We can use DAGs as an intermediate representation in a compiler, using the same data structure as with a tree representation. A possible C data structure for the DAG in Fig. 4.3(b) is shown in Fig. 4.4.

DAG intermediate representations are somewhat harder to construct (we have to find out what is common), but give an obvious saving of space. They also highlight equivalent bits of code, e.g. common sub-expressions, which we

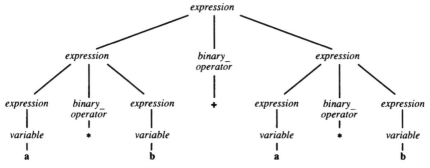

Figure 4.3(a)   Parse tree for a VSL expression

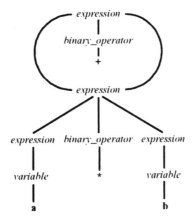

Figure 4.3(b)   Directed acyclic graph for a VSL expression

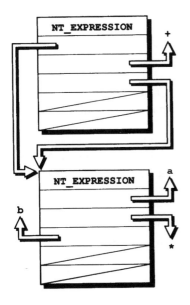

Figure 4.4   C data structure for a directed acyclic graph

need only evaluate once when translating. They are thus a first level of optimization in translation.

4.1.2 THREE-ADDRESS CODE

The major alternatives to trees or DAGs are representations based on *three-address code* or *TAC*. The basic form of a TAC instruction is:

$$res := arg_1 \ op \ arg_2$$

In other words a binary operator where we specify the address of both source operands and the result (hence three-address code). These addresses are typically variable names from the source program, compiler-generated temporary variables, or constants. Variable names are always represented symbolically, their resolution into machine addresses is a problem for the code generator.

For example, we would use:

```
a := b + c
```

to specify that the values in locations b and c should be added and the result placed in location a. There are several variants on this basic TAC instruction format, to handle unary operators, branching, and so forth, but they can all be expressed as an operator with up to three addresses.

Any parse tree can be translated into TAC. For example the VSL parse tree of Fig. 4.3(a) might be translated as:

```
t₁ := a * b
t₂ := a * b
c  := t₁ + t₂
```

Just as a DAG shared common code of a tree, so we can write TAC where common code is shared. For example, the DAG of Fig. 4.3(b) might also be translated as:

```
t₁ := a * b
c  := t₁ + t₁
```

Types of TAC instructions

Each compiler writer will select his or her own set of TAC instructions. The important point is that there should only be a small set, and they should be relatively simple.

The set we use in the VSL compiler and throughout this book is exceptionally simple because VSL has no types and no logical or relational operators. However, it will serve to illustrate the techniques involved. There are six groups of instructions.

Binary operators   These are for the four binary arithmetic operators. They comprise:

```
a := b + c
a := b − c
a := b * c
a := b / c
```

Unary operators   There is only one unary operator in VSL, negation. Its TAC instruction only uses two addresses and is:

```
a := -b
```

Assignment   This is an instruction to copy a value from one address to another. Its form is:

```
a := b
```

Unconditional jump   This has the form:

```
goto a
```

a is the TAC code to branch to. This may be a pointer to the actual TAC instruction, or an index into the TAC code array.

Conditional jump   This is much simpler with VSL than in other languages, because all conditions are solely dependent on an expression being zero or non-zero. There are two such instructions to jump according to whether a particular value is zero or non-zero.

```
ifz b goto a
ifnz b goto a
```

Function call and return   There are three instructions to handle this in VSL which have the form:

```
arg a
a := call b
return a
```

A series of `arg` instructions is used to specify each argument in turn, then a `call` instruction specifies which function to call and where to put the result. For example, the VSL statement d := fn(a, b, c) would be translated as:

```
arg a
arg b
arg c
d := call fn
```

Returning results from a function is handled by the `return` instruction, which simply returns its argument as the function's value.

Representation of TAC

The obvious way to present a TAC instruction is as a struct with four fields:

```
struct tac
{
        int          op ;
        struct tacarg a ;
        struct tacarg b ;
        struct tacarg c ;
} ;
```

The individual instructions are represented as small integers in the op field. The arguments cannot be represented so simply. There are three possible types of argument—constants, names or labels. Of these, names can be of a number of types—variable names, function names, or compiler-generated temporary variable names. To handle all these we could use a pointer to a discriminated union:

```
struct tacarg
{
        int     disc ;
        union
        {
                int                const ;
                struct symbtab     name ;
                struct tac         *label ;
        }       data ;
} ;
```

The disc field identifies the type of argument. Constants are simply represented as integers and labels are pointers to TAC instructions. Names are identified by their symbol table entry, rather than just their textual representation. The symbol table is used to hold all the details of a variable name and is discussed in detail in the next chapter.

Discriminated unions do require extra space for the discriminant. If we are prepared to put constants and TAC labels in the symbol table, then we can just use symbol table entries for all TAC arguments:

```
struct tac
{
        int             op ;
        struct symbtab *a ;
        struct symbtab *b ;
        struct symbtab *c ;
} ;
```

It is up to the designer to choose which is more appropriate for a particular compiler.

To represent the complete body of TAC we could use an array of these structures, either declared explicitly:

```
struct tac  icode[10000] ;
```

or allocated dynamically with malloc(). A TAC label can then be just an index into this array.

As an example the following TAC would lead to the data structure shown in Fig. 4.5:

$$t_1 := a * b$$
$$t_2 := a * b$$
$$c := t_1 + t_2$$

TAC is conveniently generated using syntax-directed translation. Typical semantic rules might use a routine tacgen() to set up the TAC quadruples:

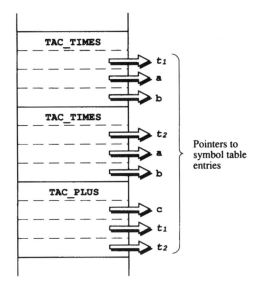

Figure 4.5 Part of a TAC array

```
void tacgen( int              op,
             struct symbtab *a,
             struct symbtab *b,
             struct symbtab *c )
{
        icode[pc].op = op ;
        icode[pc].a  = a ;
        icode[pc].b  = b ;
        icode[pc].c  = c ;

        pc++ ;
}
```

pc, an integer variable, is used to hold the index of the next available slot in the code array. When generating TAC we make use of an attribute *place* to hold the address where the result of a calculation has been put. So for example:

assignment_statement → *variable* := *expression*
    { tacgen(TAC_COPY, *variable.entry*, NULL,
    expression.place) ; }

The *entry* attribute used is the variable's symbol table entry. Note that using this approach we must have a depth-first left-to-right evaluation of semantic rules if the code is to be generated in the correct order.

A more flexible approach is to represent TAC not as a fixed array but as a linked list. To do this we add a field to the TAC data structure allowing TAC instructions to be linked together. Under these circumstances the destinations of TAC branches should be pointers to TAC instructions. This is the approach used in the VSL compiler described in Chapter 12.

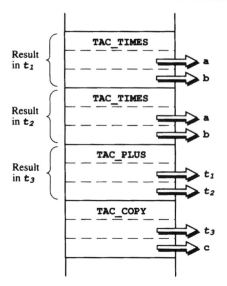

Figure 4.6 Triple representation of TAC

Other representations of TAC

This use of quadruples is not the only representation of TAC. One alternative is
to use only triples. This is achieved by omitting the result field. Results are
always put into a temporary variable with the name t_n, where n is the index of
the instruction in the TAC array. For example, to encode the TAC quadruple
example above as triples we should use:

$$
\begin{aligned}
t_1 &:= a \ * \ b \\
t_2 &:= a \ * \ b \\
t_3 &:= t_1 + t_2 \\
c &:= t_3
\end{aligned}
$$

For the first three statements, the destination is implied. The data structure is
shown in Fig. 4.6.

In general this saves space, although in the example above this was lost
because of the need to use an additional instruction. However, there is a key
disadvantage to this representation. In an optimizing compiler, we wish to
optimize the intermediate code by moving TAC instructions around, as is
discussed in Chapter 11. But when we move a TAC instruction using this triple
representation, the temporary variable into which the result goes is changed and
all references to it must also be changed.

A compromise is to use *indirect triples*. In this case we use triples to represent
the code, but have a separate array, giving the sequence in which these triples are
executed. This is shown for the example below in Fig. 4.7.

$$
\begin{aligned}
t_1 &:= a \ * \ b \\
t_2 &:= t_1 + t_1 \\
c &:= t_2
\end{aligned}
$$

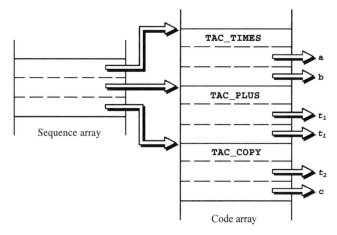

Figure 4.7   Indirect triple representation of TAC

This saves a little space over quadruples by sharing of common triples (as is the case in the example shown). However, a more important advantage is that moving code is a question of just changing an index in the sequence array, which is more efficient than changing complete quadruples.

These alternative representations are now of relatively little importance, since space savings of at most 25 per cent are not particularly significant in a modern compiler.

4.2   Abstract machines

Intermediate codes of the forms described in the previous section are clearly suited primarily to conveying information from syntax analyser to semantic analyser. They are not particularly suitable for direct interpretation, e.g. by a hybrid compiler/interpreter system, because they contain many unresolved references such as explicit function and variable names.

The term *abstract machine* in general refers to a representation much closer to a typical target machine, with variable references all converted to memory addresses and often with target machine features such as registers. Abstract machines are not usually used as an interface between syntax and semantic analysis, but as the output from general-purpose code generators. They are then either interpreted or go through a specialist code generator to produce code for a specific target machine. UCSD PCODE, an abstract machine for Pascal compilers, is an example of an interpreted code. VAM, the target machine throughout this book, is another such interpreted code. OCODE, produced by BCPL compilers, is an example of output from a general-purpose code generator that is intended for subsequent translation into a specific machine code. There are some abstract machines that serve both purposes, e.g. CINT-CODE for BCPL.

All such abstract machines have the same general design. They are very similar to typical real target machines. All semantic information must have been resolved—variable names turned into addresses and so on. In general, an interpreter for such machines is both small and fast.

Exercises

PRACTICAL PROBLEMS

4.1. Write semantic rules to translate VSL expressions into a tree intermediate representation. Make use of routines such as mknode() and mkvalnode().

4.2. Consider how you would modify the semantic rules of the previous question to generate a DAG.

4.3. What TAC might be generated for the VSL code:

```
FUNC main()
{
    VAR    i

    i := 10

    WHILE i
    DO
    {
        PRINT fac( i )
        i := i - 1
    }
    DONE
}

FUNC fac( n )
    IF n
    THEN
        RETURN n * fac( n - 1 )
    ELSE
        RETURN 1
    FI
```

4.4. Devise semantic rules for translation of the VSL WHILE statement into TAC. Use of attributes to hold labels marking the start and end of the loop would be appropriate.

ESSAY TITLES

4.1. Compare and contrast different intermediate representations used to convey information from the syntax analyser to the semantic analyser.

4.2. What use are abstract machines?

4.3. How might a C programmer implement three-address code as an intermediate representation used to convey information from the syntax analyser to the semantic analyser?

4.1. Investigate different abstract machines and compare their use.

4.2. Look at the use of quadruples in the IBM FORTRAN H Compiler.

Further reading

The best source of information on intermediate codes is to look at specific examples. OCODE, the intermediate code for BCPL is described by Richards (see the further reading section, Chapter 1). This is of particular interest, since OCODE is itself generated from a tree representation produced by the syntax analyser.

Quadruples used by the FORTRAN H Compiler are described in 'Object Code Optimization' by E. S. Lowry and C. W. Medlock, *Communications of the ACM*, **12**, 13–22 (1969).

5
Lexical analysis

Lexical analysis is the first of two stages in the analysis of the structure of a source program. In this chapter we consider why this division into two stages is appropriate, the data structures needed to support lexical analysis, and two methods of constructing lexical analysers. The first of these is a straight programming approach. The second makes use of finite state machines and is the basis of the LEX and FLEX lexical analyser generators described at the end of the chapter.

5.1 Why have a separate lexical analyser?

Why do we choose to separate the structural analysis into two stages, when the syntax of a programming language is a single grammar? The prime reasons are efficiency and clarity. The complete parse tree for a typical program has the characters making up the program at each leaf. However, this is not particularly helpful, and it is easier to think of the terminal symbols of the grammar as complete entities—such as integers, variable names, or complete keywords— rather than the individual characters of which they are made. For example, a VSL parse tree would have leaves such as `1729`, `loopvar`, and `WHILE`. Figure 5.1(a) shows part of a VSL parse tree for the expression `nel+496` with characters at its leaves. Figure 5.1(b) shows the same tree with characters grouped into simple entities.

The lexical analyser reads the individual characters of the source language, grouping them into basic entities or *tokens*. A block diagram showing the action of a lexical analyser is given in Figure 5.2. The lexical analyser takes as input source language, and produces as output a stream of tokens, the source language for the syntax analyser. In addition, the lexical analyser may produce error messages and diagnostic information. There are only a small number of tokens for any language, and they are conveniently represented by small integers. As an example the VSL statement:

```
a := b + 3
```

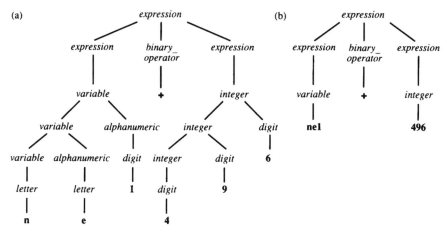

Figure 5.1   Parse tree with: (a) characters at nodes; (b) simple entities at nodes

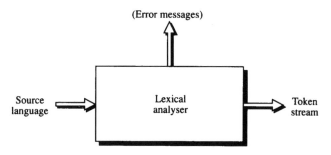

Figure 5.2   Block diagram of a lexical analyser

would yield the stream of tokens: variable, assignment symbol, variable, plus symbol, constant.

The pattern describing each token is often expressed informally, but it can always be expressed as a conventional type 3 grammar. For convenience, the formal specification may be as a type 2 grammar, which can be trivially converted to a (more verbose) type 3 grammar. For example, in VSL an integer is informally a sequence of one or more decimal digits, although it can be expressed formally as the type 3 grammar:

integer → **0** | **1** | **2** | **3** | **4** | **5** | **6** | **7** | **8** | **9** | *integer* **0** | *integer* **1** | *integer* **2** |
            integer **3** | *integer* **4** | *integer* **5** | *integer* **6** | *integer* **7** | *integer* **8** |
            integer **9**

For convenience this may be written as the trivially equivalent, but clearer type 2 grammar:

$$integer \rightarrow digit \mid integer\ digit$$

$$digit \quad \rightarrow \textbf{0} \mid \textbf{1} \mid \textbf{2} \mid \textbf{3} \mid \textbf{4} \mid \textbf{5} \mid \textbf{6} \mid \textbf{7} \mid \textbf{8} \mid \textbf{9}$$

Table 5.1   Some tokens, patterns, and lexemes

integer	a string of decimal digits	`1729,561,0`
variable	an alphanumeric string beginning with a letter	`loopvar,t1,x`
operator	one of '+', '−', '*', or '/'	`+,/`
VAR	the letters 'V', 'A', 'R'	`VAR`

Tokens are themselves general concepts such as *integer*. In carrying out lexical analysis we will read in particular instances of these tokens, such as `1729` or `561`. Such specific instances are called *lexemes*. For some tokens, such as those associated with a keyword, there will be only a single possible lexeme. A lexeme can be thought of as an attribute of the token. Table 5.1 shows some tokens, their patterns, and some example lexemes.

Most lexemes have a simple representation. For example, the lexeme associated with an integer is a number, and the lexeme associated with a text string a character array. Tokens such as keywords with a single lexeme need no explicit representation for the lexeme at all. The one awkward case is variable names. Invariably we will want to hold more information about a variable than just its textual representation. To do this we use a symbol table.

5.1.1   SYMBOL TABLES

The symbol table is used throughout a compiler to build up information about names used throughout the source program. At the lexical analyser stage it may hold no more information than the text of a variable's name. However, during syntax and semantic analysis, e.g. information about the variable's type and scope, will be added. In VSL, for example, names may be used both as variable names and function names, and we need to store this information at some stage. Similarly we may wish to store information about the block in which a variable was declared. Eventually during code generation we may wish to associate an address with a variable.

The symbol table may be used for information about symbols other than those explicitly declared. It may be useful to hold information about compiler-generated temporary variables, labels, and even constants.

Typically such data will be held in a C struct:

```
struct symbtab
{
        char *name ;
        int    type ;
        int    blockno ;
        int    addr ;
} ;
```

We could allow a fixed space for the name string, but this would be wasteful for the majority of variable names, which are short. Rather than using `malloc()`

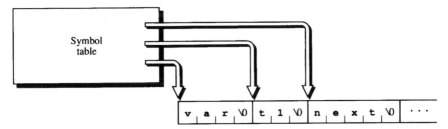

Figure 5.3   Allocation of string space for a symbol table

to allocate space for each string in turn, which would be slow, we allocate a single array for all strings at the start of compilation and carve it up as is required (see Fig. 5.3).

Throughout compilation we will need to be able to look up names in the symbol table, e.g. to check if variables have been declared. This must be done efficiently and so linear representations of the symbol table, e.g. as an array of structs or a linked list, are inappropriate. The natural data structure to use is a hash table, where the hash index is derived from the name. Open hash tables, in which names with the same hash index are linked in a list, are to be preferred, since the problem of the symbol table filling up is avoided. We therefore add a link field to our symbol table data structure:

```
struct symbtab
{
        struct symbtab *link ;
        char           *name ;
        int            type ;
        int            blockno ;
        int            addr ;
} ;
```

Part of such a hash table is shown in Fig. 5.4.

A little thought needs to be given to the hashing function. It is important that it uses all the information in the name. Functions that hash on only the first few characters will be caught out by programmers using a lot of variables such as temp1, temp2, temp3, temp4, etc. Relying too much on the length of the variable name is not wise—many programmers use a majority of single-character variable names. A simple function used in BCPL treats the length (up to 255 characters) and first three characters of the name as a single 32-bit integer and takes this value *mod* the size of the hash table as the hash value. Other authors have suggested shifting the bottom 4 bits of each character into a word and taking this value *mod* the size of the hash table. In all cases choosing the hash table size to be a prime number (as with any hash table) is sensible. The function used in the VSL compiler is as shown on the following page.

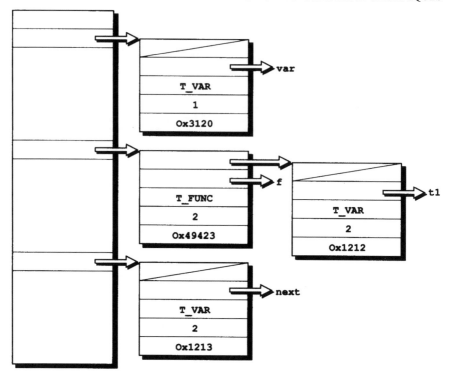

Figure 5.4   Symbol table implemented as an open hash table

```
#define HASHSIZE 997

int hash ( char *s )

{
        int   hv = 0 ;
        int   i ;

        for( i = 0 ; s[i] != EOS ; i++ )
        {
                int v = (hv >> 28)  ^ (s[i] & Oxf) ;

                hv = (hv << 4) | v ;
        }

        hv = hv & Ox7fffffff ;                  /* Ensure positive */
        return hv % HASHSIZE ;

}       /* int hash ( char *s ) */
```

This uses the bottom 4 bits of each character of the name and rotates them
into the hash value. It represents a good compromise between efficiency and
effectiveness.

The symbol table structure described above is typical of a compiler. In the VSL compiler described in Chapter 13 we use a rather simpler structure with just two data fields in addition to the link and type fields. These fields are implemented as a union for efficiency, their use being discriminated by the type field.

```
typedef struct symb                     /* Symbol table entry */
{
        struct symb *next ;             /* Next in chain */
        int         type ;              /* What is this symbol */
        union                           /* Primary value */
        {
                int         val ;       /* For integers */
                char        *text ;     /* For var names */
        } val1 ;
        union                           /* Secondary value */
        {
                int         val ;       /* For offsets etc */
                struct tac *label ;     /* For branches */
        } val2 ;
} SYMB ;
```

5.1.2 ADDITIONAL FUNCTIONS OF A LEXICAL ANALYSER

The lexical analyser is often a convenient place to carry out many administrative chores. The most common of these is stripping out comments and white space between tokens. Comments are often not even formally defined in the language grammar. Their use is often intuitively obvious, but including them in the grammar may at best make the grammar more verbose, and at worst may not be possible with a type 2 grammar. Individual symbols may be separated by arbitrary white space (i.e. spaces and tabs), which is also tedious to specify in a formal grammar.

In addition to stripping out comments as they are read in and handling white space separators, lexical analysers may do a certain amount of preprocessing, handling conditional compilation, macros, and the like. If this is at all complex, however, it is more likely to be carried out by a separate preprocessor, which filters the input before it reaches the lexical analyser.

5.1.3 EFFICIENCY CONSIDERATIONS IN LEXICAL ANALYSERS

Lexical analysis can be the most time-consuming part of a compiler's execution. This is primarily because it handles all the input. A prime consideration in separating lexical and syntax analysis is that effort can be put into handling input/output (I/O) effectively. Because lexical analysis reads input a character at a time, it is essential that buffering is used. In our examples with C we use the routine getchar() which under Unix is a buffered I/O routine. With different operating systems it may be necessary to provide explicit buffering within the lexical analyser.

There is a further efficiency gain to be had by separating lexical and syntax analysis. Tokens can invariably be described using type 3 grammars. These are inherently easier and hence quicker to parse than type 2 grammars. We

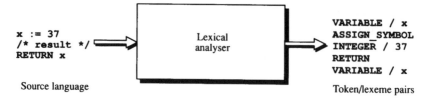

Figure 5.5 Action of a lexical analyser

now give examples of two different ways of constructing efficient lexical analysers.

5.2 *Ad hoc* lexical analysers

Lexical analysers are often sufficiently simple that they can be written straight down as a C program. Such a lexical analyser consists of a loop containing a single switch statement, which decides what the next token being read in is by looking at the next character. It takes as input the source text and produces as output a list of token/lexeme pairs. The block diagram is shown in Fig. 5.5.

A variant is to implement the lexical analyser as a subroutine, which when called from the syntax analyser returns the next token/lexeme pair from the source program. An example of the design of such a lexical analyser for VSL is given below.

5.2.1 AN *AD HOC* LEXICAL ANALYSER FOR VSL

Tokens are conveniently represented by small integers. We use a global variable, ch, to hold the next source program character to be analysed. We must be consistent in our use of ch, it is all too easy for it to become the character just analysed, leading to bugs in which characters are lost or duplicated. Our lexical analyser is an integer-valued function, yylex() which returns the next token from the source program. We use a global variable to hold the associated lexeme. Since this may be an integer or a text string we define two global variables, yylval and yytext, to hold integer and character arrays, respectively. The rather bizarre names of these variables is historical, but matches the equivalent names used by the LEX lexical analyser generator described in the following section. The header for our *ad hoc* lexical analyser might look something like:

```
#define  T_BRA       '('   /* Single char tokens */
#define  T_KET       ')'
#define  T_COMMA     ','
#define  T_ASSIGN    256   /* Multi char tokens */

#define  T_FUNC      257   /* Reserved words */
#define  T_PRINT     258
#define  T_RETURN    259
#define  T_VARIABLE  268   /* Complex tokens */
#define  T_INTEGER   269
```

```
#define   T_TEXT       270
#define   T_EOF        271   /* End of file */
#define   T_UNKNOWN    272   /* Unknown token */

int       ch ;                /* Next char */
int       yylval ;            /* Integer lexeme */
char      yytext[255] ;       /* Textual lexeme */
```

Note how we represent single character tokens by their ASCII value, using integers above 255 for multi-character tokens. The token T_UNKNOWN is returned if the lexical analyser fails to recognize a character sequence as a valid token.

Before compilation a certain amount of setting up that is specific to the lexical analyser needs to be done. A key part of this is the setting up of a look-up table for the reserved words. A simple hash table will suffice. In addition we need to initialize ch.

This initialization might look something like:

```
void lex_init ()
{
       /* Set up the lookup table */

       clear_reserved () ;

       add_reserved( T_FUNC,     "FUNC" ) ;
       add_reserved( T_PRINT,    "PRINT" ) ;
       add_reserved( T_RETURN,   "RETURN" ) ;

       . . .

       ch = getchar () ;

}      /* init_lex() */
```

This assumes the existence of three functions with which to handle the look-up table: clear_reserved() sets up an empty hash table; add_reserved (t, str) adds token t whose character string is str to the table; lookup_reserved (str) returns the token corresponding to the given string if it is a reserved word or else returns T_UNKNOWN if the string is not a reserved word.

We can now build the outline of our main routine, yylex():

```
int  yylex()
{
       switch( ch )
       {
                . . .
       /* cases for each different token */
                . . .
       }

}      /* yylex() */
```

The code with each case must ensure that `ch` is left pointing to the next character to be analysed and that `yylval` and `yytext` are set up as appropriate. We now look at one or two of the cases that have to be handled. White space is skipped and then `yylex()` called recursively to return a token. Comments are introduced by `//` and if we see this we must read through until we find newline and then use a recursive call to `yylex()` to return a token. However, in skipping comments we must look first for a `/` and then a second `/`. If we do not find a `/` then we did not have a comment, so the `/` must be returned as the token `T_DIVIDE` without reading a further character (since `ch` now holds the character after the first `/`):

```
case ' ':
case '\n':
case '\t':

        while( isspace( ch = getchar()))
                ;
        return yylex() ;

case '/':

        ch = getchar() ;

        if( ch != '/' )
                return T_DIVIDE ;

        . . .
        /* code to skip a comment */
        . . .
```

Single-character tokens are just passed through as themselves. The multiple character token `:=` must be checked for. Capital letters introduce a reserved word (all variables in VSL are in lower case). We read the characters into `yytext` and then look it up. In all these cases there is only a single possible lexeme and we need not set `yylval` or `yytext`:

```
case '(':
case ')':
case ',':
        . . .
        yylval = ch ;
        ch     = getchar() ;
        return yylval ;

case ':':

        if((ch = getchar()) != '=')
                return T_UNKNOWN ;

        ch = getchar() ;
        return T_ASSIGN ;
case 'A':
case 'B':
case 'C':
        . . .

        yytext[0] = ch ;
```

```
for( i = 0 ; isupper(ch = getchar()) ; yytext[i++] = ch )
        ;

yytext[i++] = EOS ;

return lookup_reserved( yytext ) ;
```

Similar code is used to read in a variable name, introduced by a lower-case letter or a text string introduced by *' '*. Integers are introduced by a digit and read in, building up the number in yylval. Finally EOF (end of file) must be recognized. Any other character will then be unexpected and we can return T_UNKNOWN, having saved the offending character in yylval and called getchar() to get the next character:

```
case '0':
case '1':
       . . .
       yylval = ch - '0' ;

       while( isdigit( ch = getchar())
               yylval = yylval * 10 + ch - '0' ;

       return T_INTEGER ;

case EOF:

       return T_EOF ;

default:

       yylval = ch ;
       ch = getchar() ;
       return T_UNKNOWN ;
}
```

5.3 Lexical analysis with finite state machines

The languages generated by type 3 grammars can always be recognized by a *finite state machine (FSM)*, sometimes also called a *finite automaton (FSA)*. That is to say, for any type 3 grammar we can build a finite state machine, which given a string as input will tell us whether that string is a sentence of the grammar.

What are finite state machines?

5.3.1 FINITE STATE MACHINES

A finite state machine consists of a number of *states* controlling its operation, together with rules for moving from one state to another. It takes as input a string of symbols and produces outputs giving information about the input string. An example will make this clear. Figure 5.6 shows a finite state machine to recognize VSL variable names. The machine starts off in state 0, its *initial state*, and under the guidance of successive characters in the input string moves from state to state following the appropriately labelled arrows between states. If

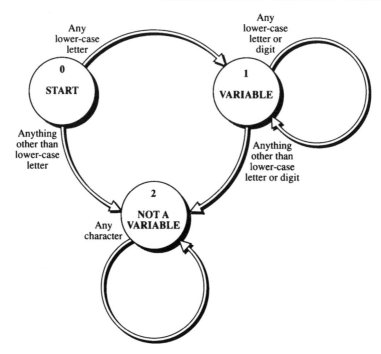

Figure 5.6 A finite state machine to recognize VSL variables

it ends up in state 1 it has recognized a VSL variable name, i.e. a lower-case letter followed by a number of lower-case letters and digits. If it ends up in state 2 it has failed to recognize a valid variable name. For example, consider the string v10. The character v moves the machine to state 1, following the arrow from state 0 labelled 'Any lower-case letter'. This is what we want, since v is a valid variable name. The character 1 keeps the machine in state 1 (v1 is also a valid variable name) and the character 0 keeps the machine in state 1 (v10 is yet another valid variable name). By comparison, the string VAR would move the machine straight to state 2 since V is not a lower-case letter. This again is what we want, since none of V, VA, or VAR are valid VSL variable names.

Finite state machines are easily represented in C by a two-dimensional *transition array* of state against character, with the new state as entry. For each state we also have an *output array*. So for Fig. 5.6 the transition array would be:

```
int trans[][] =
      {{ 2, 2, 2 },    /* '^@' */
       { 2, 2, 2 },    /* '^A' */
        . . .
       { 2, 1, 2 },    /* '0' */
       { 2, 1, 2 },    /* '1' */
        . . .
       { 1, 1, 2 },    /* 'a' */
       { 1, 1, 2 },    /* 'b' */
       { . . .  }} ;
```

and the output array would be:

```
int  output[] = { T_UNKNOWN, T_VARIABLE, T_UNKNOWN } ;
```

The code using the finite state machine is then:

```
state = 0 ;  /* Initial state */

for( ; ; )
{
        state = trans[ch][state] ;
        printf( "%d", output[state] ) ;
        ch    = getchar() ;
}
```

We can use finite state machines in lexical analysers by using the source program as input string and emitting tokens as output. We need one finite state machine for each token to be recognized, and conceptually we need to run them in parallel on the same input. However, we can always construct an equivalent single finite state machine that will recognize the same set of tokens as the group of finite state machines running in parallel. Figure 5.7(a) shows the FSM to recognize a VSL variable name and Fig. 5.7(b) shows the FSM to recognize a VSL integer. Figure 5.7(c) is a single FSM to recognize both variable names and integers.

Building the tables to drive a FSM to do lexical analysis for a complete computer language by hand would be extremely tedious. Instead we use tools to construct automatically a finite state machine from descriptions of all the tokens involved.

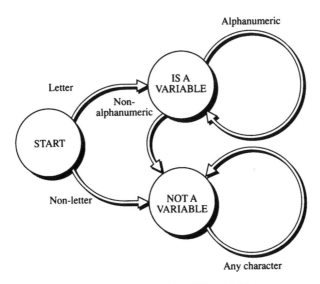

Figure 5.7(a) FSM for VSL variables

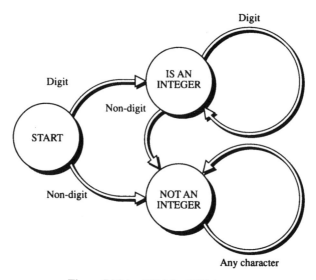

Figure 5.7(b)   FSM for VSL integers

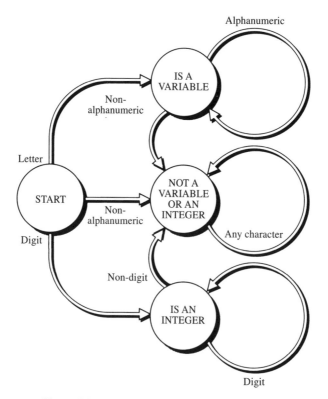

Figure 5.7(c)   FSM for VSL integers and variables

Table 5.2   The basic operations

Concatenation	x y	The pattern consists of x followed by y
Alternation	x | y	The pattern consists of either x or y
Arbitrary repetition	x *	The pattern consists of the string x repeated zero or more times

5.3.2 TOOLS FOR BUILDING LEXICAL ANALYSERS

LEX is a lexical analyser generator widely available under the Unix operating system. From a description of the grammars for tokens it generates transition and output tables for a FSM and a driving program in C.

FLEX is an alternative to LEX freely available from the Free Software Foundation, which runs on PCs as well as Unix. It offers a few minor extensions to, and variations from LEX, and often generates faster parsers, but is otherwise the same. It can be made to mimic LEX fairly closely by use of the -l flag.

In this book all the examples show the use of LEX, but FLEX can be freely substituted throughout.

The conventional BNF form for grammars is not particularly compact. Instead LEX uses *regular expressions* to describe the syntax of each token. This is an alternative way of describing the set of sentences that make up the grammar. Regular expressions make use of three basic operations as shown in Table 5.2.

Bracketing is used for grouping. So, for example, the pattern:

(0 | 1 | 2 | 3 | 4 | 5 | 6 | 7 | 8 | 9) (0 | 1 | 2 | 3 | 4 | 5 | 6 | 7 | 8 | 9)*

(a digit followed by zero or more digits) recognizes VSL integers.

Regular expressions are exactly equivalent to type 3 grammars (hence the name regular grammar). Any type 3 language may be described by a regular expression and vice versa. Thus regular expressions can be recognized by finite state machines. Regular expressions have the advantage of compactness and being easily understood. A number of extensions to the basic notation are used by LEX as shown in Table 5.3. A number of other practical extensions are needed to deal with expressions involving characters such as * that have a specific meaning. These are shown in Table 5.4.

A LEX program has the general form

Definitions
%%
Rules
%%
User subroutines written in C

After processing with LEX this will produce a C program, defining an integer-valued routine called yylex() which when called will return the next token from the input.

Table 5.3 The extensions to the basic notation that are used by LEX

Character classes	[0-9]	This means alternation of the characters in the range listed, in this case $0\|1\|2\|3\|4\|5\|6\|7\|8\|9$. More than one range may be specified, e.g. alphanumeric characters would be [0-9A-Za-z]
Not operator	^	The first character in a character class may be ^ to indicate the complement of the set of characters specified. Thus [^0-9] matches any non-digit
Arbitrary character	.	The period matches any single character except newline
Single repetition	x?	This means zero or one occurrence of x
Non-zero repetition	x+	This means x repeated one or more times. Thus it is equivalent to xx*
Specified repetition	x{n,m}	This means x repeated between n and m times
Beginning of line	^x	Match x at the beginning of line only
End of line	x$	Match x at the end of a line only
Context sensitivity	ab/cd	Match ab, but only when followed by cd

Table 5.4 Extensions to the notation that involve characters with a specific meaning

Literal strings	"x"	This means x even if x would normally have a special meaning. Thus "b*" may be used to match b followed by an asterisk. This is also useful for including space characters
Literal characters	\x	Where x is an operator means x itself. Thus b* could also be used to match b followed by an asterisk. For non-operators, these escapes have their usual C meaning, \n for newline, \t for tab, and so on
Definitions	{varname}	Subpatterns may be defined. This means substitute the predefined pattern called varname

LEX definitions

The definitions section allows us to predefine strings that will prove useful in the rules section. For example, the VSL lexical analyser includes the following definitions:

```
comment        "//".*
delimiter      [ \t\n]
whitespace     {delimiter}+
uc_letter      [A-Z]
lc_letter      [a-z]
letter         {lc_letter}|{uc_letter}
ascii_char     [^\"\n]
escaped_char   \\n|\\\"
digit          [0-9]
variable       {lc_letter} ({lc_letter}|{digit})*
integer        {digit}+
text           \"({ascii_char}|{escaped_char})*\"
```

Each definition consists of a name being defined on the left and its definition on the right. Thus we define a comment as being // (quoted because of their special meaning otherwise) followed by an arbitrary number of characters other than newline. A delimiter character is a space, tab, or newline and whitespace is one or more delimiters. Note how the definition of whitespace uses the earlier definition of a delimiter.

LEX rules

The rules section is where we define the patterns corresponding to each token. The VSL lexical analyser includes the following rules:

```
{whitespace}    {                               }
{comment}       {                               }
{variable}      { mkname() ;
                  return VARIABLE ;             }
{integer}       { mkval() ;
                  return INTEGER ;              }
{text}          { mktext() ;
                  return TEXT ;                 }
":="            { return ASSIGN_SYMBOL ;        }
FUNC            { return FUNC ;                 }
PRINT           { return PRINT ;                }
RETURN          { return RETURN ;               }
CONTINUE        { return CONTINUE ;             }
IF              { return IF ;                   }
THEN            { return THEN ;                 }
ELSE            { return ELSE ;                 }
FI              { return FI ;                   }
WHILE           { return WHILE ;                }
DO              { return DO ;                   }
DONE            { return DONE ;                 }
VAR             { return VAR ;                  }
.               { return yytext [0] ;           }
```

Rules consist of a pattern to match, followed by some C code to obey if that match succeeds. The simplest option is to do nothing, as is the case with whitespace or a comment. The input is merely discarded and LEX tries to match something against the new input. Note the use of the predefined pattern for whitespace and comment. For a variable we call a routine, mkname(), to save the variable name in the symbol table. LEX holds the lexeme just matched in the array yytext. mkname() can use this information to save the name in the symbol table if appropriate. We then return the token T_VARIABLE from this routine. Similarly, the routine mkval() will convert the string in yytext into an integer in yylval when recognizing an integer and yytext() is used for text strings. We then see the use of explicit pattern matches for the assignment symbol := and the reserved keywords. Finally, we use a single-character match to pick up any single characters and return them as tokens (which will be in the range 0–225). We do not do any error checking here, leaving it to the syntax analyser to decide the validity of tokens.

User subroutines

This is where we might have included the subsidiary routines, mkname(), mkval(), and mktext(). This section is used for any subsidiary code that the user needs.

Ambiguity in LEX

LEX does not worry about ambiguity. It will always select the longest possible match. If two matches are the same length, the first is used. This is why we could use a single-character match to pick up any unknown characters at the end of our list of rules. All other valid tokens are longer and would have been picked up earlier. The fact that the longest match is used means that the pattern for a comment:

"//".*

will match from // right to the end of the line.

The full LEX source for the VSL lexical analyser is given in Chapter 13 (Section 13.2.3). Now is a good time to take a look at this program.

Exercises

PRACTICAL PROBLEMS

5.1. Code up various hashing functions for an open hash table and compare their effectiveness by compiling a histogram of hash chain lengths. Consider their performance with the following sets of variables:
(a) 100 random alphanumeric strings of up to 10 characters.
(b) 100 random alphanumeric strings of exactly 6 characters.
(c) 100 strings of the form variable0, variable1, variable2, ..., variable99.
5.2. Code up the *ad hoc* lexical analyser for VSL, and test its performance.
5.3. Compare the performance of the LEX lexical analyser for VSL with the *ad hoc* version.

ESSAY TITLES

5.1. Why separate lexical and syntactic analysis in a compiler?
5.2. Compare and contrast hand-coded lexical analysers with those generated using LEX.
5.3. What are the key elements of a LEX program?

DISCUSSION TOPICS

5.1. Investigate the algorithm for combining a number of finite state machines running in parallel into a single FSM.
5.2. Investigate some of the additional features of LEX not covered in this book.

Further reading

There is relatively little more to be said on *ad hoc* lexical analysers. Symbol tables can become very complex if they have to deal with different scoping rules for different languages. They are a subject best studied by practical example.

LEX is described in all Unix manuals. Its description is also available as 'Lex—A Lexical Analyzer Generator' by M. E. Lesk, Computer Science Technical Report 39, AT&T Bell Laboratories, Murray Hill, NJ, USA.

The standard distribution of FLEX comes with its own manual. Details of how to obtain FLEX are given in Appendix B.

Regular expressions and finite state machines have been much studied by Kleene, as described in *Automata Studies* by C. Shannon and J. McCarthy, published by Princeton University Press, USA (1956). Any textbook on computation theory will cover this. A particularly useful text is *Computation Finite and Infinite Machines* by M. L. Minsky, published by Prentice Hall (1967).

6
Syntax analysis methods

During syntax analysis we determine whether the stream of tokens from the lexical analyser form a valid sentence in our programming language grammar. If so, we must unambiguously derive its parse tree. Many different approaches to this problem exist, and in this chapter we concentrate on the two most widely used.

6.1 Approaches to parsing

There are two obvious ways of building up a parse tree. One is to start with the sentence symbol and build down towards the terminals; the other is to start at the terminals and build up towards the sentence symbol. These are known as *top-down* and *bottom-up* parsing methods respectively. Figure 6.1(a) shows a top-down parse and Figure 6.1(b) a bottom-up parse of the VSL phrase, 2+2.

Many algorithms based on these two approaches are known. Algorithms exist to parse any type 2 language, but efficient parsers exist only for subsets of type 2. Fortunately most programming language grammars fall into one of these subsets and can thus be parsed efficiently. In Sec. 6.2 we look at the most commonly used top-down method and its derivatives. In Sec. 6.3 we look at the most commonly used bottom-up method and an alternative which is also in widespread use.

6.1.1 CRITERIA FOR AN EFFECTIVE PARSING ALGORITHM

The primary criterion for a parsing algorithm is that it must be efficient. In general we want algorithms whose parsing time is proportional to the size of the program parsed.

A second criterion related to efficiency is that a parser should be able to determine its action by considering only a fixed number of tokens, k, ahead in the token stream. It is inefficient to have to allow for arbitrary lookahead. Practical parsing methods use only a single token lookahead, i.e. $k = 1$.

An important practical criterion is that a parser should not backtrack. At all stages it should operate deterministically. A number of authors have described

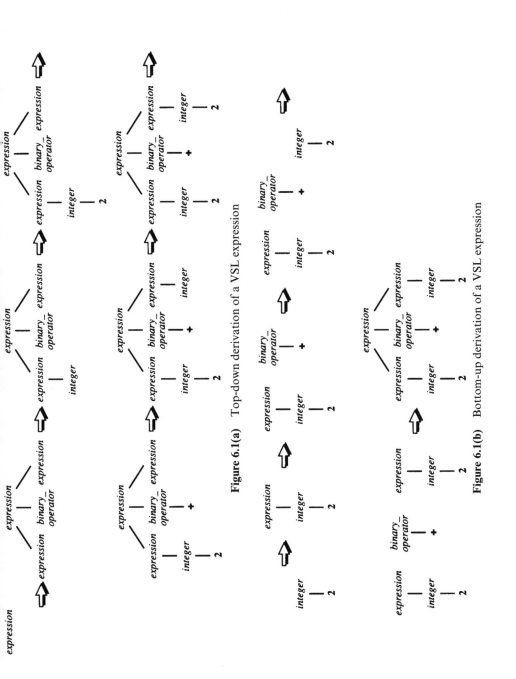

Figure 6.1(a) Top-down derivation of a VSL expression

Figure 6.1(b) Bottom-up derivation of a VSL expression

81

backtracking parsers, but these are rarely used in practice. It is difficult to undo semantic actions carried out by the parser as is necessary if it has to backtrack.

In the past it was important that parsers were small, because of the small size of machine memories. This is now less important, and some parsing methods may use tables occupying many hundreds of kilobytes. In cases where memory is limited this may restrict the compiler writer in his or her choice of parsing method.

The bottom line is that the parsing method must be powerful enough for the language being parsed. Different methods parse different subsets of type 2 grammars. If a parser is not suitable for the grammar under consideration, then either a different parser must be used, or the grammar must be rewritten.

6.1.2 CLASSIFICATION OF PARSING METHODS

A common way of classifying parsing methods is by the type of derivation (left-most or right-most) they give and the number of tokens lookahead they require. In addition, we specify the direction in which we read the source language. Although with most computers it is only convenient to read from left to right (reading files backwards is not usually done efficiently), there is no theoretical reason why we should not have parsers that use right-to-left reading. So, for example, we talk of an LR(1) parser to mean a parser in which we read the source from the left (the L), produce a right-most derivation (the R) and require at most one token lookahead during parsing (the 1). We describe a grammar that can be parsed by an LR(1) parser as an LR(1) grammar.

6.2   Top-down parsing methods

In this section we consider in detail a widely used LL(1) parsing method, *predictive recursive descent*. By predictive we mean that we need no back-tracking—we can always tell which bit of the parse tree to construct next by looking at the next token in the input. In the following description we shall refer loosely to recursive descent meaning specifically predictive recursive descent.

Recursive descent involves writing a small C routine for each non-terminal in the grammar. We will also introduce a variant method, *table-driven, top-down parsing*, in which all the information for parsing is contained in a single table. This is not so suitable for hand coding, but is appropriate for parser generators that can generate the table from the grammar.

Both these top-down methods are unable to handle left recursive grammars, something that occurs in most programming language grammars. In the next section on bottom-up parsing we discuss the use of *operator precedence parsing*, which is often combined with recursive descent to solve this problem.

6.2.1   RECURSIVE DESCENT PARSING

In top-down parsing we recognize non-terminals in turn, starting with the sentence symbol, to form the parse tree. A recursive descent parser is constructed by writing routines to recognize each non-terminal in turn, calling other routines to recognize other non-terminals. We start with the sentence symbol. In VSL this is defined by the production:

$$program \rightarrow function\_list$$

The corresponding C routine would be

```
void program()
{
        function_list() ;

}       /* program() */
```

This is trivial, but for productions with more than one symbol on the right-hand side we must call routines to recognize them in turn. If there is a terminal symbol, we must check that it matches the next token in the source program. We use a global variable, nextsymb, to hold the next token in the source program. Having verified that the token is correct, we must call yylex() to obtain the next token in the input stream. So, for example, the production:

$$function \rightarrow \textbf{FUNC}\ variable\ (\ parameter\_list\ )\ statement$$

would be implemented as:

```
void function()
{
        if( nextsymb != T_FUNC )
        {
                printf( "syntax error\n" ) ;
                exit( 0 ) ;
        }
        else
                nextsymb = yylex() ;

        variable() ;

        if( nextsymb != '(' )
        {
                printf( "syntax error\n" ) ;
                exit( 0 ) ;
        }
        else
                nextsymb = yylex() ;

        parameter_list() ;

        if( nextsymb != ')' )
        {
                printf( "syntax error\n" ) ;
                exit( 0 ) ;
        }
        else
                nextsymb = yylex() ;

        statement() ;

}       /* function() */
```

If we do not find the appropriate tokens in the correct places we must have a syntax error. In this example we just print out an error message and stop, but a real parser would attempt to be more informative in its error messages and try to recover. Statements to check that tokens are correct clutter up the program. For clarity we define a small routine to do this:

```
void checkfor( int token )
{
        if( token != nextsymb )
        {
                printf( "Syntax Error\n" ) ;
                exit( 0 ) ;
        }
        else
                nextsymb = yylex() ;

}       /* checkfor( int token ) */
```

Our routine to recognize a function then becomes:

```
void  function()
{
        checkfor( T_FUNC ) ;
        variable() ;
        checkfor( '(' ) ;
        parameter_list() ;
        checkfor( ')' ) ;
        statement() ;

}       /* function() */
```

We thus build up a collection of routines to recognize all the parts of the grammar. We run the parser by calling the routine to recognize the sentence symbol, in this case program(). This will call routines for each part of the parse tree, until at the leaves routines (such as function() above) read the individual tokens. In this way we read in and parse the complete source program.

Two problems need to be resolved: how to deal with alternatives and how to handle recursion.

Alternatives

An *if_statement* in VSL is defined by the productions:

> *if_statement* → **IF** *expression* **THEN** *statement* **FI** |
> **IF** *expression* **THEN** *statement* **ELSE** *statement* **FI**

When we come to the routine to recognize an *if_statement* we need to decide which alternative to recognize. This is not immediately possible. The next token on the input should be **IF** in both cases and so this cannot be used to decide between the expansions. However, we note that left factoring is possible:

if_statement → **IF** *expression* **THEN** *statement if_right_part*

if_right_part → **FI** |
               ELSE *statement* **FI**

We have deferred the decision until we come to the right part of the *if_statement*. At this stage we are presented with two easily distinguished alternatives. If the next token is **FI** then we must use the first production for *if_right_part*, otherwise we check that the next token is **ELSE** and use the second production. This illustrates a key principle of LL(1) recursive descent. It must always be possible to distinguish between alternatives purely by looking at the next source token. Note that we only look at the next token, we do not call yylex() at this stage to read past the token. We are looking ahead a single token, hence the 1 in LL(1). The routines would be coded as:

```
void   if_statement()
{
        checkfor( T_IF ) ;
        expression() ;
        checkfor( T_THEN ) ;
        statement() ;
        if_right_part() ;

}      /* if_statement() */

void   if_right_part()
{
        if( nextsymb = T_FI )

                /* First production */

                nextsymb = yylex() ;

        else
        {
                /* Second production */

                checkfor( T_ELSE ) ;
                statement() ;
                checkfor( T_FI ) ;
        }

}      /* if_right_part() */
```

There is no real need for if_right_part() to be a separate routine, since it is not called from anywhere else. We should combine the two routines as:

```
void   if_statement()
{
        checkfor( T_IF ) ;
        expression() ;
        checkfor( T_THEN ) ;
        statement() ;

        if( nextsymb = T_FI )

                /* First production */

                nextsymb = yylex() ;
```

```
        else
        {
                /* Second production */

                checkfor( T_ELSE ) ;
                statement() ;
                checkfor( T_FI ) ;
        }

}       /* if_statement() */
```

It is good practice to combine routines like this where a non-terminal appears on the right of only one production.

Not all alternatives are quite so easy to sort out as this. How, for example, do we code up the routine to recognize:

$$statement \rightarrow assignment\_statement \mid return\_statement \mid$$
$$print\_statement \mid null\_statement \mid$$
$$if\_statement \mid while\_statement \mid block$$

This is only going to be possible if the tokens that could start an *assignment_statement, return_statement, print_statement, null_statement, if_statement, while_statement,* or *block* are all different. In this case it is true. Inspection of the grammar shows us that an *assignment_statement* must begin with a variable, a *return_statement* with **RETURN**, a *print_statement* with **PRINT**, a *null_statement* with **CONTINUE**, an *if_statement* with **IF**, a *while_statement* with **WHILE** and a *block* with {. We can distinguish which choice by looking at the next token. This is a single token lookahead—we do not call yylex() to read past the token.

We can formalize this identification of the terminal symbols that could start the right-hand side of a production. We define the *left terminal set* of a sequence of symbols, $\bar{u}$, written as $\mathbb{L}_T(\bar{u})$ to be the set of terminals which start all the sequences of symbols derivable from $\bar{u}$. This is conveniently defined in a recursive fashion. Suppose $\bar{u}$ has the form:

$$X_1 X_2 \cdots X_n$$

If X_1 is a terminal, then add X_1 to $\mathbb{L}_T(\bar{u})$, otherwise add $\mathbb{L}_T(X_1)$ to $\mathbb{L}_T(\bar{u})$. This is not quite sufficient, because, for example, if there is a derivation of X_1 that could give the null symbol, ε, then we must consider the terminals that could start X_2. Thus for each $i(i = 2, \ldots, n)$ such that each $X_k(k = 1, \ldots, i - 1)$ has a derivation $X_k \Rightarrow \varepsilon$ we add $\mathbb{L}_T(X_i)$ to $\mathbb{L}_T(\bar{u})$. If X_i could derive ε for all $i(i = 1, \ldots, n)$ then we add ε to $\mathbb{L}_T(\bar{u})$.

As an example consider constructing $\mathbb{L}_T(assignment\_statement)$ in VSL. *assignment_statement* is a non-terminal and so we must add the left terminal sets of its derivations, in this case only one, $\mathbb{L}_T(variable := expression)$. The first symbol in this is a terminal (it is a token returned by the lexical analyser) and so we add it to $\mathbb{L}_T(assignment\_statement)$. This completes the process and so we can say that $\mathbb{L}_T(assignment\_statement)$ is {*variable*}.

Given a production with a number of alternatives:

$$A \rightarrow \bar{u}_1 \mid \bar{u}_2 \mid \cdots$$

We can write a recursive descent routine only if all the sets $\mathbb{L}_T(\bar{u}_i)$ are disjoint. The general form of such a routine will be:

```
void  A()
{
        switch( nextsymb )
        {
        case Lт(ū1) :
                /* routines to recognise ū1  */
                return ;

        case Lт(ū2) :
                /* routines to recognise ū2  */
                return ;

                /* etc. */

        default:

                printf( "Syntax error\n" ) ;
                exit( 0 ) ;
        }

}       /* A() */
```

If we discover that the left terminal sets are not disjoint, then we cannot use recursive descent to parse the grammar as it stands. We must either rewrite the language grammar or use a different parsing method, at least for this non-terminal.

If one of the left terminal sets contains ε, then we may have a problem. In this case A could be replaced by nothing at all and the next token would be the first token of the symbol following A in the sentence being parsed. To deal with this we introduce the *lookahead set* or *follow set* of A, $\mathbb{F}_T(A)$. This is the set of terminal symbols which can start symbols that could follow A. We compute this as follows:

- Put EOF in $\mathbb{F}_T(S)$ where S is the sentence symbol.
- If there is a production $B \rightarrow \bar{w}A\bar{z}$, add everything except ε in $\mathbb{L}_T(\bar{z})$ to $\mathbb{F}_T(A)$.
- If there is a production $B \rightarrow \bar{w}A$ or $B \rightarrow \bar{w}A\bar{z}$ where $\bar{z} \Rightarrow \varepsilon$, then add everything in $\mathbb{F}_T(B)$ to $\mathbb{F}_T(A)$.

For example, we compute $\mathbb{F}_T(statement)$ in VSL as follows. *statement* appears followed by other symbols in the right-hand side of productions for *if_statement* and *while_statement*. We therefore add $\mathbb{L}_T(\textbf{FI})$, $\mathbb{L}_T(\textbf{ELSE})$, and $\mathbb{L}_T(\textbf{DONE})$ to $\mathbb{F}_T(statement)$. None of these contain ε so this part is complete. *statement* also appears at the right-hand end of productions for *statement_list* and *function*. We therefore add $\mathbb{F}_T(statement\_list)$ and $\mathbb{F}_T(function)$. $\mathbb{F}_T(statement\_list)$ yields the set $\{\}$. *function* itself appears at the right-hand end of a production for *function_list* and so we add $\mathbb{F}_T(function\_list)$. This in turn gives $\mathbb{F}_T(program)$, which is the sentence symbol, and so we add **EOF** to $\mathbb{F}_T(statement)$. The complete follow set is therefore {**FI, ELSE, DONE,**}, **EOF**}.

We can now generalize our handling of recursive descent for the production

$$A \rightarrow \bar{u}_1 \mid \bar{u}_2 \mid \cdots$$

If there is a derivation from $\bar{u}_i$ that could yield ε then we must distinguish that case by using $\mathbb{L}_T(\bar{u}_i) \cup \mathbb{F}_T(A)$. That is:

```
void  A()
{
        switch( nextsymb )
        {
        case 𝕃_T(ū_1) :
                /* routines to recognise ū_1  */
                return ;

        case 𝕃_T(ū_2) :
                /* routines to recognise ū_2  */
                return ;

                /* etc. */

        case 𝕃_T(ū_i) ∪𝔽_T(A) :
                /* routines to recognise ū_i  */
                return ;

                /* etc. */

        default:

                printf( "Syntax error\n" ) ;
                exit( 0 ) ;
        }

}       /* A() */
```

It is clear that at most we can have one case where $\bar{u}_i \Rightarrow \varepsilon$.

Recursion

Most recursion causes no problem with recursive descent (hence the name). For example, when parsing an *if_statement*, we call the routine to parse a *statement*, which in turn might call recursively the routine to parse an *if_statement*. Parsing of a VSL routine such as:

```
FUNC main()
{
        VAR  a, b, c

        a := f1()
        b := f2()
```

```
IF a
THEN
    IF b
    THEN
            c := 1
    ELSE
            c := 0
    FI
  FI
}
```

could cause such behaviour.

Left recursive productions, however, cause trouble. Consider the production for a *function_list* in VSL:

$$function\_list \rightarrow function \mid function\_list\ function$$

This cannot be parsed since the left terminal sets are not disjoint. $\mathbb{L}_T(function\_list)$ must include $\mathbb{L}_T(function)$. Indeed any left recursive production:

$$A \rightarrow \bar{u} \mid A\bar{v}$$

is not parsable because $\mathbb{L}_T(A\bar{v})$ must include $\mathbb{L}_T(\bar{u})$ or if $\bar{u} \Rightarrow \varepsilon$ then both $\mathbb{F}_T(A)$ and $\mathbb{L}_T(A\bar{v})$ must include $\mathbb{L}_T(\bar{v})$.

We can be more general about this, since there are other forms of recursion that can cause trouble. We cannot have any production where the routine to recognize the production could recurse without having consumed any source tokens, i.e. without having called `yylex()`. Such a routine could get into a recursive loop. In general we must exclude productions of the general form:

$$A \rightarrow X_1 X_2 \cdots X_n$$

Where there is some X_i with a derivation $X_i \Rightarrow A\bar{u}$ and each $X_k, k = 1, \ldots, i - 1$ has a derivation $X_k \Rightarrow \varepsilon$.

If we have a grammar with left recursion it cannot be parsed using recursive descent without being rewritten using the techniques of Chapter 3. For example, we might rewrite the production for a *function_list* in VSL as:

$$function\_list \rightarrow function \mid function\ function\_list$$

This is now right recursive and suitable for parsing with recursive descent.

A key point to remember with rewriting is that it changes the structure of the parse tree, which may be carrying semantic information. For example, the unambiguous grammar for VSL expressions is left recursive:

$$
\begin{aligned}
expression &\rightarrow expression\ term\_operator\ term \mid term \\
term\_operator &\rightarrow + \mid - \\
term &\rightarrow term\ factor\_operator\ factor \mid factor \\
factor\_operator &\rightarrow * \mid / \\
factor &\rightarrow unary\_operator\ expression \mid (\ expression\ ) \mid integer \mid \\
&\quad\quad variable \mid variable\ (\ argument\_list\ ) \\
unary\_operator &\rightarrow -
\end{aligned}
$$

This grammar is useful because its parse trees reflect the precedence and left associativity of the binary arithmetic operators. To rewrite it would change the structure of the parse tree and we would lose the precedence information.

If we cannot rewrite the parse tree then we must resort to alternative methods of parsing, at least for those parts of the grammar that contain left recursion. An important method in this respect is operator precedence parsing, which is discussed at the end of this chapter.

6.2.2 ATTRIBUTE GRAMMARS AND RECURSIVE DESCENT

The top-down approach of recursive descent is well suited for use with many types of attribute grammar. Synthesized attributes can be used because recursive descent gives us a depth-first construction of the parse tree. Inherited attributes can be used in an L-attributed grammar, because the construction is also left to right.

Synthesized attributes

Synthesized attributes are easily handled by making the parse routines return a pointer to a list of attributes as a result. We need to create a struct with one field for each attribute. For efficiency each routine uses a static copy of this struct, rather than creating a new copy with `malloc()` each time the routine is called. Attribute values that need to be kept must be copied explicitly. A typical such struct to hold a value attribute and a name attribute might be:

```
struct attr
{
        int    value ;
        char *name ;
} ;
```

A typical routine to recognize a non-terminal, A, defined by the production $A \rightarrow \mathbf{x}B\mathbf{y}$ and return synthesized attributes would be:

```
struct attr *A()
{
        static struct attr res ;
        struct attr       *t ;

        checkfor( x ) ;
        t = B() ;
        checkfor( y ) ;

        /* Code to synthesise new attributes, possibly
           using attributes passed back by B() and set
           up the appropriate fields in res */

        return &res ;

}        /* A() */
```

Inherited attributes

We handle inherited attributes by passing a pointer to struct attr as an argument to each routine. So, for example, our routine to recognize *A* might become:

```
struct attr *A( struct attr *arg )
{
        static struct attr  res ;
        struct attr         targ ;
        struct attr         *t ;

        checkfor( x ) ;

        /* Code to set up inherited attributes for B() in
           targ, possibly using inherited attributes passed
           into A() */

        t = B( &targ ) ;
        checkfor( y ) ;

        /* Code to synthesize new attributes in res, possibly
           using attributes passed back by B() and inherited
           by A() */

        return &res ;

}       /* A( struct attr *arg ) */
```

Single attribute grammars

In practice such complexity is not needed. A large proportion of parsers only use one attribute, the parse tree being constructed. The parser builds the parse tree, leaving semantic actions to a separate phase which will walk over the parse tree. To achieve this we require our parsing routines just to return the piece of the parse tree they have built. A suitable structure might be the following, which is described in Chapter 4:

```
struct node
{
        int             nodetype ;
        union
        {
                int             value ;     /* integers·*/
                char            *name ;     /* variable names */
                struct node *ptr ;          /* subtrees */
        }               field1 ;
        struct node *field2 ;
        struct node *field3 ;
        struct node *field4 ;
        struct node *field5 ;
} ;
```

The routine to recognize *A* would then be:

```
struct node *A()
{
        struct node *res = (struct node *)malloc(
                              sizeof( struct node )) ;

        checkfor( x ) ;
        res->field1.ptr = B() ;
        checkfor( y ) ;

        res->nodetype = NT_A ;
        res->field2    = NULL ;
        res->field3    = NULL ;
        res->field4    = NULL ;
        res->field5    = NULL ;

        return res ;

}       /* A() */
```

6.2.3 TABLE-DRIVEN, TOP-DOWN PARSING

All recursive descent parsing routines do one of two things:

● They call yylex() to read tokens.
● They call other routines to recognize other non-terminals.

In addition, some routines have to make a choice between various possible expansions by considering the next input token.

A logical extension is to encapsulate this data in a table and have a single routine to carry out the appropriate actions according to the next token to be parsed and the information in the table. It is beyond the scope of this book to describe the construction of these parsing tables (although it is not that difficult), but we describe their use. Table-driven parsing is particularly suitable when the parser is generated automatically from a description of the grammar.

The predictive parsing program makes use of a stack, containing in order the symbols we are trying to recognize. Initially this contains the sentence symbol of the grammar. It takes as input a stream of tokens from the lexical analyser and produces as output a list of the productions used to build a left-most derivation of the parse tree. The actions of the parser are controlled by a parse table M. This table contains entries, $M[X,a]$ for each non-terminal in the grammar, X, and each terminal, a. This details the action to take when we encounter a as the next token on the input stream and X is on the top of the stack ready to be recognized. Figure 6.2 shows a schematic diagram of the parsing program.

We commence with the sentence symbol alone on the stack. The parser then loops considering the symbol, X, on the top of the stack, using **EOF** if the stack is empty and a, the next token from the lexical analyser. It carries out one of the four following actions:

● If both X and a are **EOF** we have successfully recognized the sentence symbol and parsing is complete.

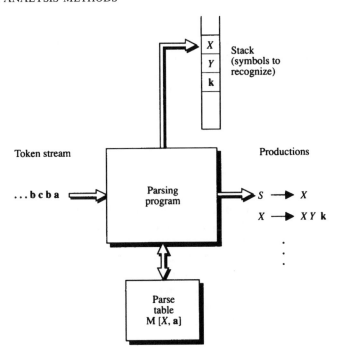

Figure 6.2   Table-driven, top-down parser

- If X and a are the same (but not **EOF**) then we wish to recognize this token. Pop X off the stack since it is now recognized and call `yylex()` to get a new token, a.
- If X is a token, but not the same as a we were expecting to find an X but got an a instead. This is an error, and we call an error-recovery routine. A simple error message might be 'a found where X expected'.
- We consult $M[X,a]$. If we have a valid source program this will be a production of the form $X \to Y_1 Y_2 \cdots Y_n$. This means that we wish to recognize $Y_1 Y_2 \cdots Y_n$ in turn. We pop X off the stack and replace it by $Y_1 Y_2 \cdots Y_n$, with Y_1 on the top. We output that production $X \to Y_1 Y_2 \cdots Y_n$ has been used. Alternatively we find $M[X,a]$ has an error entry, meaning that if we are trying to recognize X it cannot start with a, i.e. a is not in $\mathbb{L}_T(X)$. We call an error-recovery routine, possibly with a message such as 'X cannot start with a'.

This illustrates the simple behaviour of table-driven recursive descent, which as can be seen is no longer recursive. It is often just referred to as table-driven, top-down parsing.

Top-down parsing is now almost completely restricted to handling trivial grammars, without left recursion, where it is simple to write a set of recursive descent routines by hand. A typical case might be a simple command interpreter for an application. In general, shift-reduce LR parsing, as described in Sec. 6.3, is more powerful than table-driven LL(1) parsing. The availability of good shift-reduce parser tools in the public domain means that only in specialized cases is LL(1) to be preferred. This is invariably in cases where it is essential that productions are resolved from the top down, possibly so that inherited attributes can be properly handled, or because semantic actions must be invoked before a complete parse can be achieved.

6.3 Bottom-up parsing

The alternative approach to parsing is to construct the parse tree from the bottom up. We will consider principally one class of parsers, the *LR shift-reduce parsers*. These parsers are too large to construct by hand but are well suited to construction by automatic parser generators. Because of their size it is only in the last fifteen to twenty years that these parsers have become popular. We will also briefly consider *operator precedence parsing*. This is only suitable for a very restricted class of grammars, but has the advantage of being easily constructed by hand. Its particular value is in combination with recursive descent to recognize left recursive productions.

6.3.1 SHIFT-REDUCE PARSING

Shift-reduce parsing makes use of a stack and parsing table in the same fashion as table-driven, top-down parsing. It takes as input a stream of tokens and produces as output a list of productions to use in building the parse tree. However, with shift-reduce parsing the productions come out in reverse order. We would need to start with the last one to reconstruct the parse tree from the sentence symbol. In addition they yield a right-most derivation. Such parsers are thus LR(k) parsers. In general, we are interested in the case where $k = 1$.

With shift-reduce parsing we use the stack to hold symbols that we are trying to combine to give non-terminals further up the parse tree. It is thus the inverse of table-driven, top-down parsing. At any stage we have principally two options:

- Push the current token onto the top of the stack and call the lexical analyser to get a new token. We say we *shift* the token onto the stack.
- Decide that the tokens on the top of the stack form a valid right-hand side of a production. Pop them off the stack and replace them with the non-terminal on the left-hand side of the production. If the production is:

$$A \rightarrow X_1 X_2 \cdots X_n$$

and the symbols $X_1 X_2 \cdots X_n$ are on the top of the stack we remove them and replace them by A. We say that we *reduce* using the production $A \rightarrow X_1 X_2 \cdots X_n$. Note that in LR(1) parsing we may look at the next token without reading it (i.e. one symbol lookahead) in making the decision whether to reduce or shift.

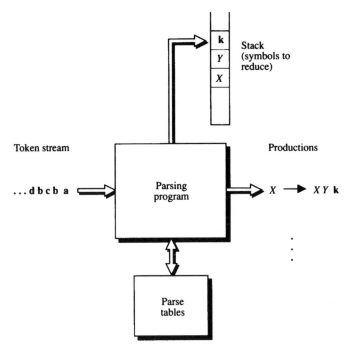

Figure 6.3   Shift-reduce parser

There are two further subsidiary possibilities, *accept* on successful completion of parsing and *error* when we reach a state where the current token cannot be part of a valid program. Figure 6.3 shows a schematic diagram of a shift-reduce parser.

In bottom-up parsing we simplify initially a sentence and then successive sentential forms using productions of the grammar. In LR parsing we are attempting to carry out a right-most derivation in reverse. Consider the grammar:

$$S \rightarrow AB$$

$$A \rightarrow \mathbf{x} \mid A\mathbf{y}$$

$$B \rightarrow \mathbf{z}$$

Figure 6.4 shows a right-most derivation of the sentence **xyz** in this grammar. At each stage in the derivation we expand the right-most non-terminal by replacing the non-terminal by the right-hand side in a production defining it to give a new sentential form. Thus we have the series of derivations:

$$S \underset{rm}{\Rightarrow} AB \underset{rm}{\Rightarrow} A\mathbf{z} \underset{rm}{\Rightarrow} A\mathbf{yz} \underset{rm}{\Rightarrow} \mathbf{xyz}$$

Reduction is the opposite of derivation. We introduce the concept of a *handle* to mean the right-hand side of a production which must be reduced in the reverse

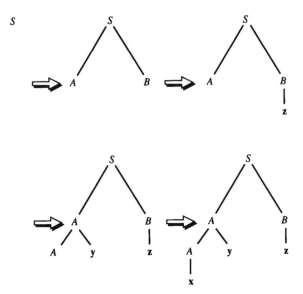

Figure 6.4   Right-most derivation of **xyz**

of one step of a right-most derivation. For example, the last step in the derivation of **xyz** was to use the production $A \rightarrow$ **x**. Correspondingly, in shift-reduce parsing of this sentence we would say that **x** was the handle by which to reduce the sentence **xyz**. The next step would be to reduce the handle **yz** in the sentential form A**yz**.

In our stack-based shift-reduce parser we push tokens onto the stack until we have a handle to reduce. The essence of shift-reduce parsing is building the tables that tell us when there is a handle on the top of the stack that can be reduced.

Not all type 2 grammars can be parsed by a shift-reduce parser. There are some grammars for which a shift-reduce parser could get into a state where it could not tell whether to shift or reduce (a *shift-reduce conflict*) or even by which production to reduce (a *reduce-reduce conflict*). Such grammars are not LR(1) grammars.

Ambiguous grammars are never LR grammars, because by definition there must be more than one handle under some circumstances. However, shift-reduce parsers can readily be modified to handle such grammars in a consistent manner. Typically the parser may resolve shift-reduce conflicts by always shifting and reduce-reduce conflicts by always reducing in favour of the earlier production in the definition of the grammar (which then makes the order in which productions are written down significant).

A common case in which shift-reduce conflicts occur is with IF statements in many programming languages (including C). The problem occurs if the IF statement has an optional ELSE part, so that we may have a dangling ELSE. A typical grammar for such statements would be:

$$S \rightarrow \textbf{if } E \textbf{ then } S \mid$$
$$\textbf{if } E \textbf{ then } S \textbf{ else } S$$

Imagine a shift-reduce parser given the following:

if E **then if** E **then** S **else** S

At some stage the parser will end up with a stack containing:

if E **then if** E **then** S

with **else** as the next token on the input stream. Should it reduce by the first production for S to give:

if E **then** S

or should it shift the **else** onto the stack to give:

if E **then if** E **then** S **else**

If we resolve in favour of shifting then we get a parse in which an **else** is always associated with its nearest **if**. This is what is done in the case of C. Note that this problem does not occur in VSL because IF statements are terminated by FI and are thus unambiguous.

Reduce-reduce conflicts are much less common. Although there are places where they validly occur in language grammars, they are more usually indicative of a problem in the definition of the language.

6.3.2 LR PARSERS

LR parsers are a particular style of shift-reduce parser. It is clear that determining the handle to reduce in a sentential form depends on the symbols to the left of the handle. In an LR parser we use a state machine to hold this information. Rather than reading and shifting symbols to reduce on the top of the stack, we shift states describing what is on the stack so far. The state on the top of the stack combined with the next input token enables us to deduce whether we have a handle to reduce, or whether we need to read the next input token and shift a new state onto the top of the stack.

For such a parser we need two tables. The *action* table, $A[s,a]$, tells whether to shift, reduce, accept, or flag an error when state s is on the top of the stack and a is the next input token. The *goto* table, $G[s,X]$, gives the new state to put on the top of the stack after a shift or reduce action. After a shift action $G[s,a]$ is the new state to shift on the top of the stack and we call the lexical analyser to get a new a. After a reduction by $X \rightarrow \bar{u}$, we pop the states due to the handle $\bar{u}$ from the stack (there will be one for each symbol in $\bar{u}$) to expose states s'. We then output $X \rightarrow \bar{u}$ and push $G[s',X]$ as the new state on the top of the stack. Figure 6.5 shows a schematic diagram for an LR shift-reduce parser.

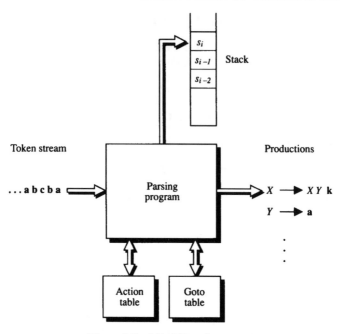

Figure 6.5   LR shift-reduce parser

We start with the *initial state* s_0 on the stack. Part way through a parse we will have the stack containing:

$$s_0 s_1 s_2 \cdots s_i$$

The next input token is a. The action of the parser is to loop, doing one of the following:

- If $A[s_i, a]$ is shift we consult $G[s_i, a]$ to get a new state, s_{i+1} to put on the top of the stack. The stack then looks like:

$$s_0 s_1 s_2 \cdots s_i s_{i+1}$$

  We then call the lexical analyser to get a new a.
- If $A[s_i, a]$ is reduce by $Y \to X_1 \cdots X_k$ then we pop the k states $s_{i-k+1} \cdots s_i$ off the stack leaving s_{i-k} on the top of the stack. We then consult $G[s_{i-k}, Y]$ to find a new state s_{i-k+1} to put on the top of the stack. We end up with the stack:

$$s_0 s_1 s_2 \cdots s_{i-k} s_{i-k+1}$$

  a remains as the next input token.
- If $A[s_i, a]$ is accept then parsing has succeeded.
- if $A[s_i, a]$ is error then we have a syntax error. With the current stack and the current input token we could never get a sentential form with a handle to reduce.

Table 6.1   Part of the unambiguous VSL grammar for expressions

1	*expression*	→ *expression term_operator term*
2	*expression*	→ *term*
3	*term_operator*	→ **+**
4	*term_operator*	→ **−**
5	*term*	→ *term factor_operator factor*
6	*term*	→ *factor*
7	*factor_operator*	→ *****
8	*factor_operator*	→ **/**
9	*factor*	→ **(** *expression* **)**
10	*factor*	→ **integer**
11	*factor*	→ **variable**

Table 6.1 shows part of the unambiguous VSL grammar for expressions. To keep the example simple we have left out function cells and unary minus. We have numbered each production. In the action table we will use reduce *n* to mean reduce by production numbered *n*. For shift entries in the action table we will write shift *n* to mean shift state *n* and then read a new token. This saves having separate goto table entries for tokens. We then just need goto entries for each non-terminal. Table 6.2 is the action table for this grammar.

Table 6.3 shows the goto table. We only need give this for non-terminals, since any terminals have their gotos included in the action table.

We can show the parser in action by considering parsing the expression:

variable * (integer + variable)

We show in Table 6.4 how the stack behaves as this expression is parsed.

Table 6.2   Example action table

State	+	−	*	/	(	)	integer	variable	EOF
0					shift 6		shift 15	shift 16	
1	shift 9	shift 10							accept
2					shift 6		shift 15	shift 16	
3	reduce 1	reduce 1	shift 12	shift 13		reduce 1			reduce 1
4					shift 6		shift 15	shift 16	
5	reduce 5	reduce 5	reduce 5	reduce 5		reduce 5			reduce 5
6					shift 6		shift 15	shift 16	
7	shift 9	shift 10				shift 8			
8	reduce 9	reduce 9	reduce 9	reduce 9		reduce 9			reduce 9
9						reduce 3	reduce 3	reduce 3	
10						reduce 4	reduce 4	reduce 4	
11	reduce 2	reduce 2	shift 12	shift 13		reduce 2			reduce 2
12						reduce 7	reduce 7	reduce 7	
13						reduce 8	reduce 8	reduce 8	
14	reduce 6	reduce 6	reduce 6	reduce 6		reduce 6			reduce 6
15	reduce 10	reduce 10	reduce 10	reduce 10		reduce 10			reduce 10
16	reduce 11	reduce 11	reduce 11	reduce 11		reduce 11			reduce 11

Table 6.3   Example goto table

State	expression	term_operator	term	factor_operator	factor
0	goto 1		goto 11		goto 14
1		goto 2			
2			goto 3		goto 14
3				goto 4	
4					goto 5
5					
6	goto 7		goto 11		goto 14
7		goto 2			
8					
9					
10					
11				goto 4	
12					
13					
14					
15					
16					

Table 6.4   Parsing the expression **variable * (integer + variable)**

Stack	Next token	Action
s_0	**variable**	shift s_{16}
s_0s_{16}	*	reduce by $factor \rightarrow$ **variable**
s_0s_{14}	*	reduce by $term \rightarrow$ **factor**
s_0s_{11}	*	shift s_{12}
$s_0s_{11}s_{12}$	(	reduce by $factor\_operator \rightarrow$ *
$s_0s_{11}s_4$	(	shift s_6
$s_0s_{11}s_4s_6$	**integer**	shift s_{15}
$s_0s_{11}s_4s_6s_{15}$	+	reduce by $factor \rightarrow$ **integer**
$s_0s_{11}s_4s_6s_{14}$	+	reduce by $term \rightarrow factor$
$s_0s_{11}s_4s_6s_{11}$	+	reduce by $expression \rightarrow term$
$s_0s_{11}s_4s_6s_7$	+	shift s_9
$s_0s_{11}s_4s_6s_7s_9$	**variable**	reduce by $term\_operator \rightarrow$ +
$s_0s_{11}s_4s_6s_7s_2$	**variable**	shift s_{16}
$s_0s_{11}s_4s_6s_7s_2s_{16}$	)	reduce by $factor \rightarrow$ **variable**
$s_0s_{11}s_4s_6s_7s_2s_{14}$	)	reduce by $term \rightarrow factor$
$s_0s_{11}s_4s_6s_7s_2s_3$	)	reduce by $expression \rightarrow expression\ term\_operator\ term$
$s_0s_{11}s_4s_6s_7$	)	shift s_8
$s_0s_{11}s_4s_6s_7s_8$	**EOF**	reduce by $factor \rightarrow$ ($expression$)
$s_0s_{11}s_4s_5$	**EOF**	reduce by $term \rightarrow term\ factor\_operator\ factor$
s_0s_{11}	**EOF**	reduce by $expression \rightarrow term$
s_0s_1	**EOF**	accept

Types of LR parser

There are three widely used types of LR parser: *canonical LR(k)*, *simple LR(k)*, and *lookahead LR(k)*, usually abbreviated to *LR(k)*, *SLR(k)*, and *LALR(k)*. We are usually interested in only single character lookahead, i.e. $k = 1$. The parsers only differ in how their action and goto tables are constructed, and the size of those tables.

Canonical LR parsing is the most general form of LR parsing. It will parse any language that can be parsed by a shift-reduce parser. The disadvantage is that canonical LR parsers have many thousands of states for a typical programming language and are thus large. Simple LR parsing is a variant with typically a few hundred states for a typical programming language. However, it does not parse as large a set of languages as canonical LR. In particular, there are some constructs in typical programming languages that cannot be handled by SLR. LALR parsing parses a larger set of languages than SLR but not as large a set as LR. In particular LALR can parse all the common programming language constructs. LALR parsers have the same number of states as the equivalent SLR parser, although they are rather harder to construct. LALR(1) is the parsing method used by the YACC parser generator to be discussed in Chapter 8.

As an example we shall show how to derive SLR(1) parse tables, since they are the simplest, and then show how LR(1) and LALR(1) tables may be derived in analogous fashion.

6.3.3 CONSTRUCTING SLR(1) PARSE TABLES

At the heart of the algorithm for the construction of SLR(1) parse tables is the concept of the *LR(0) configuration* (which where the context is clear will just be referred to as a configuration). A configuration is a production of the grammar with a dot at some position on its right side. For example, the VSL production:

$$expression \rightarrow expression\ term\_operator\ term$$

gives the four configurations:

$$expression \rightarrow \cdot\ expression\ term\_operator\ term$$
$$expression \rightarrow expression\ \cdot\ term\_operator\ term$$
$$expression \rightarrow expression\ term\_operator\ \cdot\ term$$
$$expression \rightarrow expression\ term\_operator\ term\ \cdot$$

In essence we shall use this dot to mark how far we have got in parsing this production. It marks the point where everything to the left has been shifted and a token in the left terminal set of the symbol after the dot is next token (or in $\mathbb{F}_T$ if everything after the dot could yield ε). The states that we put on the stack will correspond to these configurations, indicating what we have read so far. A dot at the right end of a configuration indicates that we have that configuration completely on the stack, in other words we have a handle to reduce. A dot in the middle of a configuration indicates that we need to shift a token that could start the symbol following the dot. For example, given the configuration:

$$expression \rightarrow expression \cdot term\_operator \ term$$

we wish to shift anything in $\mathbb{L}_T(term\_operator)$, i.e. $\{ +, - \}$. Overall with this configuration we are seeking to shift all the symbols that comprise a *term_operator* and then reduce them to a *term_operator*. We then can say that we are in a state corresponding to the configuration:

$$expression \rightarrow expression \ term\_operator \cdot term$$

We see that the actions we take when we are in the state corresponding to the configuration:

$$expression \rightarrow expression \cdot term\_operator \ term$$

are the same as those corresponding to the configuration where we wish to recognize the whole of a *term_operator*. That is:

$$term\_operator \rightarrow \cdot +$$

$$term\_operator \rightarrow \cdot -$$

We now have a set of three configurations corresponding to the same state of the shift-reduce parser. We call this a *configurating set* of the SLR parser. The action of adding equivalent configurations to create the configurating set we call *closure*. Our parsing tables have one state corresponding to each configurating set. We now give the formal rule for generating a configurating set from a configuration. We start with a configuration, which we put in the configurating set. For example:

$$A \rightarrow X_1 \cdots X_i \cdot X_{i+1} \cdots X_j$$

We then perform the closure operation on the configurations in the configurating set. For each configuration in the configurating set where the dot precedes a non-terminal we add configurations derived from the productions defining that non-terminal with the dot at the left of the right side if they are not already in the configurating set. So, if in the above configuration X_{i+1} was a non-terminal defined by:

$$X_{i+1} \rightarrow Y_1 \cdots Y_m$$

$$X_{i+1} \rightarrow Z_1 \cdots Z_m$$

we would add the configurations

$$X_{i+1} \rightarrow \cdot Y_1 \cdots Y_m$$

$$X_{i+1} \rightarrow \cdot Z_1 \cdots Z_m$$

We repeat this operation for all configurations in the configurating set where a dot precedes a non-terminal until no more configurations can be added. The closure operation is now complete. In our example the complete configurating set is:

$$A \quad \rightarrow X_1 \cdots X_i \cdot X_{i+1} \cdots X_j$$

$$X_{i+1} \rightarrow \cdot Y_1 \cdots Y_m$$

$$X_{i+1} \rightarrow \cdot Z_1 \cdots Z_m$$

if $Y_1\ Z_1$ are terminals. We next define the *successor function, succ*, applied to a configurating set and a grammar symbol. Given a configurating set C and a grammar symbol X we obtain a *successor configurating set, $C' = succ(C,X)$*. We take all configurations in C where there is a dot preceding X, move the dot past X and put the new configurations in C'. The successor configurating set is the closure of C'. Let us take an example from VSL. We start with the configurating set:

> *expression*   → *expression* · *term_operator term*
>
> *term_operator* → · +
>
> *term_operator* → · −

To obtain the successor configurating set on *term_operator* we first put the configuration:

> *expression* → *expression term_operator* · *term*

in the successor configurating set, C'. We then perform the closure of this set to obtain:

> *expression* → *expression term_operator* · *term*
>
> *term*   → · *term factor_operator factor*
>
> *term*   → · *factor*
>
> *factor*   → · (*expression*)
>
> *factor*   → · **integer**
>
> *factor*   → · **variable**

This is the successor configurating set.

The successor function will yield our goto table. The successor function on a grammar symbol, X, represents the action of shifting the tokens making up X and, if X is not a terminal, reducing to leave the state corresponding to X on the top of the stack. Once we have X on the top of the stack we can move to a configurating set in which the dot has moved past X.

The only thing left to do now is to construct all the configurating sets and successor functions for the grammar. At the highest level our aim is to start with a configuration with a dot before the sentence symbol and move to a configuration with a dot after the sentence symbol, since this will represent shifting and

reducing an entire sentence of the grammar. To do this we need the sentence
symbol to appear on the right of a production and so we augment our grammar.
If our grammar, G, has the sentence symbol, S, then we create an *augmented
grammar*, G', by adding the production:

$$S' \rightarrow S$$

Our aim is then to start with the initial configurating set, C_0, that is the closure
of:

$$S' \rightarrow \cdot S$$

and get to the configurating set that is the closure of:

$$S' \rightarrow S \cdot$$

i.e. we are looking for $succ(C_0, S)$.

We create the complete family of configurating sets, F, for the grammar as
follows:

1. Start with F containing just the configurating set, C_0, derived from the
   configuration $S' \rightarrow \cdot S$.
2. For each configurating set C in F and each grammar symbol X, such that
   $succ(C,X)$ is not empty, add $succ(C,X)$ to F.
3. Repeat step 2 until no more configurating sets can be added to F.

The best way of showing this is by example. The augmented grammar for VSL
expressions is shown in Table 6.5. Table 6.6 shows the family of configurating
sets derived for this grammar, together with their successor sets. We use πn for
the configuration derived from production n with the dot at the right-hand end.
Such a configuration has no successor, since we have recognized the production
as a handle.

We now have all we need for the construction of our action and goto tables.
We start by constructing F, the family of configurating sets for the augmented

Table 6.5   The augmented grammar for VSL expressions

0	*expression'*	$\rightarrow$ *expression*
1	*expression*	$\rightarrow$ *expression term_operator term*
2	*expression*	$\rightarrow$ *term*
3	*term_operator*	$\rightarrow$ *+*
4	*term_operator*	$\rightarrow$ *−*
5	*term*	$\rightarrow$ *term factor_operator factor*
6	*term*	$\rightarrow$ *factor*
7	*factor_operator*	$\rightarrow$ *
8	*factor_operator*	$\rightarrow$ /
9	*factor*	$\rightarrow$ (*expression*)
10	*factor*	$\rightarrow$ **integer**
11	*factor*	$\rightarrow$ **variable**

Table 6.6 The family of configurating sets derived for the augmented grammar

Configurating set			Successor	
C_0	expression'	$\rightarrow$ · expression	expression	$\Rightarrow C_1$
	expression	$\rightarrow$ · expression term_operator term	expression	$\Rightarrow C_1$
	expression	$\rightarrow$ · term	term	$\Rightarrow C_{11}$
	term	$\rightarrow$ · term factor_operator factor	term	$\Rightarrow C_{11}$
	term	$\rightarrow$ · factor	factor	$\Rightarrow C_{14}$
	factor	$\rightarrow$ · (expression)	(	$\Rightarrow C_6$
	factor	$\rightarrow$ · **integer**	**integer**	$\Rightarrow C_{15}$
	factor	$\rightarrow$ · **variable**	**variable**	$\Rightarrow C_{16}$
C_1	expression'	$\rightarrow$ expression ·	$\pi 0$	
	expression	$\rightarrow$ expression · term_operator term	term_operator	$\Rightarrow C_2$
	term_operator	$\rightarrow$ · +	+	$\Rightarrow C_9$
	term_operator	$\rightarrow$ · −	−	$\Rightarrow C_{10}$
C_2	expression	$\rightarrow$ expression term_operator · term	term	$\Rightarrow C_3$
	term	$\rightarrow$ · term factor_operator factor	term	$\Rightarrow C_3$
	term	$\rightarrow$ · factor	factor	$\Rightarrow C_{14}$
	factor	$\rightarrow$ · (expression)	(	$\Rightarrow C_6$
	factor	$\rightarrow$ · **integer**	**integer**	$\Rightarrow C_{15}$
	factor	$\rightarrow$ · **variable**	**variable**	$\Rightarrow C_{16}$
C_3	expression	$\rightarrow$ expression term_operator term ·	$\pi 1$	
	term	$\rightarrow$ term · factor_operator factor	factor_operator	$\Rightarrow C_4$
	factor_operator	$\rightarrow$ · *	*	$\Rightarrow C_{12}$
	factor_operator	$\rightarrow$ · /	/	$\Rightarrow C_{13}$
C_4	term	$\rightarrow$ term factor_operator · factor	factor	$\Rightarrow C_5$
	factor	$\rightarrow$ · (expression)	(	$\Rightarrow C_6$
	factor	$\rightarrow$ · **integer**	**integer**	$\Rightarrow C_{15}$
	factor	$\rightarrow$ · **variable**	**variable**	$\Rightarrow C_{16}$
C_5	term	$\rightarrow$ term factor_operator factor ·	$\pi 5$	
C_6	factor	$\rightarrow$ (· expression)	expression	$\Rightarrow C_7$
	expression	$\rightarrow$ · expression term_operator term	expression	$\Rightarrow C_7$
	expression	$\rightarrow$ · term	term	$\Rightarrow C_{11}$
	term	$\rightarrow$ · term factor_operator factor	term	$\Rightarrow C_{11}$
	term	$\rightarrow$ · factor	factor	$\Rightarrow C_{14}$
	factor	$\rightarrow$ · (expression)	(	$\Rightarrow C_6$
	factor	$\rightarrow$ · **integer**	**integer**	$\Rightarrow C_{15}$
	factor	$\rightarrow$ · **variable**	**variable**	$\Rightarrow C_{16}$
C_7	factor	$\rightarrow$ (expression ·)	)	$\Rightarrow C_8$
	expression	$\rightarrow$ expression · term_operator term	term_operator	$\Rightarrow C_2$
	term_operator	$\rightarrow$ · +	+	$\Rightarrow C_9$
	term_operator	$\rightarrow$ · −	−	$\Rightarrow C_{10}$
C_8	factor	$\rightarrow$ (expression) ·	$\pi 9$	
C_9	term_operator	$\rightarrow$ + ·	$\pi 3$	
C_{10}	term_operator	$\rightarrow$ − ·	$\pi 4$	
C_{11}	expression	$\rightarrow$ term ·	$\pi 2$	
	term	$\rightarrow$ term · factor_operator factor	factor_operator	$\Rightarrow C_4$
	factor_operator	$\rightarrow$ · *	*	$\Rightarrow C_{12}$
	factor_operator	$\rightarrow$ · /	/	$\Rightarrow C_{13}$
C_{12}	factor_operator	$\rightarrow$ * ·	$\pi 7$	
C_{13}	factor_operator	$\rightarrow$ / ·	$\pi 8$	
C_{14}	term	$\rightarrow$ factor ·	$\pi 6$	
C_{15}	factor	$\rightarrow$ **integer** ·	$\pi 10$	
C_{16}	factor	$\rightarrow$ **variable** ·	$\pi 11$	

grammar, G'. State i in our shift-reduce parser will be derived from configurating set C_i. The entries in the action and goto tables are derived as follows:

- For each terminal, a, which has a successor, $succ(C_i,a) = C_j$, set $A[i,a]$ to shift and $G[i,a]$ to j.
- For each non-terminal, X, where $succ(C_i,X) = C_j$, set $G[i,X]$ to j.
- For each configuration in C_i, $X \to \bar{u} \cdot$ where $X \neq S'$, set $A[i,a]$ to reduce by $X \to \bar{u}$ for all a in $\mathbb{F}_T(X)$.
- If the configuration $S' \to S \cdot$ is in C_i, then set $A[i,\mathbf{EOF}]$ to accept.

All unset entries are made error entries. The initial state of the parser is the one derived from the configurating set containing $S' \to \cdot S$. If any conflicting entries arise when building the action and goto tables, then the grammar is not SLR(1).

The action and goto tables derived from the family of configurating sets given in Table 6.6 are those given in Table 6.2 and 6.3, respectively. The initial state is state 0.

6.3.4 CANONICAL LR(1) PARSING

We have described the construction of SLR(1) parse tables, since they are the simplest tables to construct. For real programming languages they are often not sufficient, and so we must look to more powerful alternatives. The most general of these is canonical LR(1) parsing.

When constructing SLR(1) parse tables we do not use all the information at our disposal. When we have a configuration with a dot at the end of the form $X \to \bar{u} \cdot$ we know this must correspond to a state in which we have $\bar{u}$ as a handle on the top of the stack and we can reduce, replacing $\bar{u}$ by X. We allow such a reduction whenever the next symbol is in $\mathbb{F}_T(X)$.

In fact it may be that we should not reduce for some of the symbols in $\mathbb{F}_T(X)$, because the symbols below $\bar{u}$ on the stack preclude $\bar{u}$ being a handle for reduction in this case. In other words, SLR(1) states only tell us about the handle on the top of the stack, not what is further down on the stack. We actually need a number of states for each SLR(1) state to differentiate the possible means by which a handle has appeared on the stack.

We achieve this in canonical LR(1) parsers. Instead of starting with LR(0) configurations, we use LR(1) configurations. These have the general form:

$$A \to X_1 \cdots X_i \cdot X_{i+1} \cdots X_j, a$$

This means that we have the states corresponding to $X_1 \cdots X_i$ on the stack and are looking to put the states corresponding to $X_{i+1} \cdots X_j$, and then reduce, but only if the token following X_j is a. a is called the *lookahead* of the configuration, with the first part referred to as the *core*. The difference comes when we consider LR(1) configurations with the dot at the right end of the core:

$$A \to X_1 \cdots X_j \cdot, a$$

This means we have the states corresponding to $X_1 \cdots X_j$ on the stack, but we may only reduce when the next token to input is a. With SLR(1) parsing we would reduce if the next token was anything in $\mathbb{F}_T(A)$. With canonical LR(1) parsing we only reduce if the next token is a lookahead in a configuration for A. This must be a subset of $\mathbb{F}_T(A)$, and in many real examples will be a proper subset of $\mathbb{F}_T(A)$.

Constructing canonical LR(1) parse tables

The algorithm for constructing canonical LR(1) parse tables is broadly the same as SLR(1). However, we need to modify our algorithm for constructing configurating sets, and make a corresponding change in the successor function, *succ*.

Let us suppose we wish to form the closure of the following LR(1) configuration:

$$A \rightarrow \bar{u} \cdot B\bar{v}, a$$

This can be used only in a right-most derivation of the following form:

$$\bar{x}A\bar{y} \Rightarrow \bar{x}\bar{u}B\bar{v}a\bar{y}$$

Now from this derivation, we can only accept further derivations of B which are followed by terminals that can begin phrases derived from $\bar{v}a\bar{y}$, in other words $\mathbb{L}_T(\bar{v}a\bar{y})$. Since $\mathbb{L}_T(\bar{v}a)$ cannot derive ε (even if $\bar{v} \overset{*}{\Rightarrow} \varepsilon$, that still means $\mathbb{L}_T(\bar{v}a)$ must contain a), we have $\mathbb{L}_T(\bar{v}a) = L_T(\bar{v}a\bar{y})$.

So in forming our closure of $A \rightarrow \bar{u} \cdot B\bar{v}, a$, we must add the configurations:

$$B \rightarrow \cdot \bar{w}, b$$

where

$$b \in \mathbb{L}_T(\bar{v}b)$$

for all productions $B \rightarrow \bar{w}$.

Our method for constructing the family of configurating sets, F, is then:

1. Start with F containing just the configurating set C_0, derived from the configuration $S' \rightarrow \cdot S$, **EOF**.
2. For each LR(1) configurating set C in F and each grammar symbol X, such that $succ(C,X)$ is not empty, add $succ(C,X)$ to F.
3. Repeat step 2 until no more configurating sets can be added to F.

Once again we show this by example. We use the augmented grammar for VSL expressions of Table 6.5. Table 6.7 shows the family of LR(1) configurating sets derived for canonical LR(1) parsing. Many of the configurations in a set differ only in their lookahead, and to save space we use a shorthand notation. For example in configurating set C_0 the three configurations:

expression → · *expression term_operator term*, **EOF**

expression → · *expression term_operator term*, +

expression → · *expression term_operator term*, −

are shown as:

expression → · *expression term_operator term*, **EOF**: + :−

Table 6.7 Family of configurating sets for the canonical LR(1) parser

Configurating set			Successor	
C_0	expression′	→ · expression, **EOF**	expression	⇒ C_1
	expression	→ · expression term_operator term, $+:-:$**EOF**	expression	⇒ C_1
	expression	→ · term, $+:-:$**EOF**	term	⇒ C_{25}
	term	→ · term factor_operator factor, $+:-:*:/:$**EOF**	term	⇒ C_{25}
	term	→ · factor, $+:-:*:/:$**EOF**	factor	⇒ C_{24}
	factor	→ · (expression), $+:-:*:/:$**EOF**	(	⇒ C_6
	factor	→ · **integer**, $+:-:*:/:$**EOF**	**integer**	⇒ C_{22}
	factor	→ · **variable**, $+:-:*:/:$**EOF**	**variable**	⇒ C_{23}
C_1	expression′	→ expression · , **EOF**	π0, **EOF**	
	expression	→ expression · term_operator term, $+:-:$**EOF**	term_operator	⇒ C_2
	term_operator	→ · +, (:**integer**:**variable**	+	⇒ C_{20}
	term_operator	→ · −, (:**integer**:**variable**	−	⇒ C_{21}
C_2	expression	→ expression term_operator · term, $+:-:$**EOF**	term	⇒ C_3
	term	→ · term factor_operator factor, $+:-:*:/:$**EOF**	term	⇒ C_3
	term	→ · factor, $+:-:*:/:$**EOF**	factor	⇒ C_{24}
	factor	→ · (expression), $+:-:*:/:$**EOF**	(	⇒ C_6
	factor	→ · **integer**, $+:-:*:/:$**EOF**	**integer**	⇒ C_{22}
	factor	→ · **variable**, $+:-:*:/:$**EOF**	**variable**	⇒ C_{23}
C_3	expression	→ expression term_operator term · , $+:-:$**EOF**	π1, $+:-:$**EOF**	
	term	→ term · factor_operator factor, $+:-:*:/:$**EOF**	factor_operator	⇒ C_4
	factor_operator	→ · *, (:**integer**:**variable**	*	⇒ C_{15}
	factor_operator	→ · /, (:**integer**:**variable**	/	⇒ C_{16}
C_4	term	→ term factor_operator · factor, $+:-:*:/:$**EOF**	factor	⇒ C_5
	factor	→ · (expression), $+:-:*:/:$**EOF**	(	⇒ C_6
	factor	→ · **integer**, $+:-:*:/:$**EOF**	**integer**	⇒ C_{22}
	factor	→ · **variable**, $+:-:*:/:$**EOF**	**variable**	⇒ C_{23}
C_5	term	→ term factor_operator factor · , $+:-:*:/:$**EOF**	π5, $+:-:*:/:$**EOF**	
C_6	factor	→ (· expression), $+:-:*:/:$**EOF**	expression	⇒ C_7
	expression	→ · expression term_operator term, $+:-:$)	expression	⇒ C_7
	expression	→ · term, $+:-:$)	term	⇒ C_{14}
	term	→ · term factor_operator factor, $+:-:*:/:$)	term	⇒ C_{14}
	term	→ · factor, $+:-:*:/:$)	factor	⇒ C_{17}
	factor	→ · (expression), $+:-:*:/:$)	(	⇒ C_{13}
	factor	→ · **integer**, $+:-:*:/:$)	**integer**	⇒ C_{18}
	factor	→ · **variable**, $+:-:*:/:$)	**variable**	⇒ C_{19}
C_7	factor	→ (expression ·), $+:-:*:/:$**EOF**	)	⇒ C_8
	expression	→ expression · term_operator term, $+:-:$)	term_operator	⇒ C_9
	term_operator	→ · +, (:**integer**:**variable**	+	⇒ C_{20}
	term_operator	→ · −, (:**integer**:**variable**	−	⇒ C_{21}
C_8	factor	→ (expression) · , $+:-:*:/:$**EOF**	π9, $+:-:*:/:$**EOF**	
C_9	expression	→ expression term_operator · term, $+:-:$)	term	⇒ C_{10}
	term	→ · term factor_operator factor, $+:-:*:/:$)	term	⇒ C_{10}
	term	→ · factor, $+:-:*:/:$)	factor	⇒ C_{17}
	factor	→ · (expression), $+:-:*:/:$)	(	⇒ C_{13}
	factor	→ · **integer**, $+:-:*:/:$)	**integer**	⇒ C_{18}
	factor	→ · **variable**, $+:-:*:/:$)	**variable**	⇒ C_{19}

Table 6.7   continued

Configurating set		Successor

C_{10} *expression* → *expression term_operator term* · , $+:-:$) $\pi 1, +:-:$)
    term → *term* · *factor_operator factor*, $+:-:*:/:$)   *factor_operator* $\Rightarrow C_{11}$
    factor_operator → · *, (:integer:variable   * $\Rightarrow C_{15}$
    factor_operator → · /, (:integer:variable   / $\Rightarrow C_{16}$

C_{11} *term* → *term factor_operator* · *factor*, $+:-:*:/:$)   *factor* $\Rightarrow C_{12}$
    factor → · (*expression*), $+:-:*:/:$)   ($\Rightarrow C_{13}$
    factor → · **integer**, $+:-:*:/:$)   **integer** $\Rightarrow C_{18}$
    factor → · **variable**, $+:-:*:/:$)   **variable** $\Rightarrow C_{19}$

C_{12} *term* → *term factor_operator factor* · , $+:-:*:/:$) $\pi 5, +:-:*:/:$)

C_{13} *factor* → (· *expression*), $+:-:*:/:$)   *expression* $\Rightarrow C_7$
    expression → · *expression term_operator term*, $+:-:$)   *expression* $\Rightarrow C_7$
    expression → · *term*, $+:-:$)   *term* $\Rightarrow C_{14}$
    term → · *term factor_operator factor*, $+:-:*:/:$)   *term* $\Rightarrow C_{14}$
    term → · *factor*, $+:-:*:/:$)   *factor* $\Rightarrow C_{17}$
    factor → · (*expression*), $+:-:*:/:$)   ($\Rightarrow C_{13}$
    factor → · **integer**, $+:-:*:/:$)   **integer** $\Rightarrow C_{18}$
    factor → · **variable**, $+:-:*:/:$)   **variable** $\Rightarrow C_{19}$

C_{14} *expression* → *term* · , $+:-:$) $\pi 2, +:-:$)
    term → *term* · *factor_operator factor*, $+:-:*:/:$)   *factor_operator* $\Rightarrow C_{11}$
    factor_operator → · *, (:integer:variable   * $\Rightarrow C_{15}$
    factor_operator → · /, (:integer:variable   / $\Rightarrow C_{16}$

C_{15} *factor_operator* → * · , (:integer:variable $\pi 7$, (:integer:variable

C_{16} *factor_operator* → / · , (:integer:variable $\pi 8$, (:integer:variable

C_{17} *term* → *factor* · , $+:-:*:/:$) $\pi 6, +:-:*:/:$)

C_{18} *factor* → **integer** · , $+:-:*:/:$) $\pi 10, +:-:*:/:$)

C_{19} *factor* → **variable** · , $+:-:*:/:$) $\pi 11, +:-:*:/:$)

C_{20} *term_operator* → + · , (:integer:variable $\pi 3$, (:integer:variable

C_{21} *term_operator* → − · , (:integer:variable $\pi 4$, (:integer:variable

C_{22} *factor* → **integer** · , $+:-:*:/$:EOF $\pi 10, +:-:*:/$:**EOF**

C_{23} *factor* → **variable** · , $+:-:*:/$:EOF $\pi 11, +:-:*:/$:**EOF**

C_{24} *term* → *factor* · , $+:-:*:/$:EOF $\pi 6, +:-:*:/$:**EOF**

C_{25} *expression* → *term* · , $+:-$:EOF $\pi 2, +:-$:**EOF**
    term → *term* · *factor_operator factor*, $+:-:*:/$:EOF   *factor_operator* $\Rightarrow C_4$
    factor_operator → · *, (:integer:variable   * $\Rightarrow C_{15}$
    factor_operator → · /, (:integer:variable   / $\Rightarrow C_{16}$

We use πn, **a** for the configuration derived from production n with the dot at the right-hand end, in circumstances where it must be followed by lookahead **a**. Where several lookaheads could occur, we use the same shorthand as for configurations, separating the lookaheads by colons.

At first glance the canonical LR(1) family of configurating sets seems very similar to the SLR(1) family. However, some sets are divided into two. For example the successor on *term_operator* for C_7 is C_2 for the SLR(1) family, whereas for canonical LR(1) we must create a new set, C_9. We effectively have one set for dealing with the complete expression, and a separate set for sub-expressions (where we would not expect to encounter a completing **EOF**). One consequence of this is that some errors (for example omitting a closing bracket at the end of an expression) will be picked up sooner in the parse.

We must now slightly modify our algorithm for construction of action and goto tables, to take advantage of the lookahead information we now possess as follows:

- For each terminal, a, which has a successor, $succ(C_i,a) = C_j$, set $A[i,a]$ to shift and $G[i,a]$ to j.
- For each non-terminal, X, where $succ(C_i,X) = C_j$, set $G[i,X]$ to j.
- For each configuration in $C_i, X \rightarrow \bar{u} \cdot ,a$ except where $X = S'$ and $a = $ **EOF**, set $A[i,a]$ to reduce by $X \rightarrow \bar{u}$.
- If the configuration $S' \rightarrow S \cdot$, **EOF** is in C_i then set $A[i,$**EOF**$]$ to accept.

All unset entries are again made error entries. The initial state of the parser is the one derived from the configurating set containing $S' \rightarrow \cdot S$, **EOF**, in our example, C_0. If any conflicting entries arise when building the action and goto tables, then the grammar is not canonical LR(1).

The action and goto tables derived from the family of configurating sets given in Table 6.7 are shown in Tables 6.8 and 6.9 respectively. The initial state is state 0.

Note how we now need 26 states, where for SLR(1) we only need 17. In practice for real programming languages the difference could be a factor of ten, with canonical LR(1) requiring thousands of states, where SLR(1) would require hundreds.

6.3.5 LALR(1) PARSING

The last technique we introduce gives us more or less the best of both worlds. It can handle a wider range of grammars than SLR(1), including the few common programming language constructs that give SLR(1) trouble, and it has far fewer states than canonical LR(1).

Table 6.8 Action table for the canonical LR(1) parser

State	+	−	*	/	(	)	integer	variable	EOF
0					shift 6		shift 22	shift 23	
1	shift 20	shift 21							accept
2					shift 6		shift 22	shift 23	
3	reduce 1	reduce 1	shift 15	shift 16					reduce 1
4					shift 6		shift 22	shift 23	
5	reduce 5	reduce 5	reduce 5	reduce 5					reduce 5
6					shift 13		shift 18	shift 19	
7	shift 20	shift 21				shift 8			
8	reduce 9	reduce 9	reduce 9	reduce 9					reduce 9
9					shift 13		shift 18	shift 19	
10	reduce 1	reduce 1	shift 15	shift 16		reduce 1			
11					shift 13		shift 18	shift 19	
12	reduce 5	reduce 5	reduce 5	reduce 5		reduce 5			
13					shift 13		shift 18	shift 19	
14	reduce 2	reduce 2	shift 15	shift 16		reduce 2			
15						reduce 7	reduce 7	reduce 7	
16						reduce 8	reduce 8	reduce 8	
17	reduce 6	reduce 6	reduce 6	reduce 6		reduce 6			
18	reduce 10	reduce 10	reduce 10	reduce 10		reduce 10			
19	reduce 11	reduce 11	reduce 11	reduce 11		reduce 11			
20						reduce 3	reduce 3	reduce 3	
21						reduce 4	reduce 4	reduce 4	
22	reduce 10	reduce 10	reduce 10	reduce 10					reduce 10
23	reduce 11	reduce 11	reduce 11	reduce 11					reduce 11
24	reduce 6	reduce 6	reduce 6	reduce 6					reduce 6
25	reduce 2	reduce 2	shift 15	shift 16					reduce 2

Constructing LALR(1) parse tables

The easiest way to understand the construction of LALR(1) parse tables is to start with the canonical LR(1) family of configurating sets. If we look at our example in Table 6.7, we see that a number of configurating sets differ only in the lookahead of their configurations. C_2 and C_9 have this property, where the cores of the configurations are identical.

In LALR(1), we merge such sets, so we will create a new configurating set, $C_{2,9}$ as follows:

$$expression \rightarrow expression\ term\_operator \cdot term, +:-:):\textbf{EOF}$$

$$term \qquad\rightarrow\ \cdot\ term\ factor\_operator\ factor, +:-:*:/:):\textbf{EOF}$$

$$term \qquad\rightarrow\ \cdot\ factor, +:-:*:/:):\textbf{EOF}$$

$$factor \qquad\rightarrow\ \cdot\ (\ expression\ ), +:-:*:/:):\textbf{EOF}$$

$$factor \qquad\rightarrow\ \cdot\ \textbf{integer}, +:-:*:/:):\textbf{EOF}$$

$$factor \qquad\rightarrow\ \cdot\ \textbf{variable}, +:-:*:/:):\textbf{EOF}$$

There is then the problem of what the successor sets should be. In configurating set C_2 the successor on *term* was C_3, whereas for configurating set C_9 it was C_{10}. However, if two configurations have the same core, then their successors must also have the same core, since the core of the successor only depends on the core

Table 6.9   Goto table for canonical LR(1) parser

State	expression	term_operator	term	factor_operator	factor
0	goto 1		goto 25		goto 24
1		goto 2			
2			goto 3		goto 24
3				goto 4	
4					goto 5
5					
6	goto 7		goto 14		goto 17
7		goto 9			
8					
9			goto 10		goto 17
10				goto 11	
11					goto 12
12					
13	goto 7		goto 14		goto 17
14				goto 11	
15					
16					
17					
18					
19					
20					
21					
22					
23					
24					
25				goto 4	

of the original configuration. If these successors have the same core, then they will be merged as part of the process of creating the LALR(1) family of configurating sets.

This is clearly the case in our example, and we thus have a successor on *term* for the new configurating set $C_{2,9}$ of the new set $C_{3,10}$.

Going through our complete canonical LR(1) family of configurating sets, we find we can merge pairs of sets to create new sets $C_{2,9}$, $C_{3,10}$, $C_{4,11}$, $C_{5,12}$, $C_{6,13}$, $C_{14,25}$, $C_{17,24}$, $C_{18,22}$ and $C_{19,23}$. The complete family is shown in Table 6.10. The algorithm for creating action and goto tables remains the same as with canonical LR(1), and yields the action and goto tables of Tables 6.11 and 6.12 respectively. For clarity we have given merged states new numbers as follows:

Set:	C_0	C_1	$C_{2,9}$	$C_{3,10}$	$C_{4,11}$	$C_{5,12}$	$C_{6,13}$	C_7	C_8	C_{20}	C_{21}	$C_{14,25}$	C_{15}	C_{16}	$C_{17,24}$	$C_{18,22}$	$C_{19,23}$
State:	0	1	2	3	4	5	6	7	8	9	10	11	12	13	14	15	16

We now have tables exactly the same size as for SLR(1). There is only one difference, in state 8, where the SLR(1) parser would allow a reduction on **)**, where the LALR(1) parser would not. The LALR(1) parser is able to make the

Table 6.10 Family of configurating sets for the LALR(1) parser

Configurating set			Successor	
C_0	$expression'$	$\rightarrow$ $\cdot\,expression$, **EOF**	$expression$	$\Rightarrow C_1$
	$expression$	$\rightarrow$ $\cdot\,expression\ term\_operator\ term$, $+:-:$**EOF**	$expression$	$\Rightarrow C_1$
	$expression$	$\rightarrow$ $\cdot\,term$, $+:-:$**EOF**	$term$	$\Rightarrow C_{14,25}$
	$term$	$\rightarrow$ $\cdot\,term\ factor\_operator\ factor$, $+:-:*:/:$**EOF**	$term$	$\Rightarrow C_{14,25}$
	$term$	$\rightarrow$ $\cdot\,factor$, $+:-:*:/:$**EOF**	$factor$	$\Rightarrow C_{17,24}$
	$factor$	$\rightarrow$ $\cdot\,(\ expression\ )$, $+:-:*:/:$**EOF**	(	$\Rightarrow C_{6,13}$
	$factor$	$\rightarrow$ $\cdot\,$**integer**, $+:-:*:/:$**EOF**	**integer**	$\Rightarrow C_{18,22}$
	$factor$	$\rightarrow$ $\cdot\,$**variable**, $+:-:*:/:$**EOF**	**variable**	$\Rightarrow C_{19,23}$
C_1	$expression'$	$\rightarrow$ $expression\ \cdot\,$, **EOF**	$\pi 0$, **EOF**	
	$expression$	$\rightarrow$ $expression\ \cdot\,term\_operator\ term$, $+:-:$**EOF**	$term\_operator$	$\Rightarrow C_{2,9}$
	$term\_operator$	$\rightarrow$ $\cdot\,+$, (:**integer**:**variable**	$+$	$\Rightarrow C_{20}$
	$term\_operator$	$\rightarrow$ $\cdot\,-$, (:**integer**:**variable**	$-$	$\Rightarrow C_{21}$
$C_{2,9}$	$expression$	$\rightarrow$ $expression\ term\_operator\ \cdot\,term$, $+:-:)$**EOF**	$term$	$\Rightarrow C_{3,10}$
	$term$	$\rightarrow$ $\cdot\,term\ factor\_operator\ factor$, $+:-:*:/:)$**EOF**	$term$	$\Rightarrow C_{3,10}$
	$term$	$\rightarrow$ $\cdot\,factor$, $+:-:*:/:)$**EOF**	$factor$	$\Rightarrow C_{17,24}$
	$factor$	$\rightarrow$ $\cdot\,(\ expression\ )$, $+:-:*:/:)$**EOF**	(	$\Rightarrow C_{6,13}$
	$factor$	$\rightarrow$ $\cdot\,$**integer**, $+:-:*:/:)$**EOF**	**integer**	$\Rightarrow C_{18,22}$
	$factor$	$\rightarrow$ $\cdot\,$**variable**, $+:-:*:/:)$**EOF**	**variable**	$\Rightarrow C_{19,23}$
$C_{3,10}$	$expression$	$\rightarrow$ $expression\ term\_operator\ term\ \cdot\,$, $+:-:)$**EOF**	$\pi 1$, $+:-:)$**EOF**	
	$term$	$\rightarrow$ $term\ \cdot\,factor\_operator\ factor$, $+:-:*:/:)$**EOF**	$factor\_operator$	$\Rightarrow C_{4,11}$
	$factor\_operator$	$\rightarrow$ $\cdot\,*$, (:**integer**:**variable**	$*$	$\Rightarrow C_{15}$
	$factor\_operator$	$\rightarrow$ $\cdot\,/$, (:**integer**:**variable**	$/$	$\Rightarrow C_{16}$
$C_{4,11}$	$term$	$\rightarrow$ $term\ factor\_operator\ \cdot\,factor$, $+:-:*:/:)$**EOF**	$factor$	$\Rightarrow C_{5,12}$
	$factor$	$\rightarrow$ $\cdot\,(\ expression\ )$, $+:-:*:/:)$**EOF**	(	$\Rightarrow C_{6,13}$
	$factor$	$\rightarrow$ $\cdot\,$**integer**, $+:-:*:/:)$**EOF**	**integer**	$\Rightarrow C_{18,22}$
	$factor$	$\rightarrow$ $\cdot\,$**variable**, $+:-:*:/:)$**EOF**	**variable**	$\Rightarrow C_{19,23}$
$C_{5,12}$	$term$	$\rightarrow$ $term\ factor\_operator\ factor\ \cdot\,$, $+:-:*:/:)$**EOF**	$\pi 5$, $+:-:*:/:)$**EOF**	
$C_{6,13}$	$factor$	$\rightarrow$ $(\ \cdot\,expression\ )$, $+:-:*:/:)$**EOF**	$expression$	$\Rightarrow C_7$
	$expression$	$\rightarrow$ $\cdot\,expression\ term\_operator\ term$, $+:-:)$	$expression$	$\Rightarrow C_7$
	$expression$	$\rightarrow$ $\cdot\,term$, $+:-:)$	$term$	$\Rightarrow C_{14,25}$
	$term$	$\rightarrow$ $\cdot\,term\ factor\_operator\ factor$, $+:-:*:/:)$	$term$	$\Rightarrow C_{14,25}$
	$term$	$\rightarrow$ $\cdot\,factor$, $+:-:*:/:)$	$factor$	$\Rightarrow C_{17,24}$
	$factor$	$\rightarrow$ $\cdot\,(\ expression\ )$, $+:-:*:/:)$	(	$\Rightarrow C_{6,13}$
	$factor$	$\rightarrow$ $\cdot\,$**integer**, $+:-:*:/:)$	**integer**	$\Rightarrow C_{18,22}$
	$factor$	$\rightarrow$ $\cdot\,$**variable**, $+:-:*:/:)$	**variable**	$\Rightarrow C_{19,23}$
C_7	$factor$	$\rightarrow$ $(\ expression\ \cdot\,)$, $+:-:*:/:$**EOF**	)	$\Rightarrow C_8$
	$expression$	$\rightarrow$ $expression\ \cdot\,term\_operator\ term$, $+:-:)$	$term\_operator$	$\Rightarrow C_{2,9}$
	$term\_operator$	$\rightarrow$ $\cdot\,+$, (:**integer**:**variable**	$+$	$\Rightarrow C_{20}$
	$term\_operator$	$\rightarrow$ $\cdot\,-$, (:**integer**:**variable**	$-$	$\Rightarrow C_{21}$
C_8	$factor$	$\rightarrow$ $(\ expression\ )\ \cdot\,$, $+:-:*:/:$**EOF**	$\pi 9$, $+:-:*:/:$**EOF**	
$C_{14,25}$	$expression$	$\rightarrow$ $term\ \cdot\,$, $+:-:)$**EOF**	$\pi 2$, $+:-:)$**EOF**	
	$term$	$\rightarrow$ $term\ \cdot\,factor\_operator\ factor$, $+:-:*:/:)$**EOF**	$factor\_operator$	$\Rightarrow C_{4,11}$
	$factor\_operator$	$\rightarrow$ $\cdot\,*$, (:**integer**:**variable**	$*$	$\Rightarrow C_{15}$
	$factor\_operator$	$\rightarrow$ $\cdot\,/$, (:**integer**:**variable**	$/$	$\Rightarrow C_{16}$
C_{15}	$factor\_operator$	$\rightarrow$ $*\ \cdot\,$, (:**integer**:**variable**	$\pi 7$, (:**integer**:**variable**	
C_{16}	$factor\_operator$	$\rightarrow$ $/\ \cdot\,$, (:**integer**:**variable**	$\pi 8$, (:**integer**:**variable**	
$C_{17,24}$	$term$	$\rightarrow$ $factor\ \cdot\,$, $+:-:*:/:)$**EOF**	$\pi 6$, $+:-:*:/:)$**EOF**	
$C_{18,22}$	$factor$	$\rightarrow$ **integer** $\cdot\,$, $+:-:*:/:)$**EOF**	$\pi 10$, $+:-:*:/:)$**EOF**	
$C_{19,23}$	$factor$	$\rightarrow$ **variable** $\cdot\,$, $+:-:*:/:)$**EOF**	$\pi 11$, $+:-:*:/:)$**EOF**	
C_{20}	$term\_operator$	$\rightarrow$ $+\ \cdot\,$, (:**integer**:**variable**	$\pi 3$, (:**integer**:**variable**	
C_{21}	$term\_operator$	$\rightarrow$ $-\ \cdot\,$, (:**integer**:**variable**	$\pi 4$, (:**integer**:**variable**	

Table 6.11   Action table for the LALR(1) parser

State	+	−	*	/	(	)	integer	variable	EOF
0					shift 6		shift 15	shift 16	
1	shift 9	shift 10							accept
2					shift 6		shift 15	shift 16	
3	reduce 1	reduce 1	shift 12	shift 13		reduce 1			reduce 1
4					shift 6		shift 15	shift 16	
5	reduce 5	reduce 5	reduce 5	reduce 5		reduce 5			reduce 5
6					shift 6		shift 15	shift 16	
7	shift 9	shift 10				shift 8			
8	reduce 9	reduce 9	reduce 9	reduce 9					reduce 9
9					reduce 3		reduce 3	reduce 3	
10					reduce 4		reduce 4	reduce 4	
11	reduce 2	reduce 2	shift 12	shift 13		reduce 2			reduce 2
12					reduce 7		reduce 7	reduce 7	
13					reduce 8		reduce 8	reduce 8	
14	reduce 6	reduce 6	reduce 6	reduce 6		reduce 6			reduce 6
15	reduce 10	reduce 10	reduce 10	reduce 10		reduce 10			reduce 10
16	reduce 11	reduce 11	reduce 11	reduce 11		reduce 11			reduce 11

Table 6.12   Goto table for LALR(1) parser

State	expression	term_operator	term	factor_operator	factor
0	goto 1		goto 11		goto 14
1		goto 2			
2			goto 3		goto 14
3				goto 4	
4					goto 5
5					
6	goto 7		goto 11		goto 14
7		goto 2			
8					
9					
10					
11				goto 4	
12					
13					
14					
15					
16					

distinction between a complete parenthesized sub-expression (which could be followed by a further close bracket from a surrounding expression) and a complete parenthesized expression (which could only be followed by **EOF**), allowing detection of a missing close parenthesis slightly earlier in the parsing process.

Merging configurating sets to create LALR(1) tables does not always work, since we may get conflicts. We cannot create shift-reduce conflicts, where we have two LR(1) configurations:

$$X \rightarrow \bar{u} \cdot, a$$

$$Y \rightarrow \bar{v} \cdot a\bar{w}, \text{b}$$

A conflict such as this, where we wish to both reduce and shift on a, is due to the core of the configurations, and since the cores are identical in both the sets being merged, the conflict must have been in those sets as well.

However, we can get reduce conflicts, consider merging two sets, C_0:

$$X \rightarrow \bar{u} \cdot, a$$

$$Y \rightarrow \bar{v} \cdot, b$$

and C_1:

$$X \rightarrow \bar{u} \cdot, b$$

$$Y \rightarrow \bar{v} \cdot, a$$

The merger is valid, since the sets have common cores. However, we obtain the following merged set:

$$X \rightarrow \bar{u} \cdot, a{:}b$$

$$Y \rightarrow \bar{v} \cdot, a{:}b$$

This will lead to an action to reduce by both productions, whenever we see a or b, even though the original sets had no conflict. This is an example of a grammar which is canonical LR(1), but not LALR(1).

More efficient construction of LALR(1) parse tables

To build the complete canonical LR(1) family of configurating sets before reducing it to the LALR(1) table is far from efficient. A variety of different algorithms exist to determine tables more efficiently. They rely on two observations:

- We need not bother to write down configurations in configurating sets where the dot appears at the start of the production's right-hand side.
- We can worry about working out lookaheads after we have constructed the family of configurating sets.

We thus need only create the same number of configurating sets as with SLR(1), and those sets will have only a small number of configurations.

There are a number of different algorithms which construct LALR(1) tables efficiently this way, and which are used in parser generators such as YACC and bison, which are described in Chapter 8. Further improvements allow the action and goto tables to be held using compact representations, where space is at a premium, at the expense of some performance of the parser.

These algorithms are not particularly difficult, but are beyond the scope of an introductory text such as this.

6.3.6 ATTRIBUTE GRAMMARS AND SHIFT-REDUCE PARSING

Because shift-reduce parsing is bottom up we cannot use it directly for inherited attributes. However, it is perfectly possible to use synthesized attributes. We modify our stack so that instead of holding just states on the stack we hold state-attribute pairs. Every time we read a token and shift a state onto the stack we also shift its attribute. When we reduce a handle we also pop the attributes off the stack, calculate the synthesized attributes, and put them back with the reduced handle's state.

6.3.7 OPERATOR PRECEDENCE PARSING

Operator precedence parsing is a simple bottom-up method of parsing that can be used for a particular class of grammars, *operator grammars*. It can be used as the basis of a shift-reduce parser for such grammars. However, we shall describe it in the context of driving recursive descent when we have a left recursive grammar.

Operator grammars

An operator grammar is one in which no right side of a production contains two adjacent non-terminals. For example, the unambiguous grammar for VSL expressions used when considering LR parsers (see Table 6.1) is not an operator grammar, since the first and fifth productions contain three adjacent non-terminals. However, if we do some substitution we get the equivalent grammar as shown in Table 6.13. This is an operator grammar.

For such a grammar, we can define *operator precedence relations* between the terminal symbols of an operator grammar as follows:

- $x \doteq y$ for $x,y \in \mathbb{T}$ if there exists a production $A \rightarrow \bar{u}xy\bar{v}$ or $A \rightarrow \bar{u}xBy\bar{v}$, where $A,B \in \mathbb{N}$ and $\bar{u},\bar{v}$ are arbitrary (possibly empty) strings of symbols in $\mathbb{V}$.
- $x \gtrdot y$ for $x,y \in \mathbb{T}$ if there exists a production $A \rightarrow \bar{u}By\bar{v}$ and $B \overset{+}{\Rightarrow} \bar{w}x$ or $B \overset{+}{\Rightarrow} \bar{w}xC$, where $A,B,C \in \mathbb{N}$ and $\bar{u}, \bar{v}, \bar{w}$ are arbitrary (possibly empty) strings of symbols in $\mathbb{V}$.
- $x \lessdot y$ for $x,y \in \mathbb{T}$ if there exists a production $A \rightarrow \bar{u}xB\bar{v}$ and $B \overset{+}{\Rightarrow} y\bar{w}$ or $B \overset{+}{\Rightarrow} Cy\bar{w}$, where $A,B,C \in \mathbb{N}$ and $\bar{u}, \bar{v}, \bar{w}$ are arbitrary (possibly empty) strings of symbols in $\mathbb{V}$.

For example from the grammar of Table 6.13 we could see that $(\doteq)$ since (and) both appear in the seventh production, separated by a single non-terminal. We could also deduce that $* \gtrdot +$, from the first production, *expression → expression + term* and seeing that *expression ⇒ term ⇒ term *factor*.

We often use operator precedence to parse grammars for arithmetic expressions. In these circumstances we find an intuitive meaning to our operator precedence relations.

Table 6.13 Operator grammar for VSL expressions

expression → *expression* + *term*	
expression → *expression* − *term*	
expression → *term*	
term	→ *term* * *factor*
term	→ *term* / *factor*
term	→ *factor*
factor	→ (*expression*)
factor	→ **integer**
factor	→ **variable**

- **x** $\doteq$ **y** means **x** has the same precedence as **y**.
- **x** > **y** means **x** has greater precedence than **y**.
- **x** < **y** means **x** has lower precedence than **y**.

This can catch out the unwary. The correct relationship between + and + for example is + > +, not + $\doteq$ +, since addition is left associative, and so the left-most addition has higher precedence.

Operator precedence parse tables

An *operator precedence grammar* is an operator grammar for which only one of the relations <, $\doteq$, > holds for each pair of terminal symbols. This is the case for the grammar of Table 6.13, for which we have the relations shown in Table 6.14. We read tokens onto a stack until we build up a series of relations of the form:

$$X_i < X_{i+1} \doteq X_{i+2} \cdots \doteq X_{j-1} > X_j$$

The sequence $X_{i+1} \cdots X_{j-1}$ together with any intervening or surrounding non-terminals (which have no precedence relation) form a handle that can be reduced.

Table 6.14 Operator precedences for the grammar of Table 6.13

	+	−	*	/	(	)	integer	variable	EOF
+	>	>	<	<	<	>	<	<	>
−	>	>	<	<	<	>	<	<	>
*	>	>	>	>	<	>	<	<	>
/	>	>	>	>	<	>	<	<	>
(	<	<	<	<	<	$\doteq$	<	<	
)	>	>	>	>		>			>
integer	>	>	>	>		>			>
variable	>	>	>	>		>			>
EOF	<	<	<	<	<		<	<	

Table 6.15   VSL grammar including unary minus

expression	→ *expression term_operator term*
expression	→ *term*
term_operator	→ +
term_operator	→ −
term	→ *term factor_operator factor*
term	→ *factor*
factor_operator	→ *
factor_operator	→ /
factor	→ (*expression*)
factor	→ − *expression*
factor	→ **integer**
factor	→ **variable**

Precedence functions

Rather than building tables of precedence relations between all pairs of operators it is often possible to construct two functions, *lprec* and *rprec*, which have the property that:

$$a \lessdot b \quad \text{iff} \quad lprec(a) < rprec(b)$$

$$a \gtrdot b \quad \text{iff} \quad lprec(a) > rprec(b)$$

$$a \doteq b \quad \text{iff} \quad lprec(a) = rprec(b)$$

This is an obviously compact representation.

Operator precedence and recursive descent

A particular type of grammar that causes problems with recursive descent is the left recursive grammar used to describe expressions, e.g. the VSL grammar of Table 6.1, which is shown in Table 6.15 with unary minus. We can think of such a grammar as being a series of *basic expressions* connected by binary operators to form *complete expressions*. In general, any unary operators in the basic expressions have higher precedence than any binary operators in complete expressions. Thus in this grammar the basic expressions are given by:

$$factor \rightarrow (expression)$$

$$factor \rightarrow - expression$$

$$factor \rightarrow \textbf{integer}$$

$$factor \rightarrow \textbf{variable}$$

while the complete expressions are defined by:

$$expression \qquad \rightarrow expression \; term\_operator \; term$$

$$expression \qquad \rightarrow term$$

$$term\_operator \quad \rightarrow +$$

$$term\_operator \quad \rightarrow -$$

$$term \qquad \qquad \rightarrow term \; factor\_operator \; factor$$

$$term \qquad \qquad \rightarrow factor$$

$$factor\_operator \quad \rightarrow *$$

$$factor\_operator \quad \rightarrow /$$

The routine to parse an expression, `rexp(n)`, takes as argument a precedence (n). It parses a complete expression followed by a token whose left precedence function is less than n. This is done by calling a routine to parse a basic expression, `rbexp()`. The next token must then be a binary operator. If this token's left precedence function is less than or equal to that of the argument, n, then we call `rexp()` recursively to read the right operand of the binary operator, passing as argument the right precedence of the binary operator.

Defining the precedence functions is easy. They are only needed for the binary operators and they reflect the arithmetic precedence of the operators. Because of the use of `rbexp()` to read the left operand and `rexp()` to read the right operand of an operator we will have left associativity of operators with equal precedence, which is what we generally want. So for our VSL grammar above we will have the precedences shown in Table 6.16. A complete expression can be obtained by `rexp(0)`.

Table 6.16

Operator	lprec	rprec
+	1	1
−	1	1
*	2	2
/	2	2

The implementation is straightforward enough, `rbexp()` will have the general form:

```
void   rbexp()
{
        switch( nextsymb )
        {
        case '(':

                /* Bracketed complete expression */

                rexp( 0 ) ;
                checkfor( ')' ) ;
                return ;
```

```
        case '-':

                /* Unary - */

                nextsymb = yylex() ;
                rexp( 0 ) ;
                return ;

        case T_INTEGER:
        case T_VARIABLE:

                /* Single token */

                nextsymb = yylex() ;
                return ;
        }

    }      /* rbexp() */
```

The tree structure involved could easily be handled by making rbexp() and rexp() return a struct node for the expression read. rexp() has the form:

```
void  rexp( int n )
{
        rbexp() ;                        /* Left operand */

        /* Get the right operand */

        switch( nextsymb )
        {
        case '+':
        case '-':

                if( n >= 1 )
                        return ;         /* lprec too high */

                nextsymb = yylex() ;
                rexp( 1 ) ;              /* Call with lprec */
                return ;

        case '*':
        case '/':

                if( n >= 2 )
                        return ;         /* lprec too high */

                nextsymb = yylex() ;
                rexp( 2 ) ;              /* Call with lprec */
                return ;

        default:

                return ;                 /* Expression complete */
        }

    }      /* rexp( int n ) */
```

It is easy enough to generalize these routines to handle more complex expressions, e.g. with function calls as part of the basic expression. The routines may be called within a parser that otherwise uses recursive descent.

Exercises

PRACTICAL PROBLEMS

6.1. Write the recursive descent routines to recognize VSL statements. Assume that the routines to recognize assignment statements, return statements, print statements, null statements, if statements, and while statements have been written. Pay particular attention to the left terminal sets.
6.2. Demonstrate that the grammar for VSL expressions including unary minus shown in Table 6.15 is not SLR(1).
6.3. Extend `rbexp()` and `rexp()` so that the operator precedence parser for VSL can handle function calls.

ESSAY TITLES

6.1. Compare and contrast recursive descent and LR parsing.
6.2. What solutions are there to the problem of parsing a left recursive grammar with recursive descent?
6.3. Show by example how SLR(1) parse tables are constructed.

DISCUSSION TOPICS

6.1. Investigate the efficient construction of LALR(1) parse tables. Try them out on the example grammar of Table 6.15.
6.2. Investigate some other parsing techniques not covered in this chapter.

Further reading

There is no doubt that the standard reference work on this subject is the two-volume *The Theory of Parsing, Translation and Compiling* by V. A. Aho and J. D. Ullman, published by Prentice-Hall (1972, 1973). Although somewhat out of date, much of parsing theory, as relevant to language translation, was established by then.

As an alternative, try Gries (see the further reading section in Chapter 3), which covers a wide range of parsing methods at a simpler level.

7
Error handling

The user is generally not happy with a compiler that only accepts correct programs, and under all other circumstances stops or crashes. In the event of an error he or she expects the compiler to give constructive error messages and then recover to a consistent state, so that a single run of the compiler will find all the errors in the program.

We can identify four principle types of error which the compiler writer has to handle:

- *Lexical errors*   These are errors in the lexemes making up the program, usually mistypings of keywords, e.g. WHILE entered as HWILE.
- *Syntax errors*   These are errors in the overall structure of the program. Common examples are omitting a semicolon between statements or forgetting a closing section bracket.
- *Compile-time semantic errors*   Some semantic errors can be spotted before the program is run. The commonest examples of this are type errors, e.g. in C using a float as a character array, or in VSL trying to call a variable name as a function.
- *Run-time semantic errors*   Some errors occur only when the program is executing, e.g. dividing by zero or writing off the end of an array.

The compiler must be capable of handling and recovering from all the compile-time errors, even if it cannot as a result generate any valid code. Furthermore, error handling should not significantly slow down the compilation of correct programs. A suitable error message, comprehensible to the average user, must be provided. For example:

'missing comma on line 36'

is helpful. But:

'unable to shift in state 437'

is not. After detecting each error the compiler must recover so that it can parse the rest of the program to detect further errors. The compiler must beware of reporting spurious errors that are just a consequence of earlier errors.

The associated run-time system must have provision for trapping errors when they occur. A high-quality compiler, particularly in a teaching environment, will also detect potential problems with a program, e.g. variables that are declared but never used, statements that cannot be reached, or meaningless arithmetic such as adding constant zero.

7.1   Compile-time error handling

Lexical and syntax errors are closely related. In particular, the correction of a lexical error may lead to a syntax error if care is not taken. Compile-time type checking will be covered in Chapter 9.

7.1.1   LEXICAL ERRORS

These are very simple and mean that the lexical analyser cannot match the stream of input characters to a pattern for any token. In most cases the correct response is to return the most likely possibility, with a message stating that the lexical analyser could not recognize a token. An alternative is to return an 'error' token, and let the syntax analyser handle the error.

When we hit an error how do we recover? The simplest approach is to ignore input characters until a valid token is recognized, and for many purposes this may be adequate. A more sophisticated approach is to recognize that most lexical errors are single-character errors and to try various single-character transformations until a valid token is obtained. For example:

● Delete a single character from the input.
● Insert a single character in the input.
● Replace a single character in the input.
● Swap two adjacent characters in the input.

The most general approach is to use a series of single-character changes, choosing the shortest series of changes as the best. This is *minimum-distance error correction*. In practice this level of complexity is not needed and it is rarely implemented.

7.1.2   SYNTAX ERRORS

The first action on detecting an error is to report it. Typically the section of code where the error occurred is printed with an arrow underneath pinpointing the offending character and, if the cause of the error is clear, an appropriate message. For example, in the VSL program:

```
FUNC main()
{
        INT  a b

        a := 1
        b := 2
}
```

where there is a comma missing after the declaration of a we would hope to have
an error report of the form:

```
{
            INT a
                  ^
    ** ERROR - comma missing
```

Having reported the error, we must recover, so that any further errors can be
detected, but avoiding a cascade of derived errors. There are four types of error
recovery, which it is possible to use in combination.

Panic mode recovery

With this approach we discard input tokens until we reach a token that signifies
a consistent position. For example, in VSL we might choose to discard until we
reach a FI, DONE, CONTINUE, or closing section bracket (which means we are
about to start a new statement), or the keyword FUNC (which means we are
about to start a new function). We refer to these tokens as *synchronizing tokens*.
This method is simple and cannot get stuck in a loop since it always consumes
input tokens. However, if multiple errors between synchronizing tokens occur it
will miss some errors.

Phrase level recovery

Here we try to make local alterations to the input tokens to obtain a valid
phrase that would allow parsing to continue. Inserting, deleting, changing, and
swapping tokens are all possible. However, if we allow unlimited insertion of
tokens we can get stuck in a loop. In addition, this method works poorly when
the error was actually caused some way back in the input, e.g. by the omission of
an opening section bracket.

Error productions

If some errors (such as missing commas) are particularly common we can
augment our grammar with productions to pick up these errors and construct
our parser using this grammar. If the production is used we print out an error
message and can see clearly what corrective action is needed. Choosing a good
set of error productions can be very difficult.

Global error correction

This is like minimum-distance error correction in lexical analysis. We seek to
transform our source program to a program that can be parsed correctly. We
choose the minimum set of transformations to the input necessary. This is far
too expensive to be used for real compilers, and the closest correct program may

not always be the best correction. For example, it is often the furthest opening section bracket that is omitted.

Panic mode recovery is normally used with hand-written parsers, such as recursive descent, while error productions are common with automatically derived, table-driven parsers. For example, the YACC and Bison parser generators to be discussed in the next chapter use a type of error production for error recovery. Phrase level recovery is not often seen, while global error correction is a theoretical concept, only used in research projects.

7.2 Run-time errors

The handling of run-time errors is dependent on the target machine. The two commonest run-time errors are arithmetic errors such as divide by zero or square root of a negative number, and indirection errors, such as writing off the end of an array or trying to use an uninitialized pointer variable. On many machines such errors will be detected as traps or internal interrupts, in which case the run-time system must provide the necessary error handling and recovery. As with compile-time errors, there must be a suitable error message followed by recovery to a consistent position. Usually the only sensible recovery is to terminate execution, but it is sometimes constructive, e.g. when evaluating an arithmetic expression, to continue execution using a default value.

Trap handling is usually adequate for arithmetic errors, but may not be sufficient for indirection errors. Writing outside the bounds of a defined array may not cause a memory error, but just end up corrupting another variable. For example, in the C fragment:

```
{
        int a[2] ;
        int b ;

        a[2] = 10 ;
}
```

the attempt to use a third element of a, a[2], would quite likely just corrupt b. Improved error handling is obtained by having the compiler generate code to check array bounds at run time. In the above example whenever an element of a was indexed we would compile code to check that the index was in the range 0–1. Many target machines provide instructions to support this sort of check.

Similar code must be provided for arithmetic operations if the target machine does not detect arithmetic errors by generating a trap. So, for example, each divide instruction must be preceded by code to check that the divisor is not zero.

Such checking code seriously impairs performance and is usually provided as an option to the compiler. Once a program is debugged and running satisfactorily it can be recompiled without the checking code to give a program that runs much faster.

Exercises

PRACTICAL PROBLEMS

7.1. Investigate the error-handling capabilities of various compilers. One approach to this is to write a program of say ten lines that generates as many errors as possible. Another is to write a program illustrating particular errors and compare the messages from different compilers.

7.2. Try to add minimum-distance error correction to the *ad hoc* lexical analyser for VSL, shown in Chapter 5.

ESSAY TITLES

7.1. Compare and contrast the different possible approaches to syntax error correction in compilers.

7.2. Russian agents have just obtained a copy of the latest Star Wars software, written in VSL. Unfortunately Russian tape drives have difficulty with ASCII, and the program is read off slightly corrupted, although the position of all the lexemes is certain. Advise the Kremlin on how to reconstruct the original program. What other advice would you give if you could not even be certain of where whole lexemes occurred?

7.3. How may run-time errors be handled?

DISCUSSION TOPICS

7.1. Investigate the algorithm for global syntax error correction.

Further reading

'A Bibliography of Error Handling' by J. Ciesinger, *ACM SIGPLAN Notices*, **14**, 16–26 (1979), is a good starting point with numerous references to work on error handling in compilers.

Use of minimum-distance error correction is shown in 'A Minimum Distance Error-correcting Parser for Context-free Languages' by A. V. Aho and T. G. Peterson, *SIAM J. Computing*, **1**, 305–312 (1972).

8
Parser generators

Many types of parser are table driven. As can be seen from the example derivation of shift-reduce parse tables in Chapter 6, this is a laborious process by hand. For complete programming languages such tables are generated automatically from a specification of the grammar and associated semantic actions. The programs that perform this are known as *parser generators* or sometimes (rather incorrectly) *compiler-compilers*. Such parsers take as their input either programs in the source language, or a stream of tokens from a lexical analyser (which has to be written separately). Output is usually some intermediate representation, such as a parse tree or three-address code, for which a back end must then be written. Occasionally the output may be the target language itself, in which case the description compiler-compiler is more appropriate.

There are a wide range of parser generators, as well as tools to assist the compiler writer in analysing grammars. Some of the more interesting are discussed in Section 8.5.

The example we shall look at in detail is *YACC* (which stands for *Yet Another Compiler Compiler*) which is widely available under Unix and some other operating systems. *Bison* is a non-commercial version of YACC supplied by the Free Software Foundation. YACC takes a specification of a programming language grammar and semantic actions and produces LALR(1) parsing tables and a shift-reduce parser. The source program is read as a stream of tokens, so a lexical analyser must be provided separately, typically using the LEX lexical analyser generator.

8.1 YACC

A YACC program has the general form

Declarations

%%

Rules

%%

Support routines

After processing by YACC this will produce a shift-reduce parser written in C (typically called y.tab.c) which must be compiled by the C compiler. This provides a routine called yyparse() which is called to carry out parsing, yyparse() in turn uses yylex() which must return the next token from the input stream when it is called. yylex() can either be written by hand, or produced using the LEX lexical analyser generator.

Bison provides various extensions to YACC to make it easier to use. The only one that causes any conflict is an increased flexibility in the way output files are named (unlike YACC's fixed file names). However, by using the -y flag, Bison will behave exactly like YACC. Thus any use of YACC:

```
yacc ...
```

can be replaced by

```
bison -y ...
```

8.1.1 DECLARATIONS SECTION

In the definitions section we declare the tokens used in the grammar. There are two types of token in YACC:

- *Single characters*   These need not be declared, but are used when needed delimited by single quotes. The standard C escapes, '\n' for newline, '\t' for tab, and so on are understood.
- *Multicharacter tokens returned by the lexical analyser*   Each of these is represented by a declared name, using the %token declaration. So, for example, the reserved word 'VAR', the assignment symbol ':=', and variable names might be declared.

```
%token  VAR
%token  ASSIGN
%token  VARIABLE
```

or for conciseness

```
%token VAR ASSIGN VARIABLE
```

By convention, upper-case letters are used for tokens. Internally, each token is represented by a small integer, starting from 257 (the numbers up to 255 are used for the single ASCII characters, 256 is used as an error token). It is sometimes convenient to be able to include these definitions in other programs (such as the lexical analyser). If the -d flag is used then YACC produces a header file of C #define statements suitable for inclusion elsewhere. The above example would produce the definitions:

```
# define VAR 257
# define ASSIGN 258
# define VARIABLE 259
```

There are a number of other declarations that can appear in this section, whose effect is discussed later. In addition to YACC declarations this section can include C code for support routines, surrounded by %{ and %}. A common use of this is to include a file defining the lexical analyser routine, `yylex()`. For example:

```
%{
#include "lex.yy.c"
%}
```

8.1.2 RULES SECTION

This is where the grammar and semantic actions are defined. A production in YACC has the form:

non-terminal : *right hand side* { *actions* } ;

Rules may spread over more than one line. Typical rules for VSL might look like:

```
print_statement  :  PRINT print_list
                    {
                            $$ = $2 ;
                    }
                 ;

block            :  '{' declaration_list statement_list '}'
                    {
                            $$ = join_tac( $2, $3 ) ;
                    }
                 ;
```

The right-hand sides may include terminals and non-terminals defined elsewhere, in these examples *print_list, declaration_ list* and *statement_list*. PRINT is the token PRINT recognized by the lexical analyser. The actions have the general form of C statements, but may include variables of the form $n or $$. YACC semantic actions are the same as those permitted in S-attributed grammars with a single attribute. $n is the value of this attribute associated with the nth item on the right-hand side of the production, $$ is the attribute being synthesized and associated with the non-terminal on the left. There is only a single attribute associated with each entity in the production. In the examples above for *print_statement* and *block* the actions might be those appropriate for building a list of three-address code. So for a *print_statement* the TAC is just that created for the associated *print_list*. For a *block* we join the TAC for the declarations and statements.

If no action is specified, then there is a default action:

```
$$ = $1 ;
```

If we have multiple definitions of a non-terminal then we can use the vertical bar, |, to specify alternatives. For example:

```
function_list  :  function
               |  function_list function
                  {
                          $$ = join_tac( $1, $2 ) ;
                  }
               ;
```

By default the sentence symbol is the first non-terminal defined at the start of the rules section. An alternative sentence symbol may be specified by use of the %start statement in the declarations section. In VSL we might want to specify:

```
%start program
```

8.1.3 SUPPORT ROUTINES SECTION

C code is placed in this section to support the semantic actions defined in the rules section. For example, join_tac() would probably be defined here. In large systems support code might be defined in separate files, and this section could be empty.

We have now outlined the basic actions of YACC. There are many other commands that extend and modify the parser that is created. These are described in the following sections. As an example, however, we give here a short YACC program to recognize a VSL declaration and print out the number of variables declared:

```
%{
#include "lex.yy.c"
%}

%token VAR
%token VARIABLE            /* Handled in the lexer */

%start declaration         /* Default anyway */

%%

declaration    :  VAR variable_list
                  { printf( "%d vars\n", $1 ) ; }
               ;

variable_list  :  VARIABLE
                  { $$ = 1 ;        /* Number of vars seen */ }
               |  VARIABLE variable_list
                  { $$ = 1 + $2 ; /* Add the totals */ }
               ;

%%

main()
{
        yyparse() ;

}       /* main () */
```

We assume that lex.yy.c contains the definition of a lexical analyser capable of recognizing variables and the keyword VAR.

8.2   YACC and ambiguous grammars

8.2.1 PRECEDENCE AND ASSOCIATIVITY

The most common source of ambiguity occurs with arithmetic expressions, such as the original VSL grammar for expressions:

expression   → *expression binary_operator expression* |
                          unary_operator expression | (*expression*) | *integer* |
                          variable | *variable* (*argument_list*)
binary_operator → + | − | * | /
unary_operator → −

Rather than rewriting this unambiguously, YACC permits us to resolve the ambiguity by specifying the precedence and associativity of operators. We merely have to rewrite the grammar so that operators to be resolved appear in productions defining the same non-terminal. In the VSL case this is:

expression → *expression* + *expression* |
             expression − *expression* |
             expression * *expression* |
             expression / *expression* |
             − *expression* | (*expression*) | *integer* |
             variable | *variable* (*argument_list*)

In the declarations section we list the operators in order of precedence. This is done using the `%left` declaration for operators that associate to the left, the `%right` declaration for operators that associate to the right, and the `%nonassoc` declaration for operators (such as relational operators) that are not associative at all. Operators that have the same precedence appear in the same declaration. So for VSL we would use:

```
%left '+' '-'
%left '*' '/'
```

This is not quite sufficient, since ' − ' appears in two contexts—one as a binary operator with the same precedence and associative as ' + ', the other as a unary operator with higher precedence than any other operator and associating to the right. If unary negation were a different token there would be no problem—we could put it in the list of precedences. The solution is to define a separate token for unary negation as though it were different from the token for binary subtraction. We shall call this token UMINUS and add it to the precedence list.

```
%left  '+' '-'
%left  '*' '/'
%right UMINUS
```

UMINUS is not actually used anywhere (we do not even need to declare it as a token), but it is set up to have the same precedence as unary negation would have were it a separate token to be parsed. YACC then allows us to force any production to be parsed at a particular precedence by adding `%prec` at the end of the production. So for unary negation we can use the production:

```
expression  :  '-' expression %prec UMINUS
            ;
```

The parser created by YACC will handle this expression not as though '−' were left associative and with the precedence of '+', but with the right associativity and precedence of the imaginary token UMINUS. The %prec command has been used to override the declared precedence of '−'.

The VSL parser to generate TAC for expressions in YACC looks something like:

```
%token INTEGER
%token VARIABLE

%left  '+' '-'
%left  '*' '/'
%right UMINUS

%%

expression : expression '+' expression
               {
                       $$ = do_bin( TAC_ADD, $1, $3 ) ;
               }
           | expression '-' expression
               {
                       $$ = do_bin( TAC_SUB, $1, $3 ) ;
               }
           | expression '*' expression
               {
                       $$ = do_bin( TAC_MUL, $1, $3 ) ;
               }
           | expression '/' expression
               {
                       $$ = do_bin( TAC_DIV, $1, $3 ) ;
               }
           | '-' expression %prec UMINUS
               {
                       $$ = do_un( TAC_NEG, $2 ) ;
               }
           | '(' expression ')'
               {
                       $$ = $2 ;
               }
           | INTEGER
               {
                       $$ = mkenode( NULL, $1, NULL ) ;
               }
           | VARIABLE
               {
                       $$ = mkenode( NULL, $1, NULL ) ;
               }
           | VARIABLE '(' argument_list ')'
               {
                       $$ = do_fnap( $1, $3 ) ;
               }
           ;
```

8.2.2 SHIFT-REDUCE AND REDUCE-REDUCE CONFLICTS

Since YACC uses LALR(1) parsing it is possible for both shift-reduce and reduce-reduce conflicts to occur, as discussed in Chapter 6. YACC applies a straightforward rule in each case. With shift-reduce conflicts YACC will use a shift in favour of a reduction. With reduce-reduce conflicts YACC will reduce using the production declared first in the rules section. Both conflicts are permissible in programming language grammars, but the compiler writer should take care to check that the action obtained is that desired. As a rule of thumb, shift-reduce conflicts are quite often acceptable and YACC's resolution in favour of shift achieves the desired effect. However reduce-reduce conflicts are unusual and should be treated as an indication of probable error in the grammar specification. If in doubt, rewriting of the grammar to avoid reduce-reduce conflicts is sensible.

8.2.3 DIAGNOSTIC INFORMATION FROM YACC

To help in analysing conflicts and other errors, YACC and Bison can produce a diagnostic file. This is obtained by using the -v option, and has the name y.output. It gives the family of configurating sets, details of any conflicts, and statistical data about use of the system's internal tables. For the trivial YACC program given earlier:

```
%{
#include "lex.yy.c"
%}

%token   VAR
%token   VARIABLE        /* Handled in the lexer */

%start declaration       /* Default anyway */

%%

declaration    :  VAR variable_list
                  { printf( "%d vars\n", $$ ) ; }
               ;

variable_list :  VARIABLE
                  { $$ = 1 ;          /* Number of vars seen */ }
               |  VARIABLE variable_list
                  { $$ = $1 + $2 ;  /* Add the totals */ }
               ;
%%

main()
{
        yyparse() ;

}       /* main() */
```

the diagnostic file obtained is:

```
state 0
        $accept : _declaration $end

        VAR   shift 2
        .  error

        declaration   goto 1

state 1
        $accept :  declaration_$end

        $end  accept
        .  error


state 2
        declaration :  VAR_variable_list

        VARIABLE   shift 4
        .  error

        variable_list   goto 3

state 3
        declaration :  VAR variable_list_    (1)

        .  reduce 1

state 4
        variable_list :  VARIABLE_    (2)
        variable_list :  VARIABLE_variable_list

        VARIABLE   shift 4
        .  reduce 2

        variable_list   goto 5

state 5
        variable_list :  VARIABLE variable_list_    (3)

        .  reduce 3

4/300 terminals, 2/300 nonterminals
4/600 grammar rules, 6/750 states
0 shift/reduce, 0 reduce/reduce conflicts reported
4/350 working sets used
memory: states,etc. 33/24000, parser 2/12000
4/600 distinct lookahead sets
0 extra closures
3 shift entries, 1 exceptions
3 goto entries
0 entries saved by goto default
Optimizer space used: input 12/24000, output 8/12000
8 table entries, 3 zero
maximum spread: 258, maximum offset: 258
```

There is a slight inconvenience here, since the diagnostic file uses the underscore symbol, _, rather than a dot in items. We have used underscores in non-terminal

Table 8.1 Unclosed family of configurating sets corresponding to YACC diagnostic output

Configurating set	Successor
C_0 *declaration'* → · *declaration*	*declaration* ⇒ C_1
C_1 *declaration'* → *declaration* ·	$\pi 0$
C_2 *declaration* → **VAR** · variable_list	*variable_list* ⇒ C_3
C_3 *declaration* → **VAR** variable_list ·	$\pi 1$
C_4 *variable_list* → **VARIABLE** ·	$\pi 2$
$\quad$ *variable_list* → **VARIABLE** · *variable_list*	*variable_list* ⇒ C_5
C_5 *variable_list* → **VARIABLE** variable_list ·	$\pi 3$

symbol names (e.g. *variable_list*), and a little care is needed to tell one from the other.

The configurating sets are shown unclosed—these files are verbose enough as it is. Table 8.1 shows this output as an unclosed family of configurating sets, in the format used by Chapter 6 for comparison. The augmented grammar is constructed with the special symbol $accept, which we have translated to *declaration'*, the non-terminal on the left of the first production in the augmented grammar. The lookahead sets are not given in this output, since we have the action and goto table entries associated with each state. These are shown in Tables 8.2 and 8.3.

Table 8.2 Action table corresponding to YACC diagnostic output

State	**VAR**	**VARIABLE**	**EOF**
0	shift 2		
1			accept
2		shift 4	
3	reduce 1	reduce 1	reduce 1
4	reduce 2	shift 4	reduce 2
5	reduce 3	reduce 3	reduce 3

Table 8.3 Goto table corresponding to YACC diagnostic output

State	*declaration*	*variable_list*
0	goto 1	
1		
2		goto 3
3		
4		goto 5
5		

Finally, we are given statistics about the parser. In this example we had four terminal symbols (**VAR, VARIABLE, EOF** and the special error symbol), out of a maximum possible of 300, and two non-terminal symbols (*declaration* and *variable_list*) out of a possible 300.

If we had shift/reduce or reduce/reduce conflicts, they would have been reported, not just in the totals at the bottom of the page, but in the states where they occurred, with details of the actions that were causing the clash. This is often the best way to find out what is causing an unexpected conflict in a YACC program.

8.3   Type consistency in YACC

We have loosely used the variables holding attribute values $$, $1, $2, and so on in YACC semantic actions without any consideration of their type. In some of the examples we have used them in construction of TAC lists, and so by implication given them type TAC * (the type used by the VSL compiler for three-address code). In fact by default these attribute variables have type integer, and all values associated with them should be integer. Our use of them to hold pointers would at the very least have led to many type warnings when compiling the resulting parser y.tab.c.

All attributes used in YACC must have the same type, but that type can be specified by the user as a C union of all the types that attributes may have in the YACC program. So for VSL we use three types: SYMB * for variable names, text, and constants, all of which go in the symbol table; TAC * for three-address code lists; and ENODE * for TAC generated by expressions, which also indicates the location of the results of the expressions. We specify these in the declarations section using the %union command. For example:

```
%union
{
        SYMB    *symb ;        /* For vars, consts and text */
        TAC     *tac ;         /* For most things */
        ENODE   *enode ;       /* For expressions */
}
```

Note the similarity with a C union. This sets up a C typedef for a union YYSTYPE. If YACC is used with the -d option this definition will appear in the y.tab.h file. For example:

```
typedef union
{
        SYMB    *symb ;        /* For vars, consts and text */
        TAC     *tac ;         /* For most things */
        ENODE   *enode ;       /* For expressions */
} YYSTYPE;
```

For any token or non-terminal we can specify the type of the associated attribute as one of the fields in this union. For tokens this is done by including the type in angle brackets after %token when the token is declared. For example:

```
%token <symb> INTEGER
```

The type may also be included similarly in `%left`, `%right`, or `%nonassoc` declarations. Non-terminals have their types defined using the `%type` declaration:

```
%type <tac>   program
%type <enode> expression
```

YACC inserts the appropriate member selector for any $$ or $n reference. It is also possible to force the type in rules explicitly by putting the type in angle brackets after the first $. For example:

```
expression  :  '(' expression ')'
               { $<enode>$ = $<enode>2 ; }
            ;
```

Fortunately this is rarely needed.

8.3.1 PASSING ATTRIBUTES BACK FROM THE LEXICAL ANALYSER

The routine `yylex()` returns the next token when it is called. Any associated attribute, e.g. the symbol table entry associated with a `VARIABLE` token, is passed back using the global variable `yylval`. This has type `YYSTYPE` so that the appropriate member of the union must be used. When using LEX it is useful to know that the text of the token read is held in the character array `yytext`. *Ad hoc* lexical analysers often choose to follow the same convention.

8.4   Error handling

Error handling in YACC makes use of error productions. These have the general form:

non-terminal : `error` *synchronizing set*

The synchronizing set is a set of symbols (possibly empty). On encountering an error, YACC first pops symbols off its stack until it finds a state whose associated configurating set contains an error production with the dot at the left-hand side. It then shifts the token `error` onto the stack as though that were the next input symbol.

If the synchronizing set is empty, YACC can immediately reduce by the error production, carrying out any associated semantic actions. YACC then discards input tokens until it finds a valid one on which parsing can resume.

If the synchronizing set of the error production is not empty, YACC discards input tokens until it finds one in the synchronizing set, or, if there are non-terminals in the synchronizing set, one that can be eventually be reduced to something in the synchronizing set. It can then shift the token and eventually reduce the error production, allowing parsing to resume.

For our first example, let us consider the VSL compiler. One place where we choose to synchronize errors is in function declaration as follows:

```
            function          :      FUNC VARIABLE ' (' parameter_list ')'
                                     statement
                                     {
                                             next_tmp = 0 ;
                                             $$ = do_func( $2, $4, $6 ) ;
                                     }
                              |      error
                                     {
                                             error( "Bad function syntax" ) ;
                                             $$ = NULL ;
                                     }

                              ;
```

We have a null synchronizing set. If we encounter an error (i.e. an error entry in the action table) while trying to build a function, we will unwind the stack until we find the state whose configurating set also includes the error production. This will have derived from a configurating set with a dot just before *function*, i.e. the non-terminal we are trying to match.

We immediately reduce by the error production, i.e. behave as though we have recognized a complete *function* production. We will continue parsing, hoping that the next symbol is something appropriate with which to continue.

This could quite easily cause a cascade of errors, and so YACC refuses to recognize any more errors until at least three tokens have been shifted. Under some circumstances, we may know that parsing has resumed satisfactorily, and we may then reset error recognition, by use of the YACC statement yyerrok.

More subtle error control is possible if we use synchronizing sets. For example, a VSL WHILE statement must end in DONE. We could perform error handling for a WHILE statement as follows:

```
        while_statement : WHILE expression DO statement DONE
                        {
                                $$ = do_while( $2, $4 ) ;
                        }
                        | error DONE
                        {
                                error( "Bad WHILE syntax" ) ;
                                yyerrok ;
                                $$ = NULL ;
                        }
                        ;
```

We can be fairly confident that we have recovered this error satisfactorily if we manage to shift DONE, and so we immediately reset the error counter. Clearly this error handling may fail, if the cause of the error is omission of the synchronizing token! We also need to ensure that we return an appropriate attribute value. In this case NULL is appropriate, making an erroneous statement appear to be a continue statement.

8.5   Other parser generators and related tools

Some early parser generators were written for non-table-driven methods. *Tree-META* was a parser generator that created a recursive descent parser from a specification of the programming language grammar.

YACC and Bison effectively deal with just a single inherited attribute, although by careful use of C structs, they can effectively handle multiple attributes. BYACC is another alternative to YACC.

Ox is an extension to YACC by Kurt Bischoff, which allows both synthesized and inherited attributes to be used with a LALR(1) parser. It generates a program that builds and decorates parse trees for general attribute grammars. Rie is a similar system from the Tokyo Institute of Technology.

The Purdue Compiler Construction Tool Set (PCCTS) is a system which generates LL(k) parsers in C/C++. It is unusual in allowing backtracking. LLGen is a LL(1) parser generator, by Fisher and LeBlanc, and is described in their textbook on compiler writing. The Cocktail compiler construction system is a large set of compiler tools originating in a number of German universities, providing LALR(1) and LL(1) parser generators.

At a research level, systems under development tackle more difficult problems associated with parsing context sensitive grammars. PRECC, developed by P. T. Breuer and J. P. Bowen generates parsers for context sensitive grammars using infinite lookahead. EAG from Marc Seutter is a system for handling a range of grammars including both context free and context sensitive.

In general these systems are research oriented. Most are freely available (recent versions of Cocktail are commercial), but do not necessarily have the robustness that is found in YACC and Bison.

Exercises

PRACTICAL PROBLEMS

8.1. Get the YACC parser for VSL in Chapter 13 running without any semantic actions. Add exponentiation as a right associative binary operator in expressions.

8.2. Get the VSL parser to print out which production is being used as the semantic action for each production. Try it out on some programs. Look at how the actions used vary if left recursive productions are made right recursive.

8.3. YACC parsers can be made to print out their actions if the variable yydebug is set to 1. Modify the VSL parser by including

```
%{
#define YYDEBUG
%}
```

in the declarations section and

```
yydebug = 1 ;
```

in the code before yyparse() is called. Follow the action of the parser on some programs.

ESSAY TITLES

8.1. What is meant by a parser generator? Illustrate your answer with examples using YACC.
8.1. How are ambiguities resolved in YACC?
8.3. Show by example how errors are handled in parsers generated using YACC.

DISCUSSION TOPICS

8.1. Consider how multiple attributes could be handled in YACC.
8.2. Look at how well phrase-level error correction can be implemented using error production. This involves a degree of communication between parser and lexical analyser and use of some obscure details of YACC error handling not described in this chapter.

Further reading

YACC is described as part of the standard Unix manual. This is also available as 'YACC—Yet Another Compiler Compiler' by S. C. Johnson, Computing Science Technical Report 32, AT&T Bell Laboratories, Murray Hill, NJ, USA.

EYACC, a version of YACC with improved error handling, is also provided and documented under Unix.

Bison is freely available from the Free Software Foundation (details in Appendix B), and comes with its own comprehensive manual.

The systems available are changing all the time. While the traditional research literature is one way of following developments, a good quick source of information is the Usenet news group comp.compilers. Lists of currently available systems are regularly posted, together with details of how the software can be downloaded.

9
Semantic checking

A compiler must perform many semantic checks on a source program. Many of these are straightforward and usually done in conjunction with syntax analysis. We address these problems at the end of this chapter. Type checking is one semantic problem that is not so straightforward.

9.1 Type checking

When type checking we must perform the following tasks:

- Check that names and values are used in accordance with the type rules of the language.
- Detect implicit type conversions, inserting appropriate conversion code.

The degree of typing varies between languages. Some languages, such as BCPL, effectively have no type system at all—any value can be used anywhere that is syntactically permitted. VSL has a very simple type system. Names can be either variables holding integers or function names, and the two cannot be intermixed. It makes no sense to try to call variables as functions, nor is it profitable to perform arithmetic on function names as though they were variables. So in the VSL program:

```
FUNC main
{
    VAR   x

    main := x()
}
```

we have two type errors. We have tried to assign to `main` as though it were a variable, and we have tried to call the variable `x` as though it were a function. The types of names and values, and the rules about how they may be used, form the *type system* of a language.

C has a much more complex type system. Not only do we have a wide variety of simple types—integer, real, character, label, and so on—but we can construct new types. We may have arrays of variables of a particular type, or structures, with elements that may take arbitrary types. We can have pointers to variables of a particular type and functions that return values of arbitrary types. We can apply the rules for deriving new types recursively; so, for example, we may have an array of arrays of functions which return values that are pointers to integers:

```
int   ((*func)())[100][20] ;
```

Although it has a quite complex type system, C does not provide hard and fast rules for type checking. It is quite possible to override the type system. For example, the types of the arguments to a function need not be defined in advance, and so it is quite possible to call a function with a different type of argument to that which it was expecting. The type system is there to help the programmer avoid semantic errors, not to force his or her behaviour. We say such languages are *weakly typed*. In such languages there is a further possible role of the type checker to warn of constructs that although permitted are symptomatic of an incorrect program.

By contrast there are some languages with complete rules on how all types are declared and all interconversions between types. In principle such languages prevent the programmer making any semantic errors due to type problems. Algol 68 and Ada are good examples, and such languages are said to be *strongly typed*. If such a type system is to be flexible enough not to constrain the programmer on valid programs it must be very big and complex, with complex type checking in the compiler and possibly the run-time system.

9.1.1   IMPLEMENTING TYPE CHECKING

There are two approaches to type checking:

- *Static type checking.* Type checking is carried out at compile time. It must be possible to compute all the information required at compile time.
- *Dynamic type checking.*   Type checking is carried out while the program is running. This is obviously less efficient, but if a language permits the type of a variable to be determined at run time then we must use dynamic type checking. SNOBOL4 is an example of such a language. The type of a variable may be held in a string computed during a run of the program.

Languages rarely use exclusively dynamic type checking; static checking is used where possible by the compiler. We are concerned only with static type checking. However, similar considerations will apply when designing the run-time environment for a dynamically typed language.

Throughout we are concerned with the concept of *type equivalence*. We wish to check that entities have the same type. For example, we wish to check that the variable on the left of an assignment has the same type as the expression on the right.

9.1.2 SIMPLE TYPES

The type checking of a language such as VSL is relatively straightforward. We include a type field in the symbol table data structure. For example, in Chapter 5 we suggested the following would be appropriate:

```
struct symbtab
{
        char *name ;
        int   type ;
        int   blockno ;
        int   addr ;
} ;
```

We use small integers for the type of the variable:

```
#define  T_UNDEF  0  /* For unknown types */
#define  T_VAR    1
#define  T_FUNC   2
...
```

When a variable is declared we enter its type into the symbol table; so, for example, our YACC parser would include the rule:

```
function  :  FUNC variable '(' parameter_list ')' statement
             {
                     struct symbtab *s = lookup( $2 ) ;

                     s->type = T_FUNC ;
                     ...
             }
          ;
```

The name of the variable would have been entered into the symbol table by the lexical analyser, with type T_UNDEF. The function lookup() takes a name and yields a pointer to its symbol table entry, in which we can set the type field.

When we encounter a name in an expression we can check it has the correct type. So, for example, we might have the following code:

```
expression  :  variable
               {
               struct symbtab *s = lookup( $1) ;

               if( s->type != T_VAR )
                   error( "%s not declared as variable\n", $1 ) ;

               ...
               }
            ;
```

9.1.3 TYPE CONVERSION

In many languages it is possible to convert an expression from one type to another. In C this is done by writing the required type in parentheses before the expression. So if we wanted to convert an int to a float we might write:

```
float a ;
int   i ;

a = (float)i ;
```

Such a conversion is called a *cast*. Since ints and floats have very different representations in the target language the compiler must generate code to convert between the two. Note that casting may lose information; if we consider instead:

```
i = (int)a ;
```

we will lost the fractional part of a in the conversion.

Some conversions are so common that languages do not require them to be specified. Our previous example could equally have been written:

```
float a ;
int   i ;


a = i ;
```

since ints are automatically cast to floats. Such an implicit cast is often called a *coercion*. The type checker must detect that the two types are different, and insert the appropriate cast.

Usually there are restrictions on how types can be cast or coerced. For example, it makes little sense to coerce an array of strings to a float. C is a little unusual in that it will allow any cast, although the results will not necessarily be very meaningful.

9.1.4 TYPE TREES

In languages such as C that allow construction of complex types we need a more powerful way of describing the type of a variable or expression. A natural way to represent a complex type is as a tree showing how it is constructed from simpler types. So, for example, we might represent the type of the variables x and y declared in C as follows:

```
char  x[100] ;

struct
{
        int    i[561] ;
        char *c ;
} y[42] ;
```

by the trees given in Fig. 9.1(a) and Fig. 9.1(b), respectively.

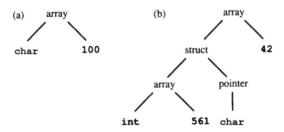

Figure 9.1 Type tree for (a) x and (b) y

The main ways of constructing complex types are as follows:

- *Pointers*   These have a single subcomponent, the type being referenced by the pointer.
- *Arrays*   These have two subcomponents—the number of elements in the array and the type of each element.
- *Records*   These have one subcomponent for each field in the record.
- *Functions*   These have two components—the type of the argument and the type of the result. However, functions may have more than one argument, and it is sensible to think of their type as being the cartesian product of their arguments. As an example of the notation:

$$\text{char} \times \text{int} \times \text{char} \rightarrow \text{float}$$

describes a function of three variables—a char, an int, and a char—which yields a float as the result. Figure 9.2 shows this as a tree.

Languages may have other type constructors, but all follow the same general principle.

The type entry in symbol table structs must now be a pointer to a typenode, a C struct suitable for holding type trees:

```
struct symbtab
{
        char             *name ;
        struct typenode *type ;
        int              blockno ;
        int              addr ;
} ;

struct typenode
{
        int              type ;
        struct typenode *comp1 ;
        struct typenode *comp2 ;
} ;

#define T_INT        1   /* Simple types */
#define T_FLOAT      2
...
#define T_POINTER  100   /* Constructors */
#define T_ARRAY    101
...
```

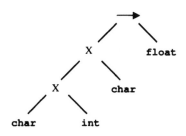

Figure 9.2   Type tree for a function

This structure can handle most C types, although with only two fields a record would be inconvenient. Equivalence of types can be tested as described earlier by a recursive walk over the two type trees:

```
int  compare( struct typenode *tree1,
              struct typenode *tree2 )
{
        /* Type fields must always agree */

        if( tree1->type != tree2->type )
                return  FALSE ;

        switch( tree1->type )
        {
        case T_INT:
        case T_FLOAT:
        ...

                /* Simple types which are the same */

                return  TRUE ;

        case T_POINTER:

                return  compare( tree1->comp1, tree2->comp1 ) ;

        case T_ARRAY:

                return  compare( tree1->comp1, tree2->comp1 ) &&
                        compare( tree1->comp2, tree2->comp2 ) ;

        ...

        }

}       /* compare() */
```

Named types

Many languages allow the naming of user-defined types. In C this is achieved by the typedef statement. For example, we might define a type for type trees:

```
typedef struct typenode tntype ;
```

tntype can then be used anywhere that an ordinary simple type could be. When checking equivalence of named types we have two possibilities:

- *Named equivalence* Treat named types as simple types, and just check that they have the same name.
- *Structural equivalence* Replace the named types by their definitions and recursively check the substituted trees.

As an example, if we define two types, list and vector:

```
typedef int[100] list ;
typedef int[100] vector ;
```

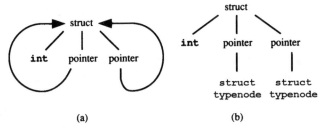

Figure 9.3 (a) Cyclic type tree for `struct typenode`; (b) Named type tree for `struct typenode`

these would be the same under structural equivalence, but different under named equivalence.

Recursive types

In many languages we can define types that refer to themselves, indeed `struct typenode` does:

```
struct typenode
{
        int             type ;
        struct typenode *comp1 ;
        struct typenode *comp2 ;
} ;
```

It might seem sensible to represent such types by cyclic graphs, as in Fig. 9.3(a). However, our recursive routine for comparing types would get into a loop with this sort of data structure. The alternative is for the pointer type constructor just to name the type to which it is pointing, as in Fig. 9.3(b). In other words we use named rather than structural equivalence. Many languages (including C) choose a compromise, using structural equivalence everywhere except when comparing pointer fields within records.

If we do wish to use structural equivalence throughout, then the type tree must be marked as it is examined to prevent looping.

9.2   Other semantic checks

As was stated in the introduction to this chapter there are many semantic checks that are routine. They are usually carried out as part of syntax analysis, or possibly during type checking. For completeness we list some of the commoner semantic checks here.

● *Label checks*   In languages with goto statements we must check that all goto labels exist, and usually that they are uniquely defined.
● *Flow of control checks*   Various flow of control constructs may only be used in the correct context. For example, in C continue statements can

only occur inside loops and break statements only inside loops or switch statements.

● *Declaration checks* This is closely related to type checking. In many languages, including VSL and C, variables must be declared before they are used. If variables are put in the symbol table by the lexical analyser, then they should be entered with an undefined type, T_UNDEF. The test for whether a variable has been declared is then just a type check test that the variable does not have the type T_UNDEF.

Checking the scope of variables is a particular problem. For block-structured languages such as C and VSL, variables may only be referenced in the block in which they are declared. Furthermore in C a declaration of a variable in an outer block may be overridden by one in an inner block. The semantic analyser must keep track of the start and end of blocks to ensure that variables are only referenced while in scope.

Exercises

PRACTICAL PROBLEMS

9.1. Draw type trees for the types of the variables in the following C declarations:

```
int     i ;
char    c[100] ;
struct  node
{
        int             data ;
        struct node *link ;
} x ;
```

9.2. Define a C struct that has a cyclic type representation. Draw the type tree as it would be seen both under structural equivalence and named equivalence.

ESSAY TITLES

9.1. What does a type checker do in a compiler for a language such as C?
9.2. What are structural and named equivalence? Why is the distinction important?

DISCUSSION TOPICS

9.1. Consider the changes needed to type checking of C if array-bound specifications could be variable rather than constant.
9.2. Investigate polymorphic typing in languages such as ML.

Further reading

Type checking of languages is currently an active research topic. Most compiling textbooks cover the subject. A good starting point for further material is ML. It is described in *Introduction to Standard ML* by Robert Harper and Kevin Mitchell, published by the Laboratory for the Foundations of Computer Science, University of Edinburgh, Scotland (1987).

10
Code generation

Having completed syntax and semantic analysis of the source program, we wish to generate the equivalent target program. As we saw in Chapter 1 this occurs typically in two stages, first to an intermediate representation, then to the target code. The techniques involved in the generation of the intermediate representation are often very similar to those involved in the generation of the target language. In Chapter 4 we classified intermediate representation into two broad groups:

- *Tree-based representations* These are closely related to the syntactic structure of the language, and we have covered the generation of such representations already.
- *Three-address codes (TAC)* These are much closer to typical machine codes, which are our usual target codes. Typically labels and names have yet to be resolved. We have only given an outline of TAC generation so far.

In this chapter we are concerned both with the generation of target machine codes (of which VAM is an example) from either of the intermediate representations above and the generation of three-address intermediate codes in the front end of the compiler. Many of the techniques are common to both.

The aim of the compiler writer is to produce as efficient a target program as possible. In this chapter we look at the basic techniques to produce a target program; the next two chapters look at how we can improve the target program to make it smaller or faster. At all stages the overriding priority is the generation of correct target code. The importance of this cannot be overstated.

The basis of code generation is simple. For each intermediate representation we have a template for the target code with fields to fill in for particular cases. So, for example, the template for a TAC addition statement:

```
a := b + c
```

to generate VAM would be something like:

```
LDI   b,R_i
LDI   c,R_j
ADD   R_i,R_j
STI   R_j,a
```

The code generator has to decide on the choice of R_i and R_j. To improve the quality of the target code additional templates can be provided to deal with special cases more efficiently.

In deciding which is the best sequence of code to generate we must consider the cost of the instructions used. If our criterion is fast code, then this cost will be related to instruction execution time; if the criterion is compact code, then this cost will be related to instruction size. For a general-purpose compiler we may want a combination of the two.

Working out the cost of instructions when the criterion is fast code may be difficult. For a simple machine it is enough to add together the times for fetching operands and evaluating the opcode. However, with pipelined machines there is a bias in favour of straight-line code, which preserves the pipeline, and with caches preserving locality of reference becomes important.

We now look at code generation for some of the constructs found in programming languages.

10.1   Declarations and storage allocation

In intermediate code generation, declarations are a matter of semantic checking only. All variables in the intermediate code appear as names or pointers into the symbol table. At target code generation time these names must be replaced by addresses in memory. Furthermore, we may need temporary variables within the generated code and these must be allocated space as though they were local variables.

10.1.1 GLOBAL AND STATIC VARIABLES

Global and static variables are very similar and are often treated identically. They both last throughout the life of the program, but static variables typically may be restricted in scope. In many languages, including C, global variables are just static variables declared outside any routine. Such variables can be allocated in their own fixed area of memory either as absolute addresses or indexed off a base register. In either case we make use of a global variable in the compiler, nextstatic, which holds the absolute address or offset of the next static location. Whenever we encounter a variable for the first time, we allocate the value of nextstatic as its address and increment nextstatic. This address is recorded in the symbol table address field:

```
struct symbtab
{
        char *name ;
        int   type ;
        int   blockno ;
        int   addr ;
} ;
```

Typically the variable will have been entered into the symbol table during syntax or lexical analysis with an invalid address such as -1 in the addr field. The first time we encounter the variable in code generation we replace the -1 by the value of `nextstatic` and increment `nextstatic`.

During code generation we may define a routine to get the address of a static variable as follows:

```
int  getstaticaddr( struct symbtab *entry )
{
        if( entry->addr == -1 )
                entry->addr = nextstatic++ ;

        return  entry->addr ;

}       /* getstaticaddr() */
```

At the end of code generation the value of `nextstatic` will tell us how much space to allow for static storage.

We need a slight modification to allow for the fact that machines (such as VAM) are often byte addressed and different types may take up different numbers of bytes. `nextstatic` is used as the byte address of the next static variable. When allocating space for a 32-bit integer we would increment `nextstatic` by 4, when allocating space for a character variable (8 bits) we would increment `nextstatic` by 1, and so on.

Many languages allow static variables to be initialized. This initial value would be held in a field in the symbol table entry, perhaps as follows:

```
struct symbtab
{
        char *name ;
        int   type ;
        int   blockno ;
        int   initval ;
        int   addr ;
} ;
```

At the end of code generation we would scan all static entries in the symbol table, generating code to initialize them where necessary.

10.1.2 LOCAL AND TEMPORARY VARIABLES

In generating code we may need to use temporary variables. When we are generating code these variables behave just as local variables. We give temporary variables unique names, typically of the form tn where n is a small integer. A simple approach is just to increment n each time we want a new temporary. This leads to more temporary variables being used than is strictly necessary. To avoid this we use a stack of temporary names, releasing temporaries for reuse when they are finished with.

Local variables of a routine, including arguments, are held on a stack frame pointed to by a stack pointer register. The stack frame will typically hold return address, dynamic, and possibly static link information as described in Chapter 2. Local variables are assigned offsets after the link information. We can do this in a manner similar to that for static and global variables, using a global variable in the code generator, `nextlocal`, to hold the offset of the next local variable to be used. At any point the value of this variable tells us how large the stack frame is. When we encounter a new local variable we give it the value in `nextlocal` as offset, and increment `nextlocal`. As with `nextstatic` we may increment by more than 1 in allowing for byte-addressed machines and different sized data types.

There is, however, a problem in block-structured languages, since local variables go out of scope at the end of the block in which they were declared, and their space on the stack can be reused. At the end of a routine all the space on the stack is freed, and `nextlocal` must be reset to start of stack for the next routine. For example, consider the VSL function:

```
FUNC demo( x, y )
{
        IF y
        THEN
        {
                VAR a, b

                a := x * 2
                b := x / 2
        }
        ELSE
        {
                VAR c, d

                c := x * 3
                d := x / 3
        }
}
```

The first two stack locations would be used for x and y. a and b would use the third and fourth stack locations. However, a and b cease to exist at the end of their block, and `nextlocal` should be decremented accordingly so that c and d use locations 3 and 4 as well.

We must keep track of which block we are in, in order to know when stack space can be reused. If we are generating code from a parse tree it is simple enough to set and reset `nextlocal` as we enter and leave the routine for handling a block. If we are working from TAC, then the block structure has been lost. An inefficient solution is to have a tree of symbol tables associated with each original block. A better approach is to partition the TAC into blocks, pushing and popping the value of `nextlocal` from a stack as blocks are entered and left. This can be done simply by having `startblock` and `endblock` instructions in the TAC. As we shall see in the next chapter, it is sensible to partition TAC into blocks for optimization, and a good representation is as linked blocks.

10.2   Expressions and assignment

Target machines provide three basic classes of opcode—for data access, data manipulation, and flow of control. Expression evaluation and assignment use the first two of these: data access in loading operands and storing the result, and data manipulation in evaluating the expression.

Expressions can be thought of as trees, with operators at the nodes and operands as subtrees or leaves. To generate code to evaluate an expression we start at the root of the tree, which will be an operator with n operands (typically $n = 1$ or $n = 2$). The following is a trivial recursive algorithm to generate code for an expression:

● Generate code to evaluate the subtrees for operands $1 - n$ into n temporary locations.
● Generate the opcode to evaluate the operator using the operands from the temporary locations, putting the result in a temporary location.

This algorithm is suitable both for the generation of TAC and for generating target code. For an assignment statement the final temporary value can be stored in the location for the assigned variable. The question arises of what to use for temporary locations. There are three main possibilities:

● Temporary local variables as discussed in the previous section. This is the approach when generating TAC.
● The machine stack if the target is a stack machine.
● Registers if the target machine has them.

For a target stack machine the code generation algorithm is trivial, since we just pop operands off the stack and push the results back there. For assignment the final result is popped off the stack into the desired location. To generate using temporary variables we might use the following routine. nextemp is a global variable containing the number of the next temporary to use. We define a routine cgexpr() which takes a tree representation of an expression and a temporary variable to store the result of evaluating the expression. In this example we just print out the TAC to evaluate the expression:

```
void   cgexpr( struct node *tree,
               int          res )
{
       switch( tree->type )
       {
       case NT_INTEGER:

               printf( "t%d := %d\n", res, tree->field1.value ) ;
               return ;

                   . . .

       case NT_ADD:

               cgexpr( tree->field1.ptr, nextemp++ ) ;
               cgexpr( tree->field2,     nextemp++ ) ;

               printf( "t%d := t%d + t%d\n", res,
                       nextemp - 1, nextemp - 2 ) ;
```

```
nextemp -=2 ;
return ;
```

. . .

This is not particularly efficient since we load everything into a temporary variable before it is used. Rather than the caller specifying the location of the result it is preferable for cgexpr () to return the location of the result.

For most binary operators the order of generation of code to evaluate operands matters. A useful rule is to evaluate the more complicated operand first. This will minimize the number of temporary variables required.

10.2.1 USING REGISTERS

When target machines have registers it is advantageous to use them to the fullest extent for two reasons:

● They are faster than main store, hence compiled code runs faster.
● Instructions using them are smaller, hence compiled code is smaller.

We use the concept of *register slaving*. All variables are associated with a location in memory. Rather than always writing a variable's value out to memory directly it is assigned, we can choose to hold the value in a register. We only write it out to memory when we need to for consistency. We say that the variable is *slaved* in the register. With modern machines having many registers it is often possible for variables to be held in registers throughout the program.

To handle registers effectively we need two data structures:

● *Register descriptor* This is a list of what can be found in each register (if anything). So, for example, R3 might hold the value of variable x and R5 might hold the constant 17. It is perfectly possible for a register to hold more than one thing simultaneously. If the variable x were to be assigned the constant 42, still using R3 as slave for the value of x, then we should know that R3 in addition to holding the value of the variable x held the constant 42. To deal with this each register descriptor must be a list of addresses held in the register. However, it is perfectly reasonable for a register descriptor to hold just a single address (perhaps the most recent) in a simple compiler.
● *Address descriptor* This is a list of the registers holding a given name (e.g. the name of a variable, or a temporary variable, or a label in the code) or constant. So, for example, given x the address descriptor would show that it was in R3 and given the constant 17 show that it was in R5. Note that a particular name or constant may be found in more than one register, but again a simple compiler may just choose to remember a single register in the address descriptor. It is even permissible not to have an address descriptor at all and rely on a search through the register descriptor to find a particular name. This is the case with the example compiler in Chapter 13.

The descriptors are used to identify the best register in which to slave values. As an example we consider the generation of VAM (a two-address instruction set) from three-address code.

The basic principle is to hold as many values in registers as possible. Values in registers are only written out to memory when we run out of registers or we cannot guarantee that the value slaved in a register is reliable. This occurs in three places:

- *On a subroutine or function call*   We do not know what the subroutine will do to the registers, so we must write out to memory any values slaved in registers that have changed since they were read from memory. Both descriptors are cleared.
- *At a branch*   We cannot easily guarantee what will be in various registers at the destination of the branch. We must again write out all slave values that have changed.
- *Before a label*   When the code branches from elsewhere we do not know what will be in registers, so we write out all slave values that have changed before the label.

The operation of ensuring a modified register is written out to memory, so that the register can be used to hold a different value, is referred to as *spilling* the register. This is an oversimplification, as we shall see in the next two chapters on code optimization. For example, we need not write a slaved value back out to memory if it is never to be read from memory again before being changed.

VAM is a two-address machine in which all data manipulation opcodes operate exclusively on registers. For a TAC instruction of the form:

```
a := b op c
```

we are going to use the corresponding VAM opcode:

```
OP   Rᵢ,Rⱼ
```

The register R_j is used for the second operand, c, and the result, a and the register R_i for the first operand, b. A simple algorithm to generate code for such a TAC instruction is as follows:

- Select register for R_j which will hold the second argument. Using the information in the descriptors we chose in order of preference a register holding c, an empty register, an unmodified register, or a modified register. If the register has been modified we spill it and if it does not already contain c we load it, adjusting the descriptors accordingly.
- We load R_i with b in similar manner, but we must not reuse R_j unless b and c are the same. With R_i there is no need to spill a register already holding b, since it will not be modified.
- Generate the instruction:

```
OP   Rᵢ,Rⱼ
```

● Update the address and register descriptors to indicate that a and not c is now held in R_j.

This algorithm can be made more complex to give better and better selection. This general approach will suffice for simple generation of either intermediate code or target language.

10.3   Flow of control

Flow of control constructs in general present little difficulty. We cover one or two techniques that are useful.

10.3.1   BACKPATCHING

A common problem is how to generate code for forward branches. At the time we generate the code we do not know the address of the label to which to branch. The solution is to generate a branch instruction without the branch address defined, and maintain a list of branches branching to the particular label. When the label is eventually defined we can walk down the list, patching in the value of its address. A particularly efficient way of doing this is to hold only the value of the most recent branch that needs its address patching in the symbol table with the label. The address field of that branch then holds the address of the previous branch that needs patching, and so on back to the first branch to reference the label. Figure 10.1 illustrates this.

There is a problem if the target instruction set has scope for branches of different sizes (as, for example, in the Motorola MC68000). We have to assume that the branches are the largest possible size, or risk not compiling some programs. The solution to this problem is a two or more pass code generation phase.

10.3.2   ROUTINE CALL AND RETURN

In Chapter 2 we discussed the format of the local stack, and attention needs to be given to how we handle routine calls. We have to ensure that the return address, dynamic link, and static link (if there is one) are set up on call and restored on return. Given the predominance of routine call, efficiency here is paramount. Typically one register is reserved as the stack pointer, in the example VSL compiler of Chapter 13 we have chosen R1 for this role. Very often this choice will be dictated by the target architecture anyway.

Routine arguments are passed as the first values on the called routine's stack frame. It is quite common to pass these values in registers and on entry to the routine initialize the register and address descriptors to indicate this. Similarly, the value returned may well be in a register. In our VSL compiler we do not pass **arguments in registers but return the result in** R4.

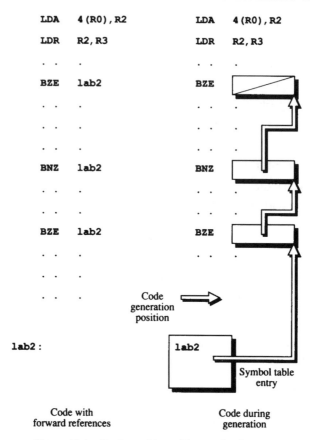

Figure 10.1 Backpatching of forward references

Routine call

The precise details of routine calling differ considerably from machine to machine. We will use the VSL calling sequence as an example. R1 is the stack pointer, R2 is used to hold the address of the called routine, and R3 will hold the return address on entering the routine. Remember R0 always holds zero. Each stack frame has two words of link information, the first at offset 0 is the dynamic link, the second at offset 4 (because VAM is byte addressed with addresses occupying 32 bits) is the return address. The calling routine will set up the dynamic link by adding nextlocal to the current stack pointer to get the new stack pointer and saving the current stack pointer there. Let us imagine we are calling a VSL function func. The address of this routine will be held in a static variable at absolute address func_add. Let us imagine that the value of nextlocal is currently 24. The code to call the routine is:

```
LDA  func_add(RO),R2    Address into R2
STI  R1,24(R1)          Save current stack pointer
LDA  24(R1),R1          Stack pointer incremented by 24
BAL  R2,R3              Call routine
```

The start of the called routine must contain code to save the return address:

```
STI  R3,4(R1)
```

Routine return

Return from the routine must include code to restore the stack pointer and then use BAL to jump to the return address. Note that we must retrieve the return address into R2 before restoring the stack pointer:

```
LDI  4(R1),R2    R2 is return address
LDI  0(R1),R1    Restore stack ptr
BAL  R2,R3       Return
```

Variations on this are numerous, but this is typical.

10.3.3 SWITCH STATEMENTS

Many languages (although not VSL) have a multiway branching construct. The C switch statement is seen in similar forms in many languages. Its general form is:

```
switch( expr )
{
case  val₁:

         statements for the first case
         break ;

case  val₂:

         statements for the second case
         break ;

         . . .

case  valₙ:

         statements for the nth case
         break ;

default:

         default statements
}
```

There are three possible ways of translating this which we will outline briefly. It is up to the compiler writer to select the best translation for each case.

Switch using if statements

The simplest way of organizing a switch statement is as a series of if statements to test each condition:

```
        if v == case1 goto l1
        if v == case2 goto l2
        . . .
        goto ld
l1:
        code for case1
        . . .
        goto lb
l2:
        code for case2
        . . .
        goto lb
        . . .
ld:
        code for default
        . . .
lb:
```

If there is no default then the `goto ld` becomes `goto lb`.

This approach is fine for a small number of cases. On average if there are n cases we have to execute $(n + 1)/2$ if instructions.

Switch using binary chop

With a larger number of cases it is worth sorting the case values into order, and then doing a binary chop on the value of the expression to find the label we want. This is more efficient if we have large numbers of cases, since we execute on average $2 \log_2(n)$ if statements. It does use rather a lot of space, needing about $2n$ conditional jumps in total, and for small switches it is very inefficient.

Switch using jump tables

If we have a number of cases all over a very narrow range, then we can use a jump table to implement the switch. This is only possible if we have indirect branches available. Once again we sort the cases into increasing numerical order. We put all the case labels into a jump table to be indexed by the switch expression. If there are unused cases we insert the default label in the corresponding place in the jump table, as shown at the top of the following page.

This style of switch implementation uses two if statements, a subtraction, and an indirect goto for any case. However, unless most of the cases between the least and the greatest are used it wastes a lot of jump table space with default label entries.

```
if v <  case1 goto 1d
if v >  casen goto 1d
t1 := v - case1
indgoto jumptab + t1

jumptab:
        address of 11
        address of 12
          .  .  .
11:
        code for case1
          .  .  .

1b:
```

10.4   Code generator generators

Just as there are parser generators, so there are code generator generators. In general they all use the same idea, to match patterns of instructions generated by the front end to patterns of instructions available on the target machine.

10.4.1   IBURG

Iburg generates a fast tree parser. It takes a grammar describing the patterns to be matched, with actions that generate the target code. The grammar is augmented by the 'cost' of the code generated, and is in general ambiguous. The Iburg generated parser finds the lowest cost parse of a given sentence. Typically the cost will be the execution time of the code, but for a compiler concerned with compact code generation, it could be the code size.

The idea of using a grammar to describe target code, and finding the lowest cost parse, in order to generate the best code predates Iburg. An early system due to Susan Graham used YACC productions to achieve the same end.

10.4.2   GNU REGISTER TRANSFER LANGUAGE

The GNU C compiler, gcc, is a highly portable optimizing C compiler. Rather than using a fixed intermediate language, gcc defines a representation called *Register Transfer Language (RTL)*. These are expression lists, describing the properties of the operation generated. RTL is also used to describe the instructions available on the target machine, in the form of patterns. Code generation is then a matter of matching the RTL generated by the front end to the RTL patterns of the machine description.

At the point of generation, RTL assumes it has an infinite number of registers available. Allocation of real registers is done in a subsequent phase.

Because they are expressions, one RTL expression can be substituted into another, and simplified to yield a new RTL expression. If this new RTL expression can match a pattern in the machine description file, we have succeeded in eliminating an instruction from the code generated.

The work of porting the compiler is thus reduced to an exercise in defining the target machine's instructions in RTL. From this the back end will be able to generate code for the target machine. Although not strictly a code generator generator, the effect is the same. Only a description of the target machine is needed to get a working code generator.

Exercises

10.1. VSL variables are local and held on a conventional stack. VSL functions are static variables holding the address of the start of the code for the function. Design the YACC semantic actions necessary to enter appropriate information in the symbol table for variables and functions.

10.2. Write the C routines to implement backpatching in the VSL compiler. Use them to implement function calling. Note that a function may be called before it is defined, and hence before the static variable holding its address is defined as in the following example:

```
FUNC a( )
{
        VAR v

        v := b( )

        PRINT "The result is", v, "\n"
}

FUNC b( )
{
        RETURN 42
}
```

10.3. Write the semantic actions for a YACC parser for VSL to translate WHILE loops into TAC.

10.1. Describe in detail backpatching of branch addresses.
10.2. How may switch statements as found in C be translated into three-address code?
10.3. What is register slaving? What data structures are needed to support it?

10.1. Consider how the algorithm for choosing VAM registers for translation of TAC may be improved.
10.2. How could function call be translated in VAM if there were no dynamic link on the stack frame?

Further reading

There are numerous approaches to code generation. A good approach to further reading is with reseach review texts. Two worth considering are 'How Hard is Compiler Code Generation?' by A. V. Aho and R. Sethi in *Lecture Notes in Computer Science*, no. 52, 1–15, published by Springer-Verlag (1977) and the more recent 'Retargetable Compiler Code Generation' by M. Ganapathi *et al.*, *Computing Surveys*, **14**, 573–592 (1982). Both these give references to papers discussing various code-generation techniques.

Both Iburg and the GNU C compiler are freely available, and incorporate documentation which describe their code generation systems. The description of RTL in the GNU C documentation is comprehensive, and not ideal for initial reading. A good summary of RTL can be found in the introduction to 'Eliminating Branches using a Superoptimizer and the GNU C Compiler' by Torbjörn Granlund and Richard Kenner, *SIGPLAN Notices*, **27** (7), 341–352 (1992).

11

Simple code optimization

Code optimization is a misnomer, since by the term we actually mean code improvement—rarely can the results be shown to be optimal in the strict sense of the word. It is a complex subject and entitled to a book in its own right. In this chapter we take an introductory look at some of the improvements possible when generating code. Unlike earlier chapters we shall not go into implementation details, since in general they are beyond the scope of an introductory text such as this.

We concentrate mainly on optimizations of three-address intermediate code. Optimizations at this stage are portable to different back ends. TAC is much more flexible than tree representations when it comes to performing optimizing transformations on the code. It is recommended that compilers that are intended to perform much optimization use TAC as their intermediate representation.

Most of these optimizations are possible on target machine codes as well. Optimizations specific to target machine codes are discussed at the end of this chapter.

11.1 Basic blocks and local optimization

A *basic block* is the fundamental unit of code. It is a sequence of consecutive statements where flow of control enters at the beginning and leaves at the end. For example, the following TAC sequence is a basic block:

```
l1:
    t1 := a * b
    t2 := t1 + c
    d  := t2 * t2
    ifz d goto l2:
```

Note that a basic block may receive control from more than one point, and control may leave in more than one direction. In the example given control may arrive at label l1 from more than one place and control leaves either to go to the next statement or to branch to l2.

This makes basic blocks an ideal unit for simple code optimization. When manipulating the TAC of a basic block to improve its efficiency, we need only worry about the effects due to the values of variables at the start of the block, or the values they have at the end of the block. This is known as *local optimization*.

The algorithm to partition a program into basic blocks is:

1. Find all the statements that start a basic block:

   ● The first statement of the program.
   ● Any labelled statement that is the target of a branch.
   ● Any statement following a branch.

   Note that branches may be conditional or unconditional.
2. For each statement starting a basic block, the block consists of that statement and all statements up to but excluding the start of the next basic block or the end of the program.

The flow of control through a program can be visualized as a directed graph of linked basic blocks called a *flow graph*. As an example consider a VSL program to sum the first 17 integers:

```
FUNC main()
{
        VAR   i, s

        i := 17
        s := 0

        WHILE i
        DO
        {
                s := s + i
                i := i - 1
        }
        DONE
}
```

This might translate into the following TAC:

```
        i := 17
        s := 0
l1:
        ifz i goto l2
        s := s + i
        i := i - 1
        goto l1:
        l2:
```

Figure 11.1 shows this as a flow graph. We have followed the convention of leaving out unconditional goto statements at the end of blocks, since the information they convey is shown by the graph. In this case it applies to the statement `goto l1:`, which terminates the third basic block.

During optimization we wish to move TAC instructions around. This can be awkward if branch addresses are to TAC instructions. Since all branch

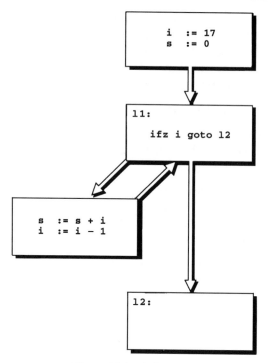

Figure 11.1 A flow graph

destinations must start basic blocks it is reasonable for branch addresses to be pointers to basic blocks. Movement of code in the basic block then does not affect the jump destination. A suitable data structure for basic blocks is a linked list, such as:

```
struct bb
{
        struct bb       *next ;
        struct taclist *tac ;
} ;
```

TAC is conveniently represented in one of the forms described in Chapter 4.

We say that a three-address statement a : = b *op* c in a basic block *references* b and c and *defines* a. A name in a basic block is said to be *live* if its value is referenced further on in the program (possibly in another basic block). A name that is not live is *dead*.

It is useful to associate with each statement in a basic block a list of where, if at all, each name in the statement is next referenced. We do this by working backwards from the end of the block. After the last statement we know that only names referenced outside the block are live. To determine exactly which these are requires dataflow analysis which is discussed later. A simple approximation is to assume that all user-defined names are live at the end of the block, and that no temporary names are. This is generally more than adequate. One point to watch is that if temporary variables are used in the control of a loop (e.g. to hold the end point of a FOR loop), such variables must also be assumed live at the end of blocks in the loop.

The algorithm for working out next reference information is as follows:

1. Enter in the symbol table entry for each variable that is live at the end of the basic block, that the variable is live, and that its next reference is at statement $N + 1$, where there are N statements in the block. Then work backwards for each statement n, a:=b op c, doing the following.
2. Associate the next reference information in the symbol table for a, b, and c with the TAC statement.
3. Mark a as dead in the symbol table.
4. Mark b and c as live in the symbol table, with next references n.

Note that liveness and next reference information is associated with each statement in the block, not just the block itself.

These definitions will help us when considering the generation of code for the basic block. A basic block can be thought of as computing a set of expressions, the values of all the variables which are live on exit from the block. Two blocks are equivalent if they compute the same set of expressions. Our optimizations will yield equivalent basic blocks which are more efficient.

We now consider the principle optimizations possible on basic blocks.

11.1.1 COMMON SUB-EXPRESSION ELIMINATION

If an expression is computed more than once we can replace the second computation by the first. Consider, for example:

```
t1 := 4 - 2
t2 := t1 / 2
t3 := a * t2
t4 := t3 * t1
t5 := t4 + b
t6 := t3 * t1
t7 := t6 + b
c  := t5 * t7
```

We can replace the duplicate computation of t3 * t1

```
t1 := 4 - 2
t2 := t1 / 2
t3 := a * t2
t4 := t3 * t1
t5 := t4 + b
t6 := t4
t7 := t6 + b
c  := t5 * t7
```

Note that the expressions must actually yield the same value. We could not use common sub-expression elimination on:

```
t1 := 4 - 2
t2 := t1 / 2
```

```
t3 := a * t2
t4 := t3 * t1
t1 := t4 + b
t6 := t3 * t1
t7 := t6 + b
c  := t5 * t7
```

since t1 is changed between the two computations of t3 * t1.

11.1.2 COPY PROPAGATION

Copy propagation is about TAC copy statements, i.e. those of the form:

```
a := b
```

After such a statement we know that a and b have the same value, and so anywhere a occurs we can replace it by b. The hope is that we will be able to replace all occurrences of a so that it becomes dead and its copy statement can then be removed. Let us take the example from the previous section after common sub-expression elimination:

```
t1 := 4 - 2
t2 := t1 / 2
t3 := a * t2
t4 := t3 * t1
t5 := t4 + b
t6 := t4
t7 := t6 + b
c  := t5 * t7
```

We can replace all occurrences of t6 after the sixth statement, t6 := t4, by t4:

```
t1 := 4 - 2
t2 := t1 / 2
t3 := a * t2
t4 := t3 * t1
t5 := t4 + b
t6 := t4
t7 := t4 + b
c  := t5 * t7
```

We note now that there is a new common sub-expression to be eliminated, t4 + b, so we can write:

```
t1 := 4 - 2
t2 := t1 / 2
t3 := a * t2
t4 := t3 * t1
t5 := t4 + b
t6 := t4
t7 := t5
c  := t5 * t7
```

And we can then again perform copy propagation:

```
t1 := 4 - 2
t2 := t1 / 2
t3 := a * t2
t4 := t3 * t1
t5 := t4 + b
```

```
t6 := t4
t7 := t5
c  := t5 * t5
```

Copy propagation has been of benefit in this example by exposing further sub-expression elimination. It is very common for one optimization technique to expose optimizations possible with another technique. We can improve the code further by using *dead-code elimination* to remove copy instructions.

11.1.3 DEAD-CODE ELIMINATION

We may have TAC statements which define a name that is in fact dead, that is it is never referenced again. There is no point in code that gives a value to such a name and so we remove the statement. For example, the TAC instruction:

```
a := b op c
```

is dead code if a has no next reference. In general, dead code arises as a consequence of other optimizations such as copy propagation and is why copy propagation is so effective.

Let us look at the code of our most recent example, assuming all non-temporary names are live at the end of the basic block:

```
t1 := 4 - 2
t2 := t1 / 2
t3 := a * t2
t4 := t3 * t1
t5 := t4 + b
t6 := t4
t7 := t5
c  := t5 * t5
```

The sixth instruction defines t6 and yet t6 has no further reference after this point. Thus the instruction may be removed. The same may be said of t7 and the seventh instruction. Thus the code we obtain is:

```
t1 := 4 - 2
t2 := t1 / 2
t3 := a * t2
t4 := t3 * t1
t5 := t4 + b
c  := t5 * t5
```

11.1.4 ARITHMETIC TRANSFORMATIONS

We can make use of some simple laws of algebra to reduce the amount of computation we need to carry out. There are three main groups of arithmetic transformation.

Constant folding

There is no point in letting target code evaluate expressions at run time that could have been computed at compile time. Instead we evaluate these expressions in the compiler and just use the constants instead. This is called *constant folding*. So in our previous example we had:

```
t1 := 4 - 2
t2 := t1 / 2
t3 := a * t2
t4 := t3 * t1
t5 := t4 + b
c  := t5 * t5
```

We can carry out the computation of t1 := 4 − 2 at compile time to give:

```
t1 := 2
t2 := t1 / 2
t3 := a * t2
t4 := t3 * t1
t5 := t4 + b
c  := t5 * t5
```

Copy propagation and dead-code elimination then yields:

```
t2 := 2 / 2
t3 := a * t2
t4 := t3 * 2
t5 := t4 + b
c  := t5 * t5
```

We can now do constant folding again to give:

```
t2 := 1
t3 := a * t2
t4 := t3 * 2
t5 := t4 + b
c  := t5 * t5
```

and again we can do copy propagation and dead-code elimination:

```
t3 := a * 1
t4 := t3 * 2
t5 := t4 + b
c  := t5 * t5
```

We have reduced six instructions to four, eliminating a subtraction and division in the process.

In practice it is easy to do constant folding in the parser. If we had a YACC parser generating a tree we might use the following code. If we find both sub-trees are integers we do the computation there and then, returning a node for an integer constant. Otherwise we return a conventional expression node.

```
expr  :  expr '+' expr
         {
             if(( $1->nodetype == T_INT ) &&
                ( $2->nodetype == T_INT ))
                return mknode( T_INT,
                              $1->field1.value +
                              $2->field1.value ) ;
             else
                return mknode( T_PLUS, $1, $2 ) ;
         }
```

A word of warning. If there is a semantic error in our constant expression, such as an attempt to divide by zero, then this error will arise in the compiler, rather than at run time.

Algebraic transformations

We can make use of algebraic identities to simplify code further. The main identities used are:

$$x + 0 \equiv 0 + x \equiv x$$
$$x - 0 \equiv x$$
$$x \cdot 1 \equiv 1 \cdot x \equiv x$$
$$x/1 \equiv x$$

Let us take our previous example:

```
t3 := a * 1
t4 := t3 * 2
t5 := t4 + b
c  := t5 * t5
```

We can replace a * 1 by a:

```
t3 := a
t4 := t3 * 2
t5 := t4 + b
c  := t5 * t5
```

And again we use copy propagation and dead-code elimination:

```
t4 := a * 2
t5 := t4 + b
c  := t5 * t5
```

These are not the only transformations possible. However, the compiler writer should be aware that most expressions occurring in programs are very simple, and there is little point in putting effort into obscure optimizations that will rarely, if ever, be used.

Reduction in strength

On most machines operations such as multiplication and division are substantially more time consuming than operations such as addition and subtraction. For example, the VAM MUL instruction is five times slower than the ADD instruction. Exponentiation, if available, is invariably much slower than multiplication and division. It is worth replacing a slow operator by a fast one where possible and this is called *reduction in strength*. Common identities used are:

$$x^2 \equiv x \times x$$
$$2 \cdot x \equiv x + x$$

In our example:

```
t4 := a * 2
t5 := t4 + b
c  := t5 * t5
```

We can use reduction in strength on the first instruction to yield:

```
t4 := a + a
t5 := t4 + b
c  := t5 * t5
```

Another common strength reduction is to use shifts when dividing or multiplying by a power of 2.

11.1.5 PACKING TEMPORARIES

We discussed in the previous chapter the reuse of temporary variables as a means of saving space. Having optimized the code, we probably have scope for further savings on use of temporaries. We use a table of available temporary names (say t1 to t9), which marks whether each temporary is live at each point in the basic block. In general, we can replace two distinct temporaries by a single temporary if there is no point where both are simultaneously live. We look at each temporary in turn and replace it by the first temporary in the table that is dead at all points where the temporary under consideration is live, using the next reference information associated with each statement. Consider our example:

```
t4 := a + a
t5 := t4 + b
c  := t5 * t5
```

t4 is defined in statement 1 and live in statement 2. We replace it by the first temporary in our table, t1:

```
t1 := a + a
t5 := t1 + b
c  := t5 * t5
```

t5 is defined in statement 2 and live in statement 3. This does not clash with the liveness of t1, and so t5 can also be replaced by t1:

```
t1 := a + a
t1 := t1 + b
c  := t1 * t1
```

This is our final optimized code. We can compare it against the original:

```
t1 := 4 - 2
t2 := t1 / 2
t3 := a * t2
t4 := t3 * t1
t5 := t4 + b
t6 := t3 * t1
t7 := t6 + b
c  := t5 * t7
```

This has eight statements involving three named variables, seven temporaries, two additions, one subtraction, four multiplications, and one division. We have replaced it by three statements involving the three named variables, one temporary, two additions, and one multiplication.

11.2 Register optimization

We can be rather more precise about register optimization than we were in the previous chapter. For simple code generation we look at putting values in registers for the duration of a basic block. At the end of the basic block live values in registers that have changed are spilled. More generally, any variable that is dead may be deleted from the register and address descriptors.

If we assume that all user-defined names are live at the end of a basic block and all temporary variables are dead, then an obvious optimization is to use registers primarily for temporary variables, to minimize spilling.

It is perfectly possible to optimize in registers between blocks. This is particularly desirable for, say, control variables in FOR loops. In this case we must use dataflow analysis to keep track of what values are in registers.

11.3 Machine-dependent optimizations

With the exception of register allocation, the optimizations we have discussed so far are available for both intermediate code and target code optimization. In general we concentrate on intermediate code optimization for portability.

Once we have optimal intermediate code there is scope for use of machine-specific optimizations in generating target code. This is achieved essentially by having a large number of templates for generating special cases of instructions. For example, in adding a constant to a variable we may normally use a generic ADD instruction in the target code. However, if the target machine has an increment instruction then this can be profitably used if the constant to be added is 1.

Another source of a wide range of optimizations is use of different addressing modes.

11.4 Peephole optimization

Target code, particularly if produced by a code generator with no optimizer, may be quite poor. A great deal of improvement can be obtained by looking at short sequences of generated instructions to remove redundant code and improve inefficient code sequences. This is *peephole optimization*, the short sequence of instructions under examination being the *peephole*.

We move the peephole along the target code seeking to replace the instructions in the peephole by a shorter or faster sequence. The following are some of the possibilities.

11.4.1 REDUNDANT LOAD ELIMINATION

If we see a code sequence where a variable is loaded immediately after it is stored, we can remove the load instruction. Thus:

```
STI   R5,32(R1)
LDI   32(R1),R5
```

could be replaced by:

```
STI   R5,32(R1)
```

The exception is if there is a label that is the target of a branch between the two instructions.

11.4.2 UNREACHABLE CODE ELIMINATION

Any unlabelled code following an unconditional branch may be removed. Thus if we have the VAM code:

```
      BRA   L7
      LDR   R5,R3
      ADD   R3,R3
L7:
      LDR   R3,R5
```

we could replace this by:

```
L7:
      LDR   R3,R5
```

11.4.3 REDUNDANT GOTO ELIMINATION

Quite often code is generated in which the target of a branch or goto is another branch or goto. In this case the first branch can jump directly. So, for example:

```
      LDR   R3,R5
      BZE   L5
      . . .
L5:
      BRA   L7
      . . .
```

could be replaced by:

```
      LDR   R3,R5
      BZE   L7
      . . .
L5:
      BRA   L7
      . . .
```

If we end up eliminating all branches to the intermediate goto, and it is preceded by an unconditional goto, then we can eliminate that goto as dead code.

```
      LDR   R3,R5
      BZE   L7
      . . .
      . . .
```

11.4.4 ARITHMETIC MANIPULATIONS

A peephole optimizer can perform constant folding, algebraic simplification, and reduction in strength. For example:

```
LDA   1(R0),R5
MUL   R5,R3
```

can be reduced to:

```
LDA   1(R0),R5
```

(remember R0 always holds zero). Using reduction in strength we can replace:

```
LDA  2(R0),R5
MUL R5,R3
```

by

```
LDA   2(R0),R5
ADD   R3,R3
```

11.4.5 MACHINE-SPECIFIC TRANSFORMATIONS

We can spot code in the peephole that could be replaced by a special opcode. For example, if VAM had an increment instruction, INC, we might replace:

```
LDA   1(R0),R5
ADD   R5,R3
```

by:

```
LDA   1(R0),R5
INC   R3
```

if INC were a faster or smaller instruction.

Exercises

PRACTICAL PROBLEMS

11.1. Write down the three-address code that might be generated for the following VSL program:

```
// A procedure to generate the n'th
// Fibonacci number

FUNC  fib( n )
{
    VAR   i          // Counter
    VAR   a, b       // Last two Fibonacci numbers

    // Special cases of n = 1

    IF n - 1
    THEN
        CONTINUE
    ELSE
        RETURN 1
    FI
```

```
// Build up the Fibonacci number,
// starting from the second

i := 2
a := 1
b := 1

// Go round until we have computed
// the n'th Fibonacci number

WHILE n - i
DO
{
    VAR  t          // Temp val

    t := a          // Save old val
    a := b          // Compute new vals
    b := t + a
    i := i + 1      // One more done
}
DONE

RETURN b
}
```

Show how the basic blocks can be optimized.

11.2. Generate VAM from the previous example and perform register allocation. Assume R1 is the stack pointer. How would register allocation differ
if VAM had only registers R0 to R5?

11.3. Take the unoptimized TAC from the first example, optimize it, and then
generate VAM. Then try generating VAM from the unoptimized TAC
and peephole optimizing the VAM. Do the results differ?

ESSAY TITLE

11.1. What is a basic block? What code optimizations are possible on a basic
block?

DISCUSSION TOPICS

11.1. Investigate directed acyclic graphs as a data structure for basic blocks.
What are their advantages?

11.2. Investigate dataflow analysis algorithms. Try them out on the VSL
program above.

Further reading

Because of the close relation of this chapter to the next, a combined further
reading list is given there. At this stage it may, however, be instructive to look at
Lowry and Medlock's paper on the FORTRAN H Compiler (see Further
Reading, Chapter 4), in which many of the local optimizations described here
were applied.

12
Advanced code optimization

The local code optimizations of the previous chapter can gain a considerable improvement in compiled code performance. However, they have limitations:

- They rely on incomplete information about liveness and availability of variables at the start and end of basic blocks.
- They cannot achieve optimizations across multiple basic blocks.

Advanced optimization techniques allow us to improve information about variables at the start and end of blocks, opening up three sources of greater optimization:

1. With more accurate information, basic block optimizations of Chapter 11 can be applied more effectively.
2. These optimizations can be extended across multiple basic blocks.
3. New optimizations, applicable to groups of basic blocks forming loops, can be used.

In addition the information gained will open up new techniques of register optimization.

All these techniques are known under the generic title of *global optimization*. We shall illustrate how four particularly useful sets of information can be obtained, and used to apply four different global optimizations. However, we are only just scratching the surface of what is possible. A recent paper surveying current research listed 57 possible optimization techniques that could be applied in the middle and back ends of modern compilers.

The increased information about the program comes from the techniques of *global dataflow analysis*. We start by further analysis of the program flow graph, in order to identify loops.

12.1 Properties of flow graphs

We introduced the idea of flow graphs in Section 11.1. Figure 12.1 shows a short program in TAC, which we will use as our main example throughout this

```
      s    := 0
      i    := 0
      n    := 10
L1:   t1   := a - b
      ifz t1 goto L2
      t2   := i * 4
      s    := s + t2
      goto L3
L2:   s    := s + i
L3:   i    := i + 1
      t3   := n - i
      ifnz t3 goto L1
      t4   := a - b
      arg t4
      call PRINTN
      arg s
      call PRINTN
```

Figure 12.1   Example TAC program

chapter. It comprises 17 statements, which form six basic blocks, making the flow graph of Fig. 12.2. For convenience we have numbered the statements and as is usual not shown unconditional goto statements.

Note that this program makes use of two variables, a and b, which are not defined elsewhere, but which are presumed to have been given values before the program is entered. The reader may find it helpful to imagine they have been read from the keyboard by a subroutine called just before statement 1. Their presence will help illustrate the behaviour of some of the optimization algorithms later, which must be able to handle variables whose value cannot be deduced at run time.

A convenient way to show which basic block is connected to which is by a *connectivity matrix*. $c_{i,j}$ is set to true if there is an edge from block i to block j. Note that in general $c_{i,j} \neq c_{j,i}$. Table 12.1 shows the connectivity matrix for the flow graph of Fig. 12.2. For clarity only true entries are shown, all others are false.

To find loops in a flow graph, we use the idea of *dominators*. We say that a block, p, dominates another node, q, if all paths from the start of the program to q go through p. In Fig. 12.2, B_5 dominates B_6, since it is impossible to reach B_6

Table 12.1   Connectivity matrix, $c_{i,j}$, for the flow graph of Fig. 12.2

$c_{i,j}$	B_1	B_2	B_3	B_4	B_5	B_6
B_1		True				
B_2			True	True		
B_3					True	
B_4					True	
B_5		True				True
B_6						

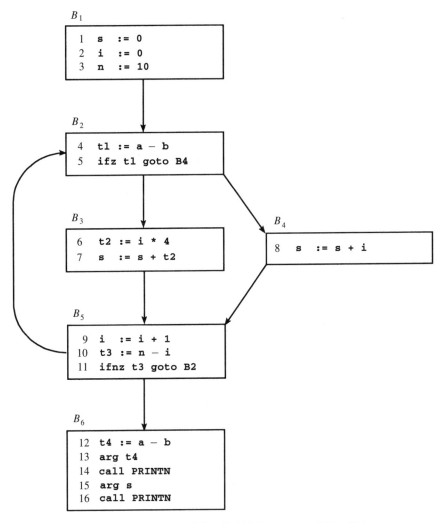

Figure 12.2 Flow graph for the TAC program of Fig. 12.1

without going through B_5. Conversely, B_3 does not dominate B_5, since it is possible to reach B_5 (via B_4), without going through B_3.

12.1.1 IDENTIFYING LOOPS

When finding loops we need to identify back edges. These are edges in the flow graph where the destination block dominates the source block. In Fig. 12.2, the only back edge is from B_5 to B_2.

A loop must have a single entry point, the *header*, and one or more back edges to the header. The header dominates all blocks in the loop (otherwise it cannot be the only entry point).

A loop is associated with each back edge, let us say $s \rightarrow d$, where d is the header of the loop. We know that s is in the loop. Since by definition, d is the only entry to the loop, a path from any block outside the loop to s (which is in the loop) must go through d. Conversely, any blocks which have a path to s without going through d are in the loop. Thus the loop associated with the back edge, $s \rightarrow d$, is the set of blocks d, s plus all blocks that can reach s without going through d.

In Fig. 12.2, we have already identified the back edge from B_5 to B_2. The loop then comprises these two basic blocks, together with B_3 and B_4, the two blocks which can reach B_5 without going through B_2.

As well as its single entry point, the header, each loop has zero or more *exit* blocks (allowing for the possibility of loops which never terminate), which have edges to blocks outside the loop. In our example B_5 is the only exit block.

12.1.2 NESTED LOOPS

If two loops do not have the same header, then either they are disjoint, or one is contained within the other. This gives a useful rule for identifying inner loops.

Shared headers are a problem, since we cannot then identify which is the inner loop. However, they tend to be infrequent, since they are a consequence of unstructured use of goto statements in programming languages and are best considered as a single loop.

12.2 Global dataflow analysis

Different global optimizations require different information, with slightly different dataflow analysis to obtain that information. For the optimizations illustrated in Sections 12.3 through 12.5 we shall require four types of information.

1. *Reaching definitions.* These are a generalization of the idea of next-reference information described in Section 11.1.
2. *Copy statements.* We shall need to know which copy statements remain unchanged across blocks, in order to extend copy propagation to more than a single basic block.
3. *Available expressions.* If we have two identical expressions in separate blocks, we shall need to know if the variables they use hold the same value, so that we can carry out common sub-expression elimination.
4. *Live variables.* The optimizations of Chapter 11 all relied on the approximation that named variables were live and temporary variables dead at the end of each basic block. We can use the dataflow analysis to compute this information exactly.

12.2.1   DETERMINING REACHING DEFINITIONS

The first technique we will describe is used to compute *reaching definitions*. These are a generalization of the idea of the next-reference information described in Section 11.1. For any TAC statement:

```
a := b op c
```

we need to know where the operands, b and c, were defined. Conversely a is defined by this TAC statement and will be of interest to future statements that reference a. However, now we are looking outside a single basic block, we must consider the possibility of not just one statement defining each operand, but the possibility of a set of defining statements.

Consider the flow graph of Fig. 12.2. The operand i is referenced in statement 6 of basic block B_3, and has *two* definitions in statement 2 of block B_1 and statement 9 of block B_5. We refer to these as *reaching definitions* of operand i in statement 6 of B_3.

Notice the effect of the loop in the graph. The first time round the loop it will be the definition of statement 2 that is referenced in statement 6, thereafter it will be the definition of statement 9 that is referenced. Statement 9 can be a preceding definition of i, even though it appears later in the program.

The precautionary principle

In dataflow analysis we always err on the side of caution. In the flow graph of Fig. 12.2, the definition of i in statement 2 only reaches statement 6 under the circumstances that a − b is non-zero on the first loop iteration. A typical use of reaching definition information will be in considering whether to carry out copy propagation. For statement 2 we must consider the *possibility* that its propagation may affect the evaluation of statement 6. We must err on the side of caution and add statement 2 to the list of definitions reaching statement 6.

In dataflow analysis we always err on the side of safety, at the expense of missing some possible optimizations. By analogy with other branches of engineering, this is referred to as the *precautionary principle* (other writers talk of conservative estimation).

The precautionary principle must also be applied to statements where we cannot be sure if a variable is being defined. In languages like C (but not VSL), we can use pointers to refer indirectly to other variables. For example:

```
int x ;
int *xp = &x ;

*xp = 42 ;
```

defines the variable x as surely as if we had just written x = 42 ;. However, in general we cannot know what address a pointer may be holding, and so any statement of the form:

```
*p = v ;
```

must be regarded as potentially defining any variable in the whole program. This can be a serious limit on the optimization possible in a program, and is one reason why strongly typed languages, where general pointer operations are not permitted can sometimes be compiled into more efficient code. The issue of resolving such problems is known as *alias analysis*, and although beyond the scope of this book is an important component of optimizing compilers for some languages.

Reaching definition information within basic blocks

We must first determine previous definition information within basic blocks. We will then combine this information for multiple basic blocks, to obtain information for a complete flow graph.

Consider a general TAC statement in a basic block:

$$n \quad \texttt{a := b op c}$$

As we saw in Section 11.1, this creates a new definition of a, and in so doing destroys all previous definitions of a for subsequent TAC statements. We can think of this in set theoretic terms, as a set of definitions *generated* by this statement, $\mathbb{G}_R$, and a set of definitions *killed* by this statement, $\mathbb{K}_R$:

$$\mathbb{G}_R = \{n\}$$
$$\mathbb{K}_R = \mathbb{U}_a - \{n\}$$

where $\mathbb{U}_a$ is the set of all definitions of a in the program. Notice that we represent definitions just by the TAC statement number (in this case n) where they occur.

We build up this information, so that we can determine $\mathbb{G}_R$ and $\mathbb{K}_R$ for a complete basic block. Suppose we have two consecutive TAC statements:

$$
\begin{array}{ll}
n & \texttt{a := b op c} \\
n+1 & \texttt{d := e op f}
\end{array}
$$

Let us suppose $\mathbb{G}_{R,n}$ and $\mathbb{K}_{R,n}$ are the sets of generated and killed definitions due to statement n, and $\mathbb{G}_{R,n+1}$ and $\mathbb{K}_{R,n+1}$ those due to statement $n+1$. The overall sets of definitions generated and killed by this pair of statements will be:

$$\mathbb{G}_R = \mathbb{G}_{R,n} - \mathbb{K}_{R,n+1} \cup \mathbb{G}_{R,n+1}$$
$$\mathbb{K}_R = \mathbb{K}_{R,n} - \mathbb{G}_{R,n+1} \cup \mathbb{K}_{R,n+1}$$

which for the example given is:

$$\mathbb{G}_R = \{n, n+1\}$$
$$\mathbb{K}_R = \mathbb{U}_a - \{n\} \cup (\mathbb{U}_a - \{n+1\})$$

Intuitively, we are adding together generated definitions for the two statements, except for the case where the second statement kills a definition in the first. Conversely, we are adding together the killed definitions, except for the case where the second statement generates a definition killed in the first.

Such equations, relating information between statements are known as *dataflow equations*. Whenever we need to construct information about a program, we will need such equations.

This is quite general, and the same logic applies if we consider the sets generated not just by two statements, but by two sequences of statements. From this comes our algorithm to build generated and killed definition sets for a complete basic block:

1. Let $\mathbb{G}_R$ and $\mathbb{K}_R$ be the sets of generated and killed definitions determined for the first n statements in the basic block which has a total of N statements. Start off with $\mathbb{G}_R = \mathbb{K}_R = \varnothing$ and $n = 0$
2. Set $n = n + 1$
3. Incorporate the definitions due to statement n in the generated and killed definition sets:

$$\mathbb{G}'_R = \mathbb{G}_R - \mathbb{K}_{R,n} \cup \mathbb{G}_{R,n}$$
$$\mathbb{K}'_R = \mathbb{K}_R - \mathbb{G}_{R,n} \cup \mathbb{K}_{R,n}$$
$$\mathbb{G}_R = \mathbb{G}'_R$$
$$\mathbb{K}_R = \mathbb{K}'_R$$

4. Repeat until $n = N$

Throughout we apply the precautionary principle. If in doubt we add a statement to the generated definition set, $\mathbb{G}_R$. Conversely, we do *not* add a statement to the killed definition set, $\mathbb{K}_R$. If in doubt we want to make sure any definition remains.

We can apply this to basic block B_1 in the flow graph of Fig. 12.2. Statement 1 generates a definition of s, and kills the other two definitions in statements 7 and 8, so we have $\mathbb{G}_R = \{1\}$ and $\mathbb{K}_R = \{7,8\}$. Statement 2 generates a definition of i and kills the other definition in statement 9, so we now have $\mathbb{G}_R = \{1,2\}$ and $\mathbb{K}_R = \{7,8,9\}$. Finally, statement 3 generates a definition of n, for which there are no other definitions that can be killed. This gives us for the complete basic block, $\mathbb{G}_R(B_1) = \{1,2,3\}$ and $\mathbb{K}_R(B_1) = \{7,8,9\}$.

Reaching definitions for complete programs

These generated and killed definition sets are not quite sufficient for our purposes, because they describe only the effect of an individual statement, or a sequence of statements within an individual basic block. We need to relate this information to the other blocks in the flow graph. We shall then be able to identify the set of definitions which reach the top of each basic block, and the set of definitions which are active at the bottom. These are known as the *top* and *bottom* sets for each basic block, $\mathbb{T}_R$ and $\mathbb{B}_R$ (other authors refer to *in* and *out* sets).

Intuitively, the definitions that reach the start of a basic block are all those which reached the end of all the blocks immediately preceding it. The definitions that reach the end of a basic block are all the definitions reaching the start, less those killed in the block plus those generated in the block.

We can write this as two new dataflow equations:

$$\mathbb{T}_R(B_j) = \bigcup_{\substack{i \\ c_{i,j}=\text{true}}} \mathbb{B}_R(B_i)$$

$$\mathbb{B}_R(B_j) = \mathbb{T}_R(B_j) - \mathbb{K}_R(B_j) \cup \mathbb{G}_R(B_j)$$

Note that unlike the generated and killed definition sets, these equations do not stand alone for a single basic block, but depend on outside information (the set of definitions active at the start of the statement). As a consequence we will not be able to generate $\mathbb{T}_R$ and $\mathbb{B}_R$ sets for individual basic blocks, until we consider the program flow graph as a whole.

We use an iterative approach, where we start with a conservative estimate of $\mathbb{T}_R$ and $\mathbb{B}_R$ sets (the precautionary principle again), and then iterate making better and better approximations until no further improvement is possible. We start by assuming that all $\mathbb{T}_R$ sets are empty, and thus all $\mathbb{B}_R$ sets comprise only those definitions generated within the basic block. We then propagate further definitions around the graph.

1. For each basic block, B_i, set $\mathbb{B}_R(B_i) = \mathbb{G}_R(B_i)$
2. For each basic block, B_j, compute

$$\mathbb{T}_R(B_j) = \bigcup_{\substack{i \\ c_{i,j}=\text{true}}} \mathbb{B}_R(B_i)$$

$$\mathbb{B}_R(B_j) = \mathbb{T}_R(B_j) - \mathbb{K}_R(B_j) \cup \mathbb{G}_R(B_j)$$

3. Repeat step 2 until there is no change in any $\mathbb{B}_R(B_j)$

Tables 12.2(a) to 12.2(c) show this computation for the flow graph of Fig. 12.2, after step 1 of the algorithm, after the first iteration of step 2 and at the end of the algorithm.

The final $\mathbb{T}_R$ and $\mathbb{B}_R$ sets can be examined in relation to the flow graph of Fig. 12.2. We see that there are no definitions that reach the top of B_1 (not surprising) while the end of that block is reached by the definitions of s, i and n in statements 1, 2 and 3. These definitions together with all other definitions in the loop defined by blocks B_2, B_3, B_4 and B_5 may reach both the top and bottom of the loop header, B_2. Note that as described earlier we are dealing with definitions that *may* reach a particular point. For example, the definition of t1 in statement 6 of B_3 will only reach B_2 if we execute the loop at least once passing through B_3.

If we look at $\mathbb{B}_R(B_3)$, we see that the definition of s in statement 1 of B_1 does not appear. It cannot reach the end of B_3, since it will always be replaced by the definition of s in statement 7 of B_3. For the same reason it does not appear in $\mathbb{B}_R(B_4)$. The definition of s in statement 1 of B_1 is also missing from both $\mathbb{T}_R(B_5)$ and $\mathbb{B}_R(B_5)$. In this case there is no redefinition of s within B_5, but whatever

Table 12.2 Computation of reaching definitions for the flow graph of Fig. 12.2: (a) after step 1; (b) after first iteration of step 2; (c) at completion

(a)

	$\mathbb{G}_R$	$\mathbb{K}_R$	$\mathbb{T}_R$	$\mathbb{B}_R$
B_1	$\{1, 2, 3\}$	$\{7, 8, 9\}$	$\varnothing$	$\{1, 2, 3\}$
B_2	$\{4\}$	$\varnothing$	$\varnothing$	$\{4\}$
B_3	$\{6, 7\}$	$\{1, 8\}$	$\varnothing$	$\{6, 7\}$
B_4	$\{8\}$	$\{1, 7\}$	$\varnothing$	$\{8\}$
B_5	$\{9, 10\}$	$\{2\}$	$\varnothing$	$\{9, 10\}$
B_6	$\{12\}$	$\varnothing$	$\varnothing$	$\{12\}$

(b)

	$\mathbb{G}_R$	$\mathbb{K}_R$	$\mathbb{T}_R$	$\mathbb{B}_R$
B_1	$\{1, 2, 3\}$	$\{7, 8, 9\}$	$\varnothing$	$\{1, 2, 3\}$
B_2	$\{4\}$	$\varnothing$	$\{1, 2, 3, 9, 10\}$	$\{1, 2, 3, 4, 9, 10\}$
B_3	$\{6, 7\}$	$\{1, 8\}$	$\{1, 2, 3, 4, 9, 10\}$	$\{2, 3, 4, 6, 7, 9, 10\}$
B_4	$\{8\}$	$\{1, 7\}$	$\{1, 2, 3, 4, 9, 10\}$	$\{2, 3, 4, 8, 9, 10\}$
B_5	$\{9, 10\}$	$\{2\}$	$\{2, 3, 4, 6, 7, 8, 9, 10\}$	$\{3, 4, 6, 7, 8, 9, 10\}$
B_6	$\{12\}$	$\varnothing$	$\{3, 4, 6, 7, 8, 9, 10\}$	$\{3, 4, 6, 7, 8, 9, 10, 12\}$

(c)

	$\mathbb{G}_R$	$\mathbb{K}_R$	$\mathbb{T}_R$	$\mathbb{B}_R$
B_1	$\{1, 2, 3\}$	$\{7, 8, 9\}$	$\varnothing$	$\{1, 2, 3\}$
B_2	$\{4\}$	$\varnothing$	$\{1, 2, 3, 4, 6, 7, 8, 9, 10\}$	$\{1, 2, 3, 4, 6, 7, 8, 9, 10\}$
B_3	$\{6, 7\}$	$\{1, 8\}$	$\{1, 2, 3, 4, 6, 7, 8, 9, 10\}$	$\{2, 3, 4, 6, 7, 9, 10\}$
B_4	$\{8\}$	$\{1, 7\}$	$\{1, 2, 3, 4, 6, 7, 8, 9, 10\}$	$\{2, 3, 4, 6, 8, 9, 10\}$
B_5	$\{9, 10\}$	$\{2\}$	$\{2, 3, 4, 6, 7, 8, 9, 10\}$	$\{3, 4, 6, 7, 8, 9, 10\}$
B_6	$\{12\}$	$\varnothing$	$\{3, 4, 6, 7, 8, 9, 10\}$	$\{3, 4, 6, 7, 8, 9, 10, 12\}$

route we take to get to B_5, we must either pass through B_3 or B_4, both of which do redefine s.

Finally, we see that the definition of t4 in statement 12 of B_6 appears only in $\mathbb{B}_R(B_6)$, since there is no route by which it can reach other blocks.

12.2.2   DETERMINING COPY STATEMENT INFORMATION

In carrying out copy propagation we will need to ensure before making a substitution of b for a in any reached statement that neither a nor b has changed. We must set up new dataflow equations to solve this problem. We introduce new generation and kill sets just for copy statements, $\mathbb{G}_C$ and $\mathbb{K}_C$.

Intuitively, $\mathbb{G}_C$ for a basic block is the set of copy statements, a := b, within the block, for which the values of a and b have not been redefined after the copy statement. $\mathbb{K}_C$ is the set of copy statements throughout the program, a := b, which are killed within the block by the redefinition of either a or b.

Because we are only going to use a copy statement if it is valid no matter by which route we enter a basic block, our precautionary principle is reversed in this case. We only add a copy statement to $\mathbb{G}_C$ if we are certain it is evaluated, while we add a copy statement to $\mathbb{K}_C$ even if we are doubtful it will be killed.

The flow graph in Fig. 12.2 has only three copy statements, 1, 2 and 3, all in basic block B_1, and so $\mathbb{G}_C(B_1) = \{1,2,3\}$. Blocks B_1 and B_2 do not reassign any of the variables in these copy statements, and so have null $\mathbb{K}_C$s. However, B_3 reassigns s, thereby killing the copy in statement 1. Thus $\mathbb{G}_C(B_3) = \{1\}$.

Like $\mathbb{G}_R$ and $\mathbb{K}_R$, $\mathbb{G}_C$ and $\mathbb{K}_C$ apply only to individual basic blocks. We define top and bottom sets, $\mathbb{T}_C$ and $\mathbb{B}_C$, defined by the dataflow equations:

$$\mathbb{T}_C(B_j) = \bigcap_{\substack{i \\ c_{i,j}=\text{true}}} \mathbb{B}_C(B_i)$$

$$\mathbb{B}_C(B_j) = \mathbb{T}_C(B_j) - \mathbb{K}_C(B_j) \cup \mathbb{G}_C(B_j)$$

Note that the definition of $\mathbb{T}_C$ depends on the *intersection* of all the preceding bottom sets. With reaching definitions, if there was a definition in any preceding block, we carried it forward. However, we can only propagate a copy if it is valid, no matter which route we took to get to its point of use. Only if the copy is in the bottom set of *all* preceding blocks, can we make use of it.

We need to modify our iterative algorithm slightly to take account of this. With reaching definitions we started with small bottom sets, which got larger as we iterated, since the top sets were the *union* of several bottom sets. With copy statements, we start with bottom sets containing all copy statements in the program (other than those killed in the block itself). Since top sets are the *intersection* of several bottom sets, this will steadily remove copy statements as they propagate around the flow graph.

We need to make one other modification. When we first execute the program, we enter the first block (B_1 in this case), bringing in no previous information. It is as though there were a preceding block with a completely empty bottom set. In evaluating the top set of B_1, we should intersect with this set, and so we must always have $\mathbb{T}_C(B_1) = \varnothing$ and thus $\mathbb{B}_C(B_1) = \mathbb{G}_C(B_1)$. Our algorithm is thus:

1. For the first basic block (i.e. the block which dominates all others), B_1, set $\mathbb{T}_C(B_1) = \varnothing$ and $\mathbb{B}_C(B_1) = \mathbb{G}_C(B_1)$
2. For each basic block, B_i, other than B_1 set $\mathbb{B}_C(B_i) = \mathbb{U} - \mathbb{K}_C(B_i)$, where $\mathbb{U}$ is the set of all copy statements in the program
3. For each basic block, B_j, other than B_1, compute

$$\mathbb{T}_C(B_j) = \bigcap_{\substack{i \\ c_{i,j}=\text{true}}} \mathbb{B}_C(B_i)$$

$$\mathbb{B}_C(B_j) = \mathbb{T}_C(B_j) - \mathbb{K}_C(B_j) \cup \mathbb{G}_C(B_j)$$

4. Repeat step 3 until there is no change in any $\mathbb{B}_C(B_j)$

Table 12.3 Computation of copy statement information for the flow graph of Fig. 12.2: (a) after step 2; (b) after first iteration of step 3; (c) at completion

(a)

	$\mathbb{G}_C$	$\mathbb{K}_C$	$\mathbb{T}_C$	$\mathbb{B}_C$
B_1	$\{1, 2, 3\}$	$\varnothing$	$\varnothing$	$\{1, 2, 3\}$
B_2	$\varnothing$	$\varnothing$	$\varnothing$	$\{1, 2, 3\}$
B_3	$\varnothing$	$\{1\}$	$\varnothing$	$\{2, 3\}$
B_4	$\varnothing$	$\{1\}$	$\varnothing$	$\{2, 3\}$
B_5	$\varnothing$	$\{2\}$	$\varnothing$	$\{1, 3\}$
B_6	$\varnothing$	$\varnothing$	$\varnothing$	$\{1, 2, 3\}$

(b)

	$\mathbb{G}_C$	$\mathbb{K}_C$	$\mathbb{T}_C$	$\mathbb{B}_C$
B_1	$\{1, 2, 3\}$	$\varnothing$	$\varnothing$	$\{1, 2, 3\}$
B_2	$\varnothing$	$\varnothing$	$\{1, 3\}$	$\{1, 3\}$
B_3	$\varnothing$	$\{1\}$	$\{1, 3\}$	$\{3\}$
B_4	$\varnothing$	$\{1\}$	$\{1, 3\}$	$\{3\}$
B_5	$\varnothing$	$\{2\}$	$\{3\}$	$\{3\}$
B_6	$\varnothing$	$\varnothing$	$\{3\}$	$\{3\}$

(c)

	$\mathbb{G}_C$	$\mathbb{K}_C$	$\mathbb{T}_C$	$\mathbb{B}_C$
B_1	$\{1, 2, 3\}$	$\varnothing$	$\varnothing$	$\{1, 2, 3\}$
B_2	$\varnothing$	$\varnothing$	$\{3\}$	$\{3\}$
B_3	$\varnothing$	$\{1\}$	$\{3\}$	$\{3\}$
B_4	$\varnothing$	$\{1\}$	$\{3\}$	$\{3\}$
B_5	$\varnothing$	$\{2\}$	$\{3\}$	$\{3\}$
B_6	$\varnothing$	$\varnothing$	$\{3\}$	$\{3\}$

Tables 12.3(a) to 12.3(c) show this computation for the flow graph of Fig. 12.2, after step 2 of the algorithm, after the first iteration of step 3 and at the end of the algorithm.

The final $\mathbb{T}_C$ and $\mathbb{B}_C$ sets can be examined in relation to the flow graph of Fig. 12.2. We see that there are no copy statements that reach the top of B_1 (not surprising) while the end of that block is reached by the copy statements 1, 2 and 3.

However, only copy statement 3 is guaranteed to reach the top of B_2 intact. Note that with copy statements we are dealing with certainty that the operands of the statement have not been altered. The first time round the loop, all three statements 1, 2 and 3 reach the top of B_2. However, on subsequent iterations, both i and s will have been reassigned, so the values they hold cannot be guaranteed to be that in the copy statements. Since n is never reassigned in the program, it is not surprising that copy statement 3 in fact reaches the $\mathbb{T}_C$ and $\mathbb{B}_C$ of all blocks.

12.2.3 DETERMINING AVAILABLE EXPRESSIONS

In carrying out common sub-expression elimination, we will wish to know where in the program there are two expressions which always yield the same value, thus allowing one to be replaced by the result of the other.

At any point in a program, a op b is an *available expression* if all routes fromthe start of the program to that point must pass through the evaluation of a op b, and subsequent to that evaluation there are no redefinitions of a or b. At such a point we could replace use of a op b by the result of its previous evaluation.

Just as with reaching definitions and copy statements, we can talk of generating and killing expressions. Intuitively, a op b is generated by a statement in which it is evaluated. a op b is killed by any statement which redefines a or b (which would therefore alter the value of a op b). We call these sets of generated and killed expressions $\mathbb{G}_E$ and $\mathbb{K}_E$.

We can create $\mathbb{G}_E$ for a basic block by the following algorithm:

1. Initially set $\mathbb{G}_E = \emptyset$
2. Starting from the top take each statement a := b op c in turn, first add b op c to $\mathbb{G}_E$, then delete any expression involving a from $\mathbb{G}_E$

Note the importance of the order of operations in step 2. If we have an expression of the form a := a op b, this will not generate a op b, since the value is immediately destroyed by assignment to a.

Once again we apply the precautionary principle. We only add an expression to the generated set if we are certain it will be evaluated, while we add to the killed set if there is a possibility that an expression will be killed.

We link these sets together for the whole program with top and bottom sets $\mathbb{T}_E$ and $\mathbb{B}_E$ for each basic block, by the following dataflow equations:

$$\mathbb{T}_E(B_j) = \bigcap_{\substack{i \\ c_{i,j}=\text{true}}} \mathbb{B}_E(B_i)$$

$$\mathbb{B}_E(B_j) = \mathbb{T}_E(B_j) - \mathbb{K}_E(B_j) \cup \mathbb{G}_E(B_j)$$

These are precisely the same equations as for copy statements. The top set is the intersection of the bottom sets of all preceding blocks. An expression is only available if it is carried forward from *all* possible routes, and so we must use intersection rather than union of the sets.

The same iterative algorithm as that for copy statements can also be used.

1. For the first basic block (i.e. the block which dominates all others), B_1, set $\mathbb{T}_E(B_1) = \emptyset$ and $\mathbb{B}_E(B_1) = \mathbb{G}_E(B_1)$.
2. For each basic block, B_i, other than B_1 set $\mathbb{B}_E(B_i) = \mathbb{U} - \mathbb{K}_E(B_i)$, where $\mathbb{U}$ is the set of all available expressions in the program

3. For each basic block, B_j, other than B_1, compute

$$\mathbb{T}_E(B_j) = \bigcap_{\substack{i \\ c_{i,j}=\text{true}}} \mathbb{B}_E(B_i)$$

$$\mathbb{B}_E(B_j) = \mathbb{T}_E(B_j) - \mathbb{K}_E(B_j) \cup \mathbb{G}_E(B_j)$$

4. Repeat step 3 until there is no change in any $\mathbb{B}_E(B_j)$

Tables 12.4(a) to 12.4(b) show this computation for the flow graph of Fig. 12.2, after step 2 of the algorithm and after the first iteration of step 3, which is the only iteration needed.

The final $\mathbb{T}_E$ and $\mathbb{B}_E$ sets can be examined in relation to the flow graph of Fig. 12.2. We see that the expression a − b appears in $\mathbb{T}_E(B_5)$. Whatever route we take to get to B_5, we will have evaluated the expression a − b, and it will have the same value. If a − b were to appear in B_5, then there is the potential to replace it by the result of the earlier evaluation.

Although B_5 leads back to B_2 and the expression a − b is in $\mathbb{B}_E(B_5)$, the expression does not appear in $\mathbb{T}_E(B_2)$. The precautionary principle insists that an expression only appears in a set if *all* routes to that point evaluate it to the same value. We will enter B_2 initially from B_1, at which point a − b will not have been evaluated. Only on subsequent iterations of the loop, during which a − b is evaluated will we then lead back from B_5 to B_2.

a − b appears commonly as an available expression, since its operands, a and

Table 12.4 Computation of available expression information for the flow graph of Fig. 12.2: (a) after step 2; (b) after first and final iteration of step 3

(a)

	$\mathbb{G}_E$	$\mathbb{K}_E$	$\mathbb{T}_E$	$\mathbb{B}_E$
B_1	$\varnothing$	{i * 4, n − i}	$\varnothing$	$\varnothing$
B_2	{a − b}	$\varnothing$	$\varnothing$	{a − b, i * 4, n − i}
B_3	{i * 4}	$\varnothing$	$\varnothing$	{a − b, i * 4, n − i}
B_4	$\varnothing$	$\varnothing$	$\varnothing$	{a − b, i * 4, n − i}
B_5	{n − i}	{i * 4, n − i}	$\varnothing$	{a − b}
B_6	{a − b}	$\varnothing$	$\varnothing$	{a − b, i * 4, n − i}

(b)

	$\mathbb{G}_E$	$\mathbb{K}_E$	$\mathbb{T}_E$	$\mathbb{B}_E$
B_1	$\varnothing$	{i * 4, n − i}	$\varnothing$	$\varnothing$
B_2	{a − b}	$\varnothing$	$\varnothing$	{a − b}
B_3	{i * 4}	$\varnothing$	{a − b}	{a − b, i * 4}
B_4	$\varnothing$	$\varnothing$	{a − b}	{a − b}
B_5	{n − i}	{i * 4, n − i}	{a − b}	{a − b, n − i}
B_6	{a − b}	$\varnothing$	{a − b, n − i}	{a − b, n − i}

b, are not altered during the program. Other expressions, i * 4 and n - i appear in only a few $\mathbb{T}_E$ and $\mathbb{B}_E$ sets, since operands are rapidly changed around, or because they are not evaluated identically in all routes through the program. For example i * 4 appears in $\mathbb{B}_E(B_3)$, but cannot propagate to B_5, since routes to B_5 via B_4 would not cause its evaluation.

12.2.4 GLOBAL LIVE VARIABLE ANALYSIS

Many of local optimizations described in Chapter 11 relied on knowledge of variables that were live at the end of a basic block. For simple optimization we relied on the assumption that all named variables were alive at the end of the block, and all temporaries dead. We can use dataflow techniques to give more precise information.

Rather than generated and killed sets, we talk of *use* and *definition sets*. $\mathbb{U}_L$ is the set of variables in a basic block which are used before they are defined, i.e. they rely on a definition prior to this block being executed. $\mathbb{D}_L$ is the set of variables which are defined prior to any use. The precautionary principle in this case means we will want to assume variables are still live if there is any doubt. Thus we add to $\mathbb{U}_L$ even if there is doubt, but add to $\mathbb{D}_L$ only if we are certain.

Our top and bottom sets then refer to variables which are live (i.e. have a subsequent use) at the top and bottom of the basic block. They are defined by the dataflow equations:

$$\mathbb{B}_L(B_i) = \bigcup_{\substack{i \\ c_{i,j}=\text{true}}} \mathbb{T}_L(B_j)$$

$$\mathbb{T}_L(B_i) = \mathbb{B}_L(B_i) - \mathbb{D}_L(B_i) \cup \mathbb{U}_L(B_i)$$

The relationships are rather the reverse of those that we have seen before in that we work backwards from succeeding blocks, rather than forwards from preceding blocks. We use a reversed form of the iterative algorithm for reaching definitions to solve these equations, propagating liveness information backwards around the flow graph.

1. For each basic block, B_i, set $\mathbb{T}_L(B_i) = \mathbb{U}_L(B_i)$
2. For each basic block, B_i, compute

$$\mathbb{B}_L(B_i) = \bigcup_{\substack{i \\ c_{i,j}=\text{true}}} \mathbb{T}_L(B_j)$$

$$\mathbb{T}_L(B_i) = \mathbb{B}_L(B_i) - \mathbb{D}_L(B_i) \cup \mathbb{U}_L(B_i)$$

3. Repeat step 2 until there is no change in any $\mathbb{T}_L(B_i)$

Tables 12.5(a) to 12.5(c) show this computation for the flow graph of Fig. 12.2, after step 1 of the algorithm, after the first iteration of step 2 and at the end of the algorithm.

The final $\mathbb{T}_L$ and $\mathbb{B}_L$ sets can be examined in relation to the flow graph of Fig. 12.2. The first thing to note is that a and b appear in all sets except $\mathbb{B}_L(B_6)$.

Table 12.5 Live variable analysis for the flow graph of Fig. 12.2: (a) after step 1; (b) after first iteration of step 2; (c) at completion

(a)

	$\mathbb{U}_L$	$\mathbb{D}_L$	$\mathbb{B}_L$	$\mathbb{T}_L$
B_1	$\varnothing$	$\{$i, n, s$\}$	$\varnothing$	$\varnothing$
B_2	$\{$a, b$\}$	$\{$t1$\}$	$\varnothing$	$\{$a, b$\}$
B_3	$\{$i, s$\}$	$\{$t2$\}$	$\varnothing$	$\{$i, s$\}$
B_4	$\{$s$\}$	$\varnothing$	$\varnothing$	$\{$s$\}$
B_5	$\{$i, n$\}$	$\{$t3$\}$	$\varnothing$	$\{$i, n$\}$
B_6	$\{$a, b, s$\}$	$\{$t4$\}$	$\varnothing$	$\{$a, b, s$\}$

(b)

	$\mathbb{U}_L$	$\mathbb{D}_L$	$\mathbb{B}_L$	$\mathbb{T}_L$
B_1	$\varnothing$	$\{$i, n, s$\}$	$\{$a, b$\}$	$\{$a, b$\}$
B_2	$\{$a, b$\}$	$\{$t1$\}$	$\{$i, s$\}$	$\{$a, b, i, s$\}$
B_3	$\{$i, s$\}$	$\{$t2$\}$	$\{$i, n$\}$	$\{$i, n, s$\}$
B_4	$\{$s$\}$	$\varnothing$	$\{$i, n$\}$	$\{$i, n, s$\}$
B_5	$\{$i, n$\}$	$\{$t3$\}$	$\{$a, b, s$\}$	$\{$a, b, i, n, s$\}$
B_6	$\{$a, b, s$\}$	$\{$t4$\}$	$\varnothing$	$\{$a, b, s$\}$

(c)

	$\mathbb{U}_L$	$\mathbb{D}_L$	$\mathbb{B}_L$	$\mathbb{T}_L$
B_1	$\varnothing$	$\{$i, n, s$\}$	$\{$a, b, i, n, s$\}$	$\{$a, b$\}$
B_2	$\{$a, b$\}$	$\{$t1$\}$	$\{$a, b, i, n, s$\}$	$\{$a, b, i, n, s$\}$
B_3	$\{$i, s$\}$	$\{$t2$\}$	$\{$a, b, i, n, s$\}$	$\{$a, b, i, n, s$\}$
B_4	$\{$s$\}$	$\varnothing$	$\{$a, b, i, n, s$\}$	$\{$a, b, i, n, s$\}$
B_5	$\{$i, n$\}$	$\{$t3$\}$	$\{$a, b, i, n, s$\}$	$\{$a, b, i, n, s$\}$
B_6	$\{$a, b, s$\}$	$\{$t4$\}$	$\varnothing$	$\{$a, b, s$\}$

These two variables are defined before we enter this flow graph are unchanged by any statement in the program and used in statement 12 of the final block B_6. Their values are therefore live throughout the program until after the evaluation of statement 12.

The variable n is defined in block B_1, and used only in statement 10 of block B_5. However, it does not die after statement 10, since even though it is not used in block B_6, it will be reused in B_5 if we go round the block again. Thus it appears in $\mathbb{B}_L(B_5)$, but not in $\mathbb{T}_L(B_6)$. Note how we keep a variable live if there is any doubt that it may be used again. The same arguments apply to the variables i and s, also defined in block B_1, and live in all blocks of the loop.

Finally, we see that no variables appear in $\mathbb{B}_L(B_6)$, since this is the end of the program. However, for many programming languages our unit of optimization is the subroutine. We may thus have semantic information (in the symbol table) about global variables, which would remain live at the end of the flow graph under consideration.

12.3   Extending basic block optimizations to complete programs

The first use of dataflow analysis data is to extend the optimizations of Section 11.1 to the complete program. We assume the local optimizations have been done, and so the global algorithms concern themselves only with benefits achievable across blocks.

12.3.1   GLOBAL COPY PROPAGATION AND DEAD-CODE ELIMINATION

As with local optimization, global copy propagation is most useful for the opportunity of subsequent dead-code elimination. By using the reaching definition information computed in Section 12.2.3 and the copy statement information computed in Section 12.2.4 we are able to combine the operations of copy propagation and dead-code elimination.

The flow graph of Fig. 12.2 has the potential for propagation and elimination of the three copy statements 1, 2 and 3 in block B_1.

We can use the reaching definition information computed in Section 12.2.3 to identify all the statements which use the definition in each copy statement. If a statement in basic block B references a, then a copy statement a : = b reaches that statement if it appears in $\mathbb{T}_R(B)$.

If a : = b, also appears in $\mathbb{T}_C(B)$, then we know that this is the only definition of a that reaches B. Provided there is no preceding definition of a or b in B itself, we can safely replace a by b.

If we replace every reference to a which is reached by a : = b, then the copy is redundant, and can be deleted.

Our complete algorithm is then:

1. Find each copy statement, a : = b
2. For each such copy statement find all uses of a that are reached by it (i.e. all references to a in basic block B where the reaching definition top set, $\mathbb{T}_R(B)$, contains a : = b and where there is no prior redefinition of a or b in B)
3. For each such use where a : = b is also in $\mathbb{T}_C(B)$, replace a by b in that use
4. If all such uses of a are replaced, then delete the copy statement, a : = b

We can apply this to the flow graph of Fig. 12.2. Copy statement 1 reaches two references in B_3 and B_4, but appears in neither $\mathbb{T}_C(B_3)$ nor $\mathbb{T}_C(B_4)$. No substitution can be made in this case. Copy statement 2 reaches three references in B_3, B_4 and B_5, but in none of these cases does it appear in the corresponding $\mathbb{T}_C$.

Copy statement 3, n : = 10, however, has a single reference, in statement 10 of block B_5. As well as appearing in $\mathbb{T}_R(B_5)$, it also appears in $\mathbb{T}_C(B_5)$ and so we can substitute for n in statement 10, which becomes:

$$t3 \; := \; 10 - i$$

Since this is the only reference reached by the copy statement definition, we know that statement 3 is now dead and it can be deleted. Figure 12.3 shows the revised flow graph.

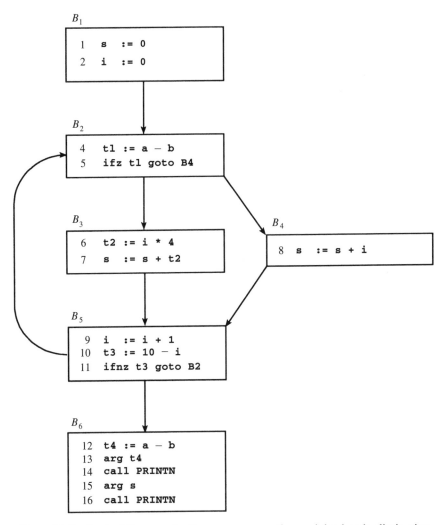

B_1

```
1   s   := 0
2   i   := 0
```

B_2

```
4   t1 := a - b
5   ifz t1 goto B4
```

B_3

```
6   t2 := i * 4
7   s   := s + t2
```

B_4

```
8   s   := s + i
```

B_5

```
9   i   := i + 1
10  t3 := 10 - i
11  ifnz t3 goto B2
```

B_6

```
12  t4 := a - b
13  arg t4
14  call PRINTN
15  arg s
16  call PRINTN
```

Figure 12.3 Revised flow graph after copy propagation and dead-code elimination

We must also update our information tables to reflect the changed flow graph. References to the deleted statement must be removed from reaching definition and copy statements. The expression in statement 10 must be altered if it appears as an available expression, and references to n must be deleted from the live variable tables. Table 12.6 shows $\mathbb{T}_R$, $\mathbb{T}_C$, $\mathbb{T}_E$ and $\mathbb{B}_L$ for the revised flow graph of Fig. 12.3.

12.3.2 GLOBAL COMMON SUB-EXPRESSION ELIMINATION

To achieve global common sub-expression elimination, we use the available expression information for the program. We look for statements a := b op c,

Table 12.6   Tables $\mathbb{T}_R$, $\mathbb{T}_C$, $\mathbb{T}_E$ and $\mathbb{B}_L$ for the revised flow graphs of Figs. 12.3 and 12.4

	$\mathbb{T}_R$	$\mathbb{T}_C$	$\mathbb{T}_E$	$\mathbb{B}_L$
B_1	$\varnothing$	$\varnothing$	$\varnothing$	{a, b, i, s}
B_2	{1, 2, 4, 6, 7, 8, 9, 10}	$\varnothing$	{a - b}	{a, b, i, s}
B_3	{1, 2, 4, 6, 7, 8, 9, 10}	$\varnothing$	{a - b}	{a, b, i, s}
B_4	{1, 2, 4, 6, 7, 8, 9, 10}	$\varnothing$	{a - b}	{a, b, i, s}
B_5	{2, 4, 6, 7, 8, 9, 10}	$\varnothing$	{a - b}	{a, b, i, s}
B_6	{4, 6, 7, 8, 9, 10}	$\varnothing$	{a - b, 10 - i}	$\varnothing$

where b op c is in the list of available expressions at the start of that block, and b and c have not been defined earlier in that block. We then search back through the flow graph, until we encounter the earlier evaluations of b op c.

Suppose we find the earlier evaluation to be d := b op c. We cannot just substitute d into the statement a := b op c, because there may be another version of the available expression from a different route, evaluated as e := b op c, for which we would wish to substitute e into a := b op c. The only solution is to follow each of the available expression evaluations by an assignment to a common variable, say t, and use that for substitution. Thus we would follow d := b op c, by t := d, and e := b op c, by t := e, allowing us to make the consistent substitution a := t, in the original statement.

This is not necessarily as inefficient as it may seem, since these copy statements will be ripe for propagation and potential dead-code elimination. Even if they are not eliminated, only one will be executed at any one time, and though the program will have increased in size, it may still be faster.
Our algorithm is then:

1. Search through the program identifying statements of the form a := b op c, in basic block B, such that a := b op c is in $\mathbb{T}_E(B)$, and there is no prior redefinition of a or b in B
2. For each such statement, allocate a new variable, t, not used elsewhere in the program. Trace back through the flow graph of the program from B searching for evaluations of the expression of the form d := b op c. Follow each such evaluation by a new statement t := d and do not search back any further along that particular path
3. Replace the original statement by a := t

Applying this to the flow graph of Fig. 12.3, we discover that only statement 12, t4 := a - b, meets the criteria of step 1 of the algorithm. Searching back we find only one evaluation, in statement 4. We follow this by a new statement, t5 := t1, and replace statement 12 by t4 := t5.

We immediately see that local copy propagation and elimination allows statement 12 to be removed, with statement 13 becoming arg t5. We have also introduced a new copy statement after statement 4, and we can apply the global

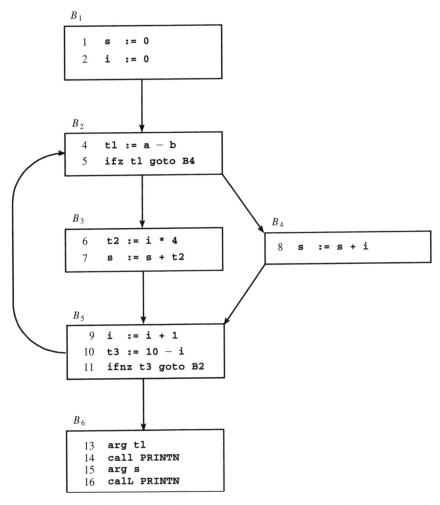

Figure 12.4 Revised flow graph after common sub-expression elimination and further copy propagation and dead-code elimination

copy propagation and dead-code elimination algorithm to remove this, with statement 13 then becoming arg t1.

Figure 12.4 shows the flow graph after all of these transformations. Although it is not generally the case after such changes, the sets $\mathbb{T}_R$, $\mathbb{T}_C$, $\mathbb{T}_E$ and $\mathbb{B}_L$ remain unchanged from Table 12.6.

12.4 Loop optimizations

Perhaps the most valuable optimizations we can make are those involving loops. Benefits from optimizing code in loops lead to gains each time round the loop.

We have seen in Section 12.1 how loops and their headers can be identified. Loop optimizations often involve moving code out of the loop, or pre-computing values for use in the loop. We need a basic block in which we can insert such code, and so before any loop optimization we create a new block for each loop, which we insert immediately before the header. Such a block is known as a *preheader*.

For the flow graph of Fig. 12.4 we shall insert a preheader, block B_{1a}, between B_1 and B_2, the header of the loop comprising B_2, B_3, B_4 and B_5.

12.4.1 CODE HOISTING

The simplest optimization is to identify statements that do not change each time a loop is executed, and move them outside the loop. For example in the VSL loop:

```
WHILE i
DO
{
        s := 0
        i := i - 1
        j := i * 4
}
DONE
```

we should clearly move the computation of s : = 0 outside the loop.

A loop consists of a set of basic blocks, identified using the method described in Section 11.2.1. A TAC statement, a := b op c, within that set of blocks will not change its value during execution of the loop, if all possible definitions of b and c are outside the loop. The reaching definition set, $\mathbb{T}_R$, for the basic block containing a := b op c gives all the statements whose definitions reach the block.

We need to recognize that if there is another statement d := a op e, where theonly definition of a or e within the loop was the definition of a := b op c now found to be invariant, then d := a op e is also invariant. This means we willneed repeated passes over the loop to identify all the possible invariants.

Our algorithm is then:

1. For each statement a := b op c whose basic block, B, lies within the loop, mark the statement as invariant if all definitions of b and c in $\mathbb{T}_R(B)$ lie outside the loop, or are invariant statements within the loop. (Note constant values of b and c meet this criterion, since they have no definitions at all!)
2. Repeat the preceding step until no more invariant statements are found.

For the flow graph in Fig. 12.4, statement 4, t1 := a − b, is the only statement in the loop that is invariant, since neither a nor b are defined in $\mathbb{T}_R(B_2)$.

We can now look at moving invariant statements out of the loop and into the preheader to be computed only once. This operation is known as *code hoisting*. Any code so moved will always be executed, irrespective of what happens within the loop and this leads to three complications which we illustrate using the following TAC.

```
            c := 10
            d := 9
            e := 8
    L1: b := d
            a := c
            d := 11
            ifnz b goto L2
            e := 561
    L2: a := 42
            c := c + 1
            ifnz c goto L1
```

This is shown as a flow graph in Fig. 12.5.

This flow graph has a loop with header B_2 and also containing B_3 and B_4, which is the sole exit block. There are three loop invariants, statements 6, 8 and 9. For convenience we have inserted a preheader, B_{1a}

Complication 1

We cannot hoist statement 8, e := 561 into the preheader, even though it is invariant. As the code stands we should execute B_1, B_{1a}, B_2 and B_4 before leaving the loop when e would have the value 8. If we were to hoist statement 8, we would execute the same blocks, but on exit e would have the value 561.

The solution is to only hoist invariant statements which are always executed in the loop. These are statements in blocks which dominate all the exit blocks.

Complication 2

Suppose we were to consider instead hoisting statement 6, d := 11. This would not appear to encounter the same problem. It is in block B_2 which dominates the exit block, B_4, and so the statement will always be executed in the loop. However, this hoisting will destroy the reaching definition from statement 2, d := 9 in B_1 to the copy statement 4, b := d in B_2. Whereas before hoisting b would have the value 9 on exit from the loop, after hoisting it would have the value 11.

The solution in this case is to only hoist a statement, a := b op c, if it is the only definition of a in the reaching definition top set, $\mathbb{T}_R(B)$, of any block, B, in the loop.

Complication 3

Finally, suppose we were to consider instead hoisting statement 9, a := 42 from B_4. This falls into neither of the two preceding problems. However, this would now make this definition precede the copy statement 5, a := c in B_2 which remains in the loop. Whereas before hoisting, a would have the value 42 on leaving the loop, after hoisting it would have the value 10.

We can avoid this problem by only hoisting a statement, a := b op c, if there is no other definition of a in the loop.

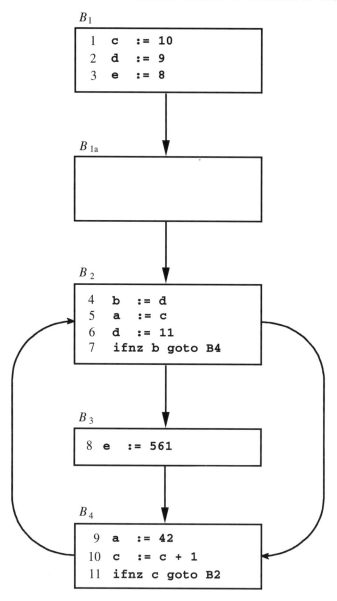

Figure 12.5 Flow graph illustrating problems with code hoisting

If an invariant, a := b op c, fails these three tests we can still use it, by combining the techniques of global sub-expression elimination and copy propagation. We treat b op c as though it were a sub-expression in the preheader, assign its value to a temporary, t := b op c, and then replace all occurrences of a := b op c by a := t in the loop. With luck copy propagation will then take some or all of these assignments out of the loop. Even if it does not, then we may have prevented multiple evaluations of the invariant expression b op c.

We can now apply these techniques to the loop invariant statement 4, t1 := a - b, from the flow graph of Fig. 12.4. This statement avoids all the three problems listed above, and so can safely be moved to the preheader, leading to the flow graph of Fig. 12.6.

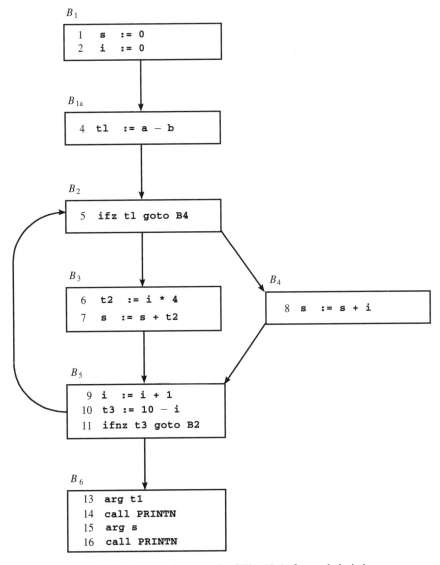

Figure 12.6 Revised flow graph of Fig. 12.4 after code hoisting

12.4.2 INDUCTION VARIABLES

Very often we see code of the form:

```
sum  := 0
n    := 10

WHILE n
DO
{
        p    := n * 2
        sum  := sum + p
        n    := n - 1
}
```

For the vast majority of computers (including VAM), multiplication is an expensive operation, and it would be significantly more efficient to note that p, being a linear function of the loop index n, is merely being incremented by a constant each time round the loop. We could write much more efficiently:

```
sum  := 0
n    := 10
p    := 20

WHILE n
DO
{
        sum := sum + p
        n   := n - 1
        p   := p - 2
}
```

The variables n and p are *induction variables* and we are applying the local optimization of strength reduction to p each time round the loop. We can use our dataflow information to identify induction variables such as p to which strength reduction can be applied, and make transformations such as the example automatically.

Our analysis depends on finding the *basic induction variables* of a loop. These are basic loop counters of the form a := a + n or a := a − n where n is a constant and which have no other definitions within the loop. A simple search of the blocks of the loop suffices for this. In the flow graph of Fig. 12.4, there is a single such basic induction variable, incremented in statement 9, i := i + 1.

Our initial algorithm for more complex induction variables deals with those which are just constant multiples of a basic induction variable.

1. Find all variables in the loop with a single definition of the form b := a * m, where m is a constant and b a basic induction variable.
2. After each occurrence of a := a + n add a statement t := t + p, where p is the constant $n*m$.
3. Replace the statement b := a * m by b := t.
4. Insert an initialization statement into the preheader t := a * m after any initial assignment to a.

We now note that this algorithm can be generalized in two ways:

1. We may vary the algorithm to deal also with induction variables which are functions of the form: b := m * a; b := a / m; b := a + m; b := a - m; b := m + a and b := m - a.
2. We may apply the algorithm not just to variables which are functions of basic induction variables, but to variables which are functions of any other induction variable. In the case of an induction variable, c, which is a function of an induction variable, b, which is in turn a function of an induction variable a, we must add two constraints. There must be no definition of a between the assignments to b and c, and there must be no definition of b outside the loop which can reach c (which requires use of information from the reaching definition top sets).

With these extensions it is usually more efficient to first identify the induction variables, and then make the substitution and code insertions. Where the same functions or constants are used it is then possible to share definitions for added efficiency.

Applying this to the flow graph of Fig. 12.6, we insert a new statement, 9a, t6 := t6 + 4 in block B_5, replace statement 6 by t2 := t6, and insert a new statement 4a, t6 := i * 4, in the preheader, B_{1a}.

Global copy propagation replaces statement 4a by t6 := 0 * 4, which local constant folding reduces to t6 := 0. Local copy propagation and dead-code elimination can be applied to new statement 6, changing statement 7 to s := s + t6, and allowing statement 6 to be eliminated.

This leaves us with the final flow graph of Fig. 12.7. The code corresponding to this graph is shown in Fig. 12.8.

In comparing this code with that of Fig. 12.1, we see that we have only reduced it in total by one statement. The main loop is reduced from nine to eight statements, but more importantly we have eliminated a multiplication from the loop. We have also eliminated all reference to one named variable.

12.5   Advanced register optimization

At this stage we could have applied the packing temporaries algorithm of Section 11.1.5. However, this may be counter-productive if we use the technique of register colouring described in Section 12.5.1 below.

If we choose not to use register colouring, our live variable analysis will help improve our register allocation. We first pack temporaries. We then use registers as needed during code generation. When we run out of registers, we must spill a value from a register in use, unless our live variable analysis shows that value is now dead.

12.5.1   REGISTER COLOURING

Register colouring is a method of handling register allocation systematically. It is particularly useful when considering global register allocation. We use two passes in generating the code. In the first pass we generate target code, but as

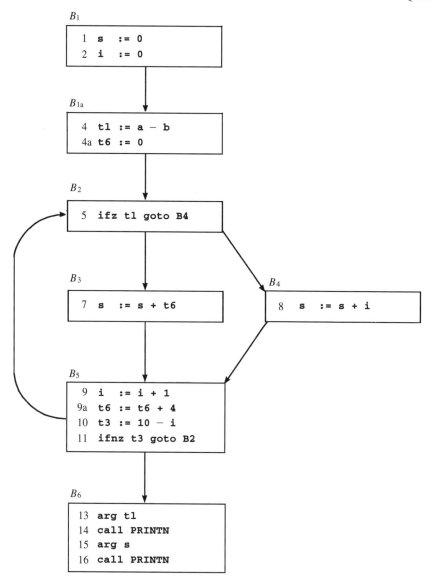

Figure 12.7 Revised flow graph of Fig. 12.6 after induction variable elimination, constant folding, copy propagation and dead-code elimination

though we had an infinite number of registers in the machine. All variable names used in the code are put in registers. In the second pass we assign physical registers to symbolic registers. We produce an *interference graph* for the symbolic registers. We have one node for each register and edges connecting registers that interfere. Registers interfere if they are both live at any point. We

```
            s   := 0
            i   := 0
            t1  := a - b
            t6  := 0
        L1: ifz t1 goto L2
            s   := s + t6
            goto L3
        L2: s   := s + i
        L3: i   := i + 1
            t6  := t6 + 4
            t3  := n - i
            ifnz t3 goto L1
            arg t1
            call PRINTN
            arg s
            call PRINTN
```

Figure 12.8   TAC program corresponding to the flow graph of Fig. 12.7

do this by looking at each statement in which a register is defined, and connecting that register to all other registers live at that point. Note that in this we are making the assumption that we only define live values, i.e. dead-code elimination has been carried out. The edges thus indicate symbolic registers that could not share a physical register.

We next attempt to colour the graph using the same number of colours as there are physical registers. By colouring a graph we mean assigning a colour to each node such that it is not connected to any node of the same colour. If we succeed then we can assign one physical register to each colour, knowing that at no point will they interfere (since that would mean two nodes of the same colour being connected).

A simple method of colouring a graph in n colours is to look for nodes with fewer than n neighbours. We can then colour that node with one of the colours not used by a neighbour. Having done that we remove the node, and its associated edges, leaving a simpler graph and repeat the process on the simpler graph. By repeating this process either we shall successfully eliminate all nodes, in which case we have achieved a colouring, or we will end up with a graph of nodes, all with n neighbours. In this latter case we must add code to spill a register, modify the interference graph accordingly, and try again. Common sense dictates spilling registers outside loops.

This is only an approximation. The general algorithm for performing graph colouring is NP-complete. A point to bear in mind is that packing temporaries is not necessarily appropriate if register colouring is used. Register colouring effectively packs temporaries anyway. By packing before colouring we introduce interferences in the graph which may make it harder to colour.

12.6 Superoptimizers

We have already seen at the start of Chapter 11 that code optimization is a misnomer. Optimizers certainly improve code considerably, but they do not in general produce optimal code, in the sense of the shortest or fastest possible code to compute a particular solution.

Superoptimizers attempt to reach this theoretical limit. In general they are machine specific, rather than based on intermediate code, since the best possible sequence will depend on the detailed functionality of individual instructions on the target computer. Typically they will take a sequence of machine code instructions and attempt to find the shortest sequence that is equivalent.

12.6.1 MASSALIN'S SUPEROPTIMIZER

Henry Massalin's superoptimizer is based on exhaustive searching of all possible shorter instruction sequences until one is found that is equivalent to the source sequence. By equivalence is meant that for any given set of values in machine registers and machine state, both sequences leave the machine with the same values in registers and in the same state. The search starts with all possible sequences of one instruction, then two instructions and so on until complete.

There are two immediate problems. First of all the search space grows exponentially as the number of instructions in the sequence increases. This is dealt with by using tree-pruning techniques to avoid pointless sequences of code. Massalin worked with the Motorola MC68020 processor. Sequences such as

```
MOVE D1, D2
MOVE D1, D2
```

which merely duplicate actions are pointless.

The much more serious problem is that of combinatorial explosion. The MC68020 has 32-bit registers. Consider testing equivalence to the single instruction sequence:

```
ADD D1, D2
```

which adds the value in register D1 to that in D2 and leaves the result in D2. To check all possible operand values would require $2^{32} \times 2^{32}$ possible input value combinations.

The first strategy is to represent all instructions as Boolean logic expressions relating their input to their output, and just check for equivalence of the two expressions. These expressions can be combined for sequences of instructions. Two sequences are identical if their expressions are the same. This would be fine, apart from mathematical operations such as addition and multiplication, which typically have 2^{31} terms in their Boolean expressions. Once again we hit combinatorial explosion.

The solution adopted is to try just a small sample of input values and see if the correct output value is generated. This does open the possibility of two different sequences appearing to be identical by chance. However, sensible choice of input values reduces this likelihood. Hand inspection of the resulting code by Massalin failed to reveal a single case where the probabilistic test failed.

A good example comes in considering the code generated for the following C function, which returns -1, 0 or $+1$, according to whether its argument is negative, zero or positive.

```
signum ( int x )
{
        if ( x > 0 )
                return 1 ;
        else if ( x < 0 )
                return -1 ;
        else
                return 0 ;
}
```

A typical C compiler will generate perhaps eight instructions for this:

```
      (x in D0)
      TST.L    D0        Test value in D0
      BLE      lab1      Skip to lab1 if D0 <= 1
      MOVE.L   #1,D1     Set result +1 for D0 positive
      BRA      lab3      Jump to end of routine
lab1: BEQ      lab2      Skip to lab2 if D0 = 0
      MOVE.L   #-1,D1    Set result -1 for D0 positive
      BRA      lab3      Jump to end of routine
lab2: CLR.L    D1        Set result 0 for D0 zero
lab3:
      (result in D1)
```

A really good optimizing compiler will get this down to six instructions:

```
      MOVE.L   #1,D1     Assume result for D0 positive
      TST.L    D0        Test value in D0
      BGE      lab2      Skip to end if D0 was positive
      BLT      lab1      Skip to lab1 if D0 < 0
      CLR.L    D1        Set result 0 for D0 zero
lab1: NEG.L    D1        Set -1 if D0 < 0, doesn't hurt
lab2:                    if D0 was 0.
```

Note that both of these involve multiple conditional branches, with serious implications for the performance of pipelined machines that are doing lookahead of instructions.

The Massalin superoptimizer discovers that the shortest equivalent sequence is just four instructions long:

```
      ADD.L    D0,D0
      SUBX.L   D1,D1
      NEGX.L   D0
      ADDX.L   D1,D1
```

This makes use of the MC68020's instructions for performing multiple precision arithmetic. These add the carry flag into the operation, which is on 32-bit unsigned quantities. The carry flag is set by these operations whenever the result would be negative.

The effect of the first instruction is that the sign bit ends up in the carry flag. The next instruction computes D1–D1–carry and puts the result in D1. Regardless of the original value in D1, this sets D1 to hold -carry. Thus D1 is -1 if D0 was negative, and zero otherwise. The carry bit remains set only if D0 was negative. The third instruction sets the carry flag unless D0 was zero, since negx (which views its argument as unsigned) will always otherwise set the flag to reflect a would-be negative result. The last instruction doubles D1 and adds the carry. If D0 was originally negative, D1 will hold −1, and the carry will be set, yielding −1 in D1. If D0 was originally positive, D1 will hold 0, and the carry will be set yielding +1 in D1. Finally, if D0 was originally zero, D1 will hold 0 and the carry will be clear, yielding 0 in D1. The code has achieved the desired result in just four instructions.

This code is all the more remarkable for needing no branch instructions. Massalin reports that a common observation is that superoptimal code makes clever use of the status flags, and tends not to use branches. It is thus particularly valuable in highly pipelined machines. A consequence is that the superoptimizer is less effective on machines with few status flags, or few instructions that set flags. Fans of the 8086 will be interested to see the superoptimizer needs just three instructions:

```
(x in ax)
cwd
neg   ax
adc   ax,dx
(result in dx)
```

Massalin gives several other examples illustrating the power of his super-optimizer. However, generated programs are limited to about 12 or 13 instructions, and because of the probabilistic test have to be checked by hand. It is not a technique that could be used directly in a general purpose compiler. In the next section we look at one approach which may be of more general use.

12.6.2 THE GNU SUPEROPTIMIZER

The GNU superoptimizer (GSO) is an extension to the GNU C compiler discussed in Chapter 10. Massalin's technique is only suitable for short sequences of code, which must be hand-checked.

There are many short sequences of code which occur very frequently in compiled code—for example code to find an absolute value, or the minimum of two values. The GNU superoptimizer works by pre-computing target code sequences for these common sequences of *goal functions*. These are then used as templates, and can be generated by the RTL code generator as required.

The goal functions are specified in C as expressions relating a number of arguments (named v0, v1 and so on) to yield a result in a variable r. Thus the goal function, eq0, which returns the value 1 if its single argument is equal to zero and 0 otherwise is specified as:

```
r = v0 == 0 ;
```

The three argument goal function, nales, performs a logical AND between its third operand and the negation of the signed comparison of its first two operands. It is specified as:

```
r = (-((signed) v0 <= (signed) v1)) & v2 ;
```

The GSO specifies a set of operations, which operate on registers. It assumes that superoptimal code will only use register-based operands. For each target architecture, GSO knows which of its set of operations are actually available, and whether in two-address or three-address form.

GSO then uses the same strategy as Massalin, pruning the search tree and using a probabilistic test for equivalence, which means that hand-checking of the results must be carried out. Like Massalin the GSO has never found a case where the probabilistic test failed.

Having found these sequences, they are then manually turned into templates, and added to the existing GNU C compiler.

Exercises

PRACTICAL PROBLEMS

12.1. Take the TAC and flow graph for the VSL program of Exercise 11.1 and compute the reaching definition, copy statement, available expression and live variable top and bottom sets.

12.2. Take the results of the previous exercise. Are any of the global optimizations described in Sections 12.3 and 12.4 possible? If so make them.

12.3. Generate VAM and construct the register interference graph for the TAC code you now have. What code would you generate if VAM were restricted to just three registers?

12.4. Peephole optimize the code you have generated. How does it compare with the code you generated for Exercise 11.3.

ESSAY TITLES

12.1. Show how dataflow equations can describe reaching definition information for a program. Give an iterative algorithm to solve these dataflow equations, justifying any initial assumptions you make.

12.2. How may common sub-expression elimination be carried out for a complete program? How does this differ from common sub-expression elimination for a single basic block?

12.3. How may program loops be identified and optimized?

DISCUSSION TOPICS

12.1. The iterative algorithms described here are general purpose, but not the most efficient methods for practical purposes. Investigate alternative methods suitable for compiling programs written in structured programming languages.

12.2. The survey by Bacon *et al.* (see Further Reading below), suggests 57 possible optimization techniques. Take one of the ones not described in this book, and investigate it further.

12.3. Investigate the particular problems associated with optimizing for (a) highly pipelined machines; (b) Very Long Instruction Word machines and (c) SIMD and MIMD parallel machines.

Further reading

As the previous chapter indicated, compiler optimization is very much an active research field. Aho, Sethi and Ullman (see Further reading, Chapter 1) were the first to give a comprehensive coverage in a general textbook. *The theory and practice of compiler writing*, by Jean-Paul Tremblay and Paul G. Sorenson also gives a good treatment. Aho, Sethi and Ullman use the terms *in* and *out* sets which are equivalent to the top and bottom sets used in this book and by Tremblay and Sorenson.

Register colouring is discussed in 'Register allocation and spilling via graph-colouring' by G. J. Chaitin, *ACM SIGPLAN Notices,* **17**, 201–207 (1982) and other papers by the same author. Massalin's superoptimizer is described in 'Superoptimizer—a look at the smallest program' by Henry Massalin, *Computer Architecture News,* **15** (5), 122–126 (1987) and the GNU superoptimizer is described in 'Eliminating branches using a superoptimizer and the GNU C compiler' by Torgjörn Granlund and Richard Kenner, *SIGPLAN Notices,* **27** (7), 341–352 (1992).

An excellent general survey is undoubtedly 'Compiler transformations for high-performance computing' by David F. Bacon, Susan L. Graham and Oliver J. Sharp, *ACM Computing Surveys,* **26**(4) (1994). This is a wide-ranging survey (the source of the 57 optimizations mentioned at the start of the chapter), with very comprehensive references to the rest of the literature. I would recommend it as a starting point for any enthusiast considering taking the subject further, and it must be a starting point for anyone contemplating the construction of a modern optimizing compiler.

13

A complete compiler for VSL

In this chapter we bring together the ideas introduced throughout this book by presenting a complete compiler to translate VSL into VAM. Both VSL and VAM are described in Appendix A. Machine-readable versions of the compiler, a VAM simulator, and a mnemonic assembler for VAM assembly code are available from the publishers via the Internet (see Appendix B). ANSI Standard C is used throughout.

13.1 The VC compiler for VSL

The compiler has a conventional three-stage structure:

1. Lexical analyser written in LEX converting source test into tokens.
2. Syntax analyser written in YACC generating three-address code.
3. Code generator for three-address code to VAM.

Each of these sections forms one source code file (`scanner.1`, `parser.y`, `cg.c`). The file `vc.h` is a header included by each section, containing general definitions and declarations. Finally, the file `main.c` contains a main program and support routines to initialize and then call the compiler. The whole system is implemented as a filter, taking source code from standard input and printing object code in the form of mnemonic VAM assembly code on standard output. The three-address code appears as comments within the VAM code. Error messages appear on the standard error stream.

13.1.1 APPROACH TO IMPLEMENTATION

Throughout the compiler we have used the most obvious, and not necessarily the most compact or efficient code. There is enormous scope for extension. There is no optimizer. The code generator has a very simple register allocator, and seldom generates particularly efficient code. Allocation of stack space for variables is wasteful of space. It is very much intended that the reader will get this compiler running on his or her own system, and modify it as a learning exercise. At the end of the chapter we suggest a number of possible changes that could be made.

13.2   Description of the compiler

The compiler is shown as a listing, but with additional comments in the code describing the strategy used by the various routines. Before the listing of each section we provide a commentary on the strategy used.

13.2.1   THE HEADER FILE, vc.h

We provide a general header for the files making up the compiler. This contains definitions of constants used throughout the code, definitions of the main data structures, and external definitions of routines used by multiple sections.

```
/**************************************************************************
 **************************************************************************


         HH   HH  EEEEEEE    AAAA    DDDDDD    EEEEEEE  RRRRRRR
         HH   HH  EEEEEEE   AAAAAA   DDDDDDD   EEEEEEE  RRRRRRRR
         HH   HH  EE        AA   AA  DD    DD  EE       RR    RR
         HHHHHHHH EEEEEE   AAAAAAAA  DD    DD  EEEEE    RRRRRRRR
         HH   HH  EE        AA   AA  DD    DD  EE       RRRRRR
         HH   HH  EE        AA   AA  DD    DD  EE       RR RR
         HH   HH  EEEEEEE   AA   AA  DDDDDDD   EEEEEEE  RR   RR
         HH   HH  EEEEEEE   AA   AA  DDDDDD    EEEEEEE  RR   RR



 **************************************************************************
 **************************************************************************


                        A Compiler for VSL
                        ==================

This is the general header file.

Modifications:
==============

22 Nov 88 JPB: First version
26 Apr 89 JPB: Version for publication
13 Jun 90 JPB: Now refers to library directory (noted by R C Shaw, Praxis).
23 Jan 96 JPB: Various minor corrections for 2nd edition publication.

 **************************************************************************
 **************************************************************************/

/* We start by defining the various constants used throughout the compiler. */

#define TRUE      1          /* Booleans */
#define FALSE     0
#define EOS       0          /* End of string */
#define HASHSIZE  997        /* Size of symbol table */
#define R_UNDEF   -1         /* Not a valid register */
```

```
/* We define the various symbol types permitted. Note the use of T_UNDEF. Many
   names are entered into the symbol table by the lexical analyser before their
   type is known, and so we give them an undefined type. */

#define T_UNDEF  0                /* Types for symbol table */
#define T_VAR    1                /* Local Variable */
#define T_FUNC   2                /* Function */
#define T_TEXT   3                /* Static string */
#define T_INT    4                /* Integer constant */
#define T_LABEL  5                /* TAC label */

/* We define constants for each of the three address code (TAC) instructions.
   For convenience we have an undefined instruction, then we specify the 12
   main TAC opcodes. */

#define TAC_UNDEF   0             /* TAC instructions */
#define TAC_ADD     1             /* a := b + c */
#define TAC_SUB     2             /* a := b - c */
#define TAC_MUL     3             /* a := b * c */
#define TAC_DIV     4             /* a := b / c */
#define TAC_NEG     5             /* a := -b */
#define TAC_COPY    6             /* a := b */
#define TAC_GOTO    7             /* goto a */
#define TAC_IFZ     8             /* ifz b goto a */
#define TAC_IFNZ    9             /* ifnz b goto a */
#define TAC_ARG    10             /* arg a */
#define TAC_CALL   11             /* a := call b */
#define TAC_RETURN 12             /* return a */

/* We then add some extra "pseudo-instructions" to mark places in the code.
   TAC_LABEL is used to mark branch targets. Its first argument will be a symbol
   table entry for a label giving a unique number for this label. TAC_VAR
   is associated with variable declarations, to help in assigning stack
   locations. TAC_BEGINFUNC and TAC_ENDFUNC mark the beginning and end of
   functions respectively. */

#define TAC_LABEL      13         /* Marker for LABEL a */
#define TAC_VAR        14         /* Marker for VAR a */
#define TAC_BEGINFUNC  15         /* Markers for function */
#define TAC_ENDFUNC    16

/* The library routines are supplied in an external file. Their entry points
   are held in a table, and we define the offsets in this table here as
   LIB_PRINTN and LTB_PRINTS. At present these are the only two library
   routines, used to print out numbers and strings in PRINT statements.

   The book assumes that the code generator library and header files are in the
   same directory as the compiler. For greater flexibility we #define a library
   directory here. This will almost certainly need changing for individual
   systems. Note the need for a / at the end of the LIB_DIR. */

#define LIB_PRINTN  0             /* Index into library entry points */
#define LIB_PRINTS  1
#define LIB_MAX     2

#define LIB_DIR "/jeremy/book/code/"  /* Library directory */
```

```
/* Many of the structures we are to use have complex unions and subfields.
   Specifying which field we want can be verbose and for convenience we
   define some of the subfields. Thus given a pointer to a symbol table entry,
   "sp" the "text" field of the "vall" union would be referred to as
   "sp->vall.text". Instead these #defines allow us to write "sp->TEXT1". */
```

```
#define VAL1    vall.val            /* Value vall */
#define TEXT1   vall.text           /* Text vall */
#define VAL2    val2.val            /* Value val2 */
#define LABEL2  val2.label          /* Label val2 */
#define ADDR2   val2.val            /* Address val2 */
#define ETYPE   res->type           /* Type of expr result */
#define EVAL1   res->vall.val       /* Value field in expr */
#define VA      a.var               /* Var result in TAC */
#define LA      a.lab               /* Label result in TAC */
#define VB      b.var               /* Var first arg in TAC */
#define LB      b.lab               /* Label first arg in TAC */
#define VC      c.var               /* Var second arg in TAC */
#define LC      c.lab               /* Label second arg in TAC */
```

```
/* This is the central structure of the compiler, the symbol table entry, SYMB.
   The symbol table takes the form of an open hash table. The entries are
   linked via the "next" field and have a "type" field. The value of this field
   determines the use made of the two value fields, which may hold text
   pointers or integers. The whole is set up using a typedef for clarity in the
   code.

   For convenience the same structure is used for items like constants and
   labels even if they do not need to be entered into the symbol table. This
   makes for a simpler TAC data structure. */
```

```
typedef struct symb                 /* Symbol table entry */
{
        struct symb *next ;         /* Next in chain */
        int         type ;          /* What is this symbol */
        union                       /* Primary value */
        {
                int     val ;       /* For integers */
                char    *text ;     /* For var names */
        } vall;
        union                       /* Secondary value */
        {
                int     val ;       /* For offsets etc */
                struct tac *label ; /* For branches */
        } val2 ;
} SYMB ;
```

```
/* TAC is stored as a doubly-linked list of quadruples. In general we will pass
   round pointers to the last generated quadruple in the syntax analyser and
   first generated quadruple in the code generator. The opcode is an integer
   and the argument and the result fields are either pointers to symbol table
   entries or pointers to other TAC quadruples (for branch instructions). The
   names of the fields are based on TAC instructions of the form

       a := b op c

   Again this is implemented as a typedef for convenience */
```

```
typedef struct tac                      /* TAC instruction node */
{
        struct tac  *next ;             /* Next instruction */
        struct tac  *prev ;             /* Previous instruction */
        int         op ;                /* TAC instruction */
        union                           /* Result */
        {
                SYMB        *var ;      /* Name */
                struct tac *lab ;       /* Address */
        } a ;
        union                           /* Operands */
        {
                SYMB        *var ;
                struct tac *lab ;
        } b ;
        union
        {
                SYMB        *var ;
                struct tac *lab ;
        } c ;
} TAC ;
```

/* When translating expressions in the syntax analyser we need to pass back as
   attribute in YACC not only the code for the expression, but where its result
   is stored. For this we use the ENODE structure. The "next" field in this
   allows it to be used for lists of expressions in function calls. typedef is
   again used for clarity */

```
typedef struct enode                    /* Parser expression */
{       struct enode *next ;            /* For argument lists */
        TAC          *tac ;             /* The code */
        SYMB         *res ;             /* Where the result is */
} ENODE ;
```

/* Global variables used throughout the compiler. "symbtab" is the hashtable.
   Each element is a list of symbol table nodes. "library" is an array holding
   the label numbers of the entry points to library routines.

   Temporary variables are given names of the form "Tnnn" where nnn is a unique
   number. "next_tmp" holds the number of the next temporary and is
   incremented each time one is used. A similar scheme with "next_label" is
   used to assign unique labels of the form "Lnnn". */

```
extern SYMB *symbtab[HASHSIZE} ;        /* Symbol table */
extern TAC  *library[LIB_MAX] ;         /* Entries for library routines */
extern int   next_tmp ;                 /* Count of temporaries */
extern int   next_label ;               /* Count of labels */
```

/* Global routines that although defined in one section may be used elsewhere.
   The majority of these are in the main section of the compiler. */

```
extern SYMB *mkconst( int n ) ;         /* In main.c */
extern SYMB *mklabel( int l ) ;
extern SYMB *mktmp( void ) ;
extern TAC  *mktac( int  op,
                    SYMB *a,
                    SYMB *b,
                    SYMB *c ) ;
extern TAC  *join_tac( TAC *c1,
                       TAC *c2 ) ;
```

```
extern void    insert( SYMB *s ) ;
extern SYMB    *lookup( char *s ) ;
extern SYMB    *get_symb( void ) ;
extern void    free_symb( SYMB *s ) ;
extern ENODE   *get_enode( void ) ;
extern void    free_enode( ENODE *expr ) ;
extern void    *safe_malloc( int n ) ;
extern void    error( char *str ) ;
extern void    print_instr( TAC *i ) ;


extern void    mkname( char *name ) ;        /* In scanner.l */


extern void    cg( TAC *tl ) ;               /* In cg.c */
```

13.2.2 THE DRIVING AND SUPPORT ROUTINES, main.c

This section contains the code to drive the stages of the compiler, together with initialization, termination, and support routines. It is the logical place to put most of the service routines that can be referenced by more than one section.

```
/*****************************************************************************
 *****************************************************************************


          MM    MM   AAAA    IIIIIIII  NN    NN
          MMM  MMM   AAAAAA  IIIIIIII  NNN   NN
          MMMMMMMM   AA   AA    II      NNNN  NN
          MM MM MM   AAAAAAAA   II      NN NN NN
          MM    MM   AA   AA    II      NN  NNNN
          MM    MM   AA   AA    II      NN  NNNN
          MM    MM   AA   AA  IIIIIIII  NN   NNN
          MM    MM   AA   AA  IIIIIIII  NN    NN


 *****************************************************************************
 *****************************************************************************


                    A Compiler for VSL
                    ==================

These are the main, initialisation, tidy up and utility routines.

Modifications:
==============

22 Nov 88 JPB: First version
26 Apr 89 JPB: Version for publication
13 Jun 90 JPB: mklabel fixed to return t
 9 May 91 JPB: mktmp fixed so as not to clobber yylval (J Johnson and K
               Schweller)
23 Jan 96 JPB: Various minor corrections for 2nd edition publication.

 *****************************************************************************
 ****************************************************************************/


/* As well as including the general header we include the header "parser.h"
   generated by YACC, which contains definitions of all the terminals. Note
   that this is the file "y.tab.h" obtained by running yacc with the -d option.
   We rename it "parser.h" when building the compiler for clarity. */
```

```c
#include <stdio.h>
#include <ctype.h>
#include "vc.h"
#include "parser.h"

/* Constants used here. CONST_MAX gives the number of small integers
   pre-initialised in the symbol table (described later). LAB_MIN is the first
   label number to be used. Label L0 is reserved for the end of code and data
   and L1 for the termination routine. Labels up to LAB_MIN - 1 may be used by
   the library routines. */

#define CONST_MAX   5
#define LAB_MIN     10

/* This is the global variable that will be set on recognition of the sentence
   symbol, <program>, by the parser. We can't make use of "yyval", since that
   is not exported by the parser if you use Bison rather than YACC. */

extern TAC *program_tac ;

/* We define a number of static variables used throughout the compiler. These
   have been declared external in the header file, and are defined here. */

SYMB  *symbtab[HASHSIZE] ;        /* Symbol table */
TAC   *library[LIB_MAX] ;         /* Entries for library routines */
int    next_tmp ;                 /* Count of temporaries */
int    next_label ;               /* Count of labels */

/* These are static variables used throughout this section. "const_tab" is the
   table of predeclared integers. "errors_found" is a flag set if the error
   routine is ever called. We do not bother to generate code if errors are
   found during parsing.

   Symbol table and expression nodes are regularly allocated, freed and
   reallocated. Rather than use the system routines "malloc()" and "free()"
   directly for this, we maintain our own freelists, held in "symb_list" and
   "enode_list". */

SYMB  *const_tab[CONST_MAX] ;     /* Small constants */
int    errors_found;              /* True if we have any errors */
SYMB  *symb_list ;                /* Freelists */
ENODE *enode_list ;

/* Prototypes of routines defined in this section. */

void   main( int    argc,
             char *argv[] ) ;
void   init_vc( int    argc,
                char *argv[] ) ;
char  *decode_args( int    argc,
                    char *argv[] ) ;
void   setup_files( char *ifile,
                    char *ofile ) ;
SYMB  *mkconst( int n ) ;
SYMB  *mklabel( int l ) ;
SYMB  *mktmp( void ) ;
SYMB  *get_symb( void ) ;
void   free_symb( SYMB *s ) ;
ENODE *get_enode( void ) ;
void   free_enode( ENODE *e ) ;
```

```
void  *safe_malloc( int n ) ;
TAC   *mktac( int    op,
                SYMB *a,
                SYMB *b,
                SYMB *c ) ;
TAC   *join_tac( TAC *c1,
                  TAC *c2 ) ;
void   insert( SYMB *s ) ;
int    hash( char *s ) ;
SYMB  *lookup( char *s ) ;
void   print_instr( TAC *i ) ;
char  *ts( SYMB *s,
            char *str ) ;
void   error( char *str ) ;


void   main( int    argc,
              char *argv[] )
```

/* The main program initialises the compiler, calls the syntax analyser and if
   this runs successfully passes the resulting TAC on for code generation.

   The program takes a single command line argument, a filename ending in
   ".vsl", which is the program to be compiled. */

```
{
        init_vc( argc, argv ) ;         /* Set up things */

        (void) yyparse() ;              /* Parse */

        if( !errors_found )
                cg( program_tac ) ;     /* Generate code from TAC */

}         /* void  main( void ) */

void  init_vc( int    argc,
                char *argv[] )
```

/* The first part of initialisation involves sorting out the arguments, and
   assigning standard input and standard output files as explained in
   decode_args and setup_files below.

   The rest involves setting various systems wide variables to sensible
   values and clearing down the symbol table. Small constants are so common we
   put them in the symbol table first and record their addresses in a table. We
   do this for the integers 0 to COUNT_MAX - 1. This will permit us efficient
   access to them throughout the compiler.

   We record the entry labels for the library routines. We happen to know from
   inspection of the library code that the entry point to PRINTN is L2 and to
   PRINTS is L4. If we rewrite the library then we may have to change these.
   This is really rather clumsy, and at the very least ought to be put in a
   single table somewhere. Note that earlier we set the first label to be used
   to L10, permitting the use of labels up to L9 for library use. */

```
{
        int  i ;                                /* General counter */

        char *ifile ;                           /* Input file */
        char *ofile ;                           /* Output file */
```

```
        /* Decode the arguments, and setup stdin and stdout accordingly */

        ofile = decode_args( argc, argv ) ;
        ifile = argv[1] ;                      /* Do after decode has checked
                                                  argument is OK */
        setup_files( ifile, ofile ) ;

        /* Give values to global variables */

        symb_list     = NULL ;                 /* Freelists */
        enode_list    = NULL ;

        errors_found = FALSE ;                  /* No errors found yet */
        next_tmp     = 0 ;                      /* No temporaries used */
        next_label   = LAB_MIN ;               /* 10 labels reserved */

        for( i = 0 ; i < HASHSIZE ; i++ )       /* Clear symbol table */
                symbtab[i] = NULL ;

        for( i = 0 ; i < CONST_MAX ; i++ )      /* Make constants */
        {
                SYMB *c = get_symb() ;         /* Node for the constant */

                c->type      = T_INT ;
                c->VAL1      = i ;
                const_tab[i] = c ;
        }

        library[LIB_PRINTN] = mktac( TAC_LABEL, mklabel( 2 ), NULL, NULL ) ;
        library[LIB_PRINTS] = mktac( TAC_LABEL, mklabel( 4 ), NULL, NULL ) ;

}       /* void  init_vc( void ) */


char  *decode_args( int    argc,
                    char *argv[] )

/* The general usage of vc is:

      vc  <file>.vsl

   The output is a file of assembler code, ending in ".vas". We check there is
   a single argument, ending in ".vsl" and construct a result ending in ".vas".
*/

{
        char *ofile ;                          /* Constructed output file */
        int   rootlen ;                        /* Length of input filename's root */

        /* First check there is a single argument */

        if( argc != 2 )
        {
                error( "single argument expected\n" ) ;
                exit( 0 ) ;
        }

        /* Find suffix, which must be ".vsl", check that it is there. */

        rootlen = strlen( argv[1] ) - strlen( ".vsl" ) ;
```

```
        if( (rootlen < 1) || (strcmp( argv[1] + rootlen, ".vsl" ) != 0) )
        {
                fprintf( stderr, "source file must end in \".vsl\"" ) ;
                exit( 0 ) ;
        }

        /* We now allocate the space for the name of the output file. Remember
           to allow a byte for the end of string marker. */

        ofile = (char *)safe_malloc( rootlen + strlen( ".vas" ) + 1 ) ;

        /* Construct the new output file by adding vas to the end of the
           existing root. Return the name of this file. */

        strncpy( ofile, argv[1], rootlen ) ;    /* Root */
        strcat( ofile, ".vas" ) ;               /* Extension */

        return  ofile ;
}       /* decode_args() */


void  setup_files( char *ifile,
                   char *ofile )

/* All our I/O is done using the standard input and standard output. We
   substitute the given files using the freopen function. */

{
        if( freopen( ifile, "r", stdin ) == NULL )
        {
                error( "setup_files: freopen of input failed" ) ;
                exit( 0 ) ;
        }

        if( freopen( ofile, "w", stdout ) == NULL )
        {
                error( "setup_files: freopen of output failed" ) ;
                exit( 0 ) ;
        }

}       /* setup_files() */


/* We now have a number of routines to set up symbol table nodes of various
   types. Memory allocation usually involves up to three routines, "mkxxx()" to
   allocate and set up the fields of a struct of type "xxx", "get_xxx()" to
   allocate space for the struct and "free_xxx()" to free up the space. */


SYMB *mkconst( int n )

/* In "mkconst()" we check if the constant is one of the predefined ones, and
   if so use it, otherwise we create a new entry for it. Note that this wastes
   space, since we should check if we have used any constant before and return
   a pointer to an existing node if possible. However the technique of just
   predefining the first few constants (which make up the majority used) is
   a good compromise that is efficient. */

{
        if((n >= 0) && (n < CONST_MAX))
```

```
                return const_tab[n] ;
        else
        {
                SYMB *c = get_symb() ;    /* Create a new node */

                c->type = T_INT ;
                c->VAL1 = n ;
                return c ;
        }

}        /* SYMB *mkconst( int n ) */


SYMB *mklabel( int 1 )

/* Make a label node with the given value */

{
        SYMB *t = get_symb() ;

        t->type = T_LABEL ;
        t->VAL1 = 1 ;

        return t ;

}        /* SYMB *mklabel( int 1 ) */


SYMB *mktmp( void )

/* Make a temporary name. This is just a var with name of the form Txxx. We
   construct a temporary name into the text buffer, "name" and
   then use the lexical analyser's name allocator "mkname()".

   Bug fix due to Jonathan Johnson 9/5/91:

   Note that yylval may not yet have been shifted, and so we must save and
   restore it after this routine. The use of a fixed size for the string where
   we build the variable would be better as a named constant. */

{
        SYMB *old_yylval = yylval.symb ;         /* Save the old yylval */
        SYMB *tmp ;                              /* Used to restore result */
        char  name[12] ;                         /* For the name of the var */

        /* Make the name with mkname */

        sprintf( name, "T%d", next_tmp++ ) ;     /* Set up text */
        mkname( name ) ;
        yylval.symb->type = T_VAR ;

        /* Hang onto this new symbol in tmp, restore yylval.symb and return
           tmp */

        tmp        = yylval.symb ;
        yylval.symb = old_yylval ;

        return tmp ;

}        /* SYMB *mktmp( void ) */
```

```
SYMB *get_symb( void )

/* Allocate space for a symbol table entry. Note the use of the freelist
   "symb_list" to hold any nodes that have been returned. If none is available
   we use "malloc()" to obtain a new node. Rather than use "malloc()" direct we
   call our own version "safe malloc()". This guarantees to return a valid
   pointer (and never NULL). If store has run out and safe_malloc() cannot
   allocate a new structure it will print an error message and exit the
   compiler. */

{
        SYMB *t ;

        if( symb_list != NULL )
        {
                t        = symb_list ;
                symb_list = symb_list->next ;
        }
        else
                t = (SYMB *)safe_malloc( sizeof( SYMB )) ;

        return t ;

}       /* SYMB *get_symb( void ) */


void  free_symb( SYMB *s )

/* This is the sister routine to "get_symb()" and just adds the symbol node to
   the freelist for reuse. */

{
        s->next   = symb_list ;
        symb_list = s ;

}       /* void  free_symb( SYMB *s ) */


ENODE *get_enode( void )

/* Allocate for ENODE. This routine and "free_enode()" are analagous to
   "get_symb()" and "free_symb()". */

{
        if( enode_list != NULL )
        {
                ENODE *expr ;

                expr      = enode_list ;
                enode_list = expr->next ;

                return expr ;
        }
        else
                return (ENODE *)safe_malloc( sizeof( ENODE )) ;

}       /* ENODE *get_enode( void ) */
```

```
void  free_enode( ENODE *expr )

/* Return an enode for reuse */

{
        expr->next = enode_list ;
        enode_list = expr ;

}         /* void  free_enode( ENODE *expr ) */


void *safe_malloc( int n )

/* Rather than have a test for a null pointer each time we call "malloc()" in
   the compiler we write our own safe version, "safe_malloc()". If memory runs
   out there is no more we can do, and so the routine aborts the entire
   compilation. */

{
        void *t = (void *)malloc( n ) ;

        /* Check we got it */

        if( t == NULL )
        {
                /* We can't use printf to put the message out here, since it
                   calls malloc, which will fail because that's why we're
                   here... */

                error( "malloc() failed" ) ;
                exit( 0 ) ;
        }
        return t ;

}         /* void *safe_malloc( int n ) */

/* A couple of routines for allocating and joining TAC lists. We need not
   maintain a freelist for TAC, since we never free a TAC quadruple once
   allocated. */


TAC *mktac( int    op,                    /* Operator */
            SYMB *a,                      /* Result */
            SYMB *b,                      /* Operands */
            SYMB *c )

/* Construct a TAC quadruple with the given fields

        a := b op c

   Note the use of #defined selectors VA, VB and VC for the TAC struct. If
   efficiency became a worry we might choose not to call "safe_malloc()" each
   time we wanted a new quadruple, but to allocate several at once. */

{
        TAC *t = (TAC *)safe_malloc( sizeof( TAC )) ;

        t->next = NULL ;                  /* Set these for safety */
        t->prev = NULL ;
        t->op   = op ;
```

```
        t->VA   = a ;
        t->VB   = b ;
        t->VC   = c ;

        return t ;

}       /* TAC *mktac( int   op,
                       SYMB *a,
                       SYMB *b,
                       SYMB *c ) */



TAC *join_tac( TAC *c1,
               TAC *c2 )

/* Join two pieces of TAC together. Remember that in the parser we always
   refer to a TAC list by the most recently generated piece of code and so we
   follow the prev pointer to get the preceding instructions. We will end up
   with a pointer to a TAC list for the parser representing the code of "c1"
   followed by that of "c2". */

{
        TAC *t ;

        /* If either list is NULL return the other */

        if( c1 == NULL )
                return c2 ;

        if( c2 == NULL)
                return c1 ;

        /* Run down c2, until we get to the beginning and then add c1 */

        t = c2 ;

        while( t->prev != NULL )
                t = t->prev ;

        t->prev = c1 ;
        return c2 ;

}       /* TAC *join_tac( TAC *c1,
                          TAC *c2 ) */


/* These are the symbol table routines. We have a routine, "insert()", to
   insert a node in the symbol table (created by one of the "mkxxx()" routines)
   and a routine, "lookup()" to find the symbol table entry, if any, for a
   given text name. Both routines use the hashing function "hash()" described
   in chapter 5. */


void  insert( SYMB *s )

/* Insert a new symbol in the symbol table. We hash on a text first argument */

{
        int hv = hash( s->TEXT1 ) ;
```

```
        s->next = symbtab[hv] ;          /* Insert at head */
        symbtab[hv]  = s ;

}       /* void  insert( SYMB *s ) */


int  hash( char *s )
```

/* Return a hashvalue from the given text. We use the bottom nybble of each
   character ORed with the top nybble of the hashvalue so far and shifted in at
   the bottom. This is then reduced mod the size of the hash table. Note the
   implicit assumption that we are on a 32 bit machine. */

```
{
        int  hv = 0 ;
        int  i ;

        for( i = 0 ; s[i] != EOS ; i++ )
        {
                int  v = (hv >> 28) ^ (s[i] & 0xf) ;

                hv = (hv << 4) | v ;
        }
        hv = hv & 0x7fffffff ;           /* Ensure positive */
        return hv % HASHSIZE ;

}       /* int  hash ( char *s ) */


SYMB *lookup( char *s )
```

/* Lookup a name in the hashtable. Return NULL if the name is not found. */

```
{
        int   hv = hash( s ) ;
        SYMB *t  = symbtab[hv] ;

        while( t != NULL )                       /* Look for the name */
                if( strcmp( t->TEXT1, s ) == 0 )
                        break ;
                else
                        t = t->next ;

        return t ;                       /* NULL if not found */

}       /* SYMB lookup( char *s ) */
```

/* We now have a couple of routines for debugging purposes. */

```
void  print_instr( TAC *i )
```

/* "print_instr()" is used to print out a TAC instruction symbolically. We use
   it in the code generator to print each TAC instruction as a comment before
   the code generated for it. The subsidiary routine, "ts()" is used to obtain
   a suitable string representation of the TAC arguments. Note the clumsy
   programming assumption that arguments can be represented in 11 characters.
*/

```
{
        char sa[12] ;                        /* For text of TAC args */
        char sb[12] ;
        char sc[12] ;

        printf( "        ", i ) ;

        switch( i->op )
        {
        case TAC_UNDEF:

                printf( "undef\n" ) ;
                break ;

        case TAC_ADD:

                printf( "%s := %s + %s\n", ts( i->VA, sa ), ts( i->VB, sb ),
                        ts( i->VC, sc )) ;
                break ;

        case TAC_SUB:

                printf( "%s := %s - %s\n", ts( i->VA, sa ), ts( i->VB, sb ),
                        ts( i->VC, sc )) ;
                break ;

        case TAC_MUL:

                printf( "%s := %s * %s\n", ts( i->VA, sa ), ts( i->VB, sb ),
                        ts( i->VC, sc )) ;
                break ;

        case TAC_DIV:

                printf( "%s := %s / %s\n", ts( i->VA, sa ), ts( i->VB, sb ),
                        ts( i->VC, sc )) ;
                break ;

        case TAC_NEG:

                printf( "%s := - %s\n", ts( i->VA, sa ), ts( i->VB, sb )) ;
                break ;

        case TAC_COPY:

                printf( "%s := %s\n", ts( i->VA, sa ), ts( i->VB, sb )) ;
                break ;

        case TAC_GOTO:

                printf( "goto L%d\n", i->LA->VA->VAL1 ) ;
                break ;

        case TAC_IFZ:

                printf( "ifz %s goto L%d\n", ts( i->VB, sb ),
                        i->LA->VA->VAL1 ) ;
                break ;
```

```
        case TAC_IFNZ:

                printf( "ifnz %s goto L%d\n", ts( i->VB, sb ),
                        i->LA->VA->VAL1 ) ;
                break ;

        case TAC_ARG:

                printf( "arg %s\n", ts( i->VA, sa )) ;
                break ;

        case TAC_CALL:

                if( i->VA == NULL )
                        printf( "call L%d\n", i->LB->VA->VAL1 ) ;
                else
                        printf( "%s = call L%d\n", ts( i->VA, sa ),
                                i->LB->VA->VAL1 ) ;

                break ;

        case TAC_RETURN:

                printf( "return %s\n", ts( i->VA, sa )) ;
                break ;

        case TAC_LABEL:

                printf( "label L%d\n", i->VA->VAL1 ) ;
                break ;

        case TAC_VAR:

                printf( "var %s\n", ts( i->VA, sa )) ;
                break ;

        case TAC_BEGINFUNC:

                printf( "beginfunc\n" ) ;
                break ;

        case TAC_ENDFUNC:

                printf( "endfunc\n" ) ;
                break ;

        default:

                /* Don't know what this one is */

                error( "unknown TAC opcode" ) ;
                printf( "unknown %d\n", i->op ) ;
                break ;
        }
        fflush( stdout ) ;

}       /* print_instr( i ) */

char *ts( SYMB *s,                  /* Symbol to translate */
          char *str )               /* String to put it in */
```

```
/* Return the string representation of the given symbol. Permissible ones are
   functions, vars, temporaries or constants */

{

        /* Check we haven't been given NULL */

        if( s == NULL )
                return "NULL" ;

        /* Identify the type */

        switch( s->type )
        {
        case T_FUNC:
        case T_VAR:

                /* Just return the name */

                return s->TEXT1 ;

        case T_TEXT:

                /* Put the address of the text */

                sprintf( str, "L%d", s->VAL2 ) ;
                return str ;

        case T_INT:

                /* Convert the number to string */

                sprintf( str, "%d", s->VAL1 ) ;
                return str ;

        default:

                /* Unknown arg type */

                error( "unknown TAC arg type" ) ;
                return "?" ;
        }

}       /* ts( SYMB *s,
                char *str ) */


void  error( char *str )

/* This is a very simple error message routine. This is just prints a message
   to the standard error stream, and sets a flag to indicate that an error has
   occurred. If this is set at the end of parsing, then we do not carry on
   further with code generation. */

{
        fprintf( stderr, "vc: %s\n", str ) ;
        errors_found = TRUE ;

}       /* void  error( char *str ) */
```

13.2.3 THE LEXICAL ANALYSER, scanner.1

This is a very simple lexical analyser. We can take advantage of the fact that all
reserved words in VSL are upper case and all variable and function names lower
case.

```
%{
/****************************************************************************
 ****************************************************************************


     SSSSSS     CCCCC    AAAA    NN    NN  NN    NN  EEEEEEEE  RRRRRR
    SSSSSSSS   CCCCCCC   AAAAAA  NNN   NN  NNN   NN  EEEEEEEE  RRRRRRR
    SS         CC        AA  AA  NNNN  NN  NNNN  NN  EE        RR    RR
     SSSSSSS   CC       AAAAAAAA NN NN NN  NN NN NN  EEEEE     RRRRRRR
          SS   CC        AA  AA  NN  NNNN  NN  NNNN  EE        RRRRRRR
          SS   CC        AA  AA  NN  NNNN  NN  NNNN  EE        RR RR
    SSSSSSSS   CCCCCCC   AA  AA  NN   NNN  NN   NNN  EEEEEEEE  RR   RR
     SSSSSS     CCCCC    AA  AA  NN    NN  NN    NN  EEEEEEEE  RR    RR


 ****************************************************************************
 ****************************************************************************

                          A Compiler for VSL
                          ==================

A scanner for VSL

Modifications:
==============

16 Nov 88 JPB:  First version
26 Apr 89 JPB:  Simple version
25 Jul 89 JPB:  Final version for publication
23 Jan 96 JPB:  Various minor corrections for 2nd edition publication.

 ****************************************************************************
 ****************************************************************************/

#include <stdio.h>
#include <ctype.h>
#include "vc.h"
#include "parser.h"

/*Routines defined here. These are in the code section below and build symbol
    table entries for variable names, integer constants and text strings
    respectively. */

void   mkname( char *name ) ;
void   mkval( void ) ;
void   mktext( void) ;

/* We define some useful patterns using regular expressions as described in
    chapter 5. Note how earlier definitions are used later (e.g. the definition
    of "delimiter" in the definition of "whitespace". These patterns are very
    straightforward, since all VSL reserved words use upper case letters and
    variable names use only lower case. */

%}
```

```
comment             "//".*
delimiter           [ \t\n]
whitespace          {delimiter}+
uc_letter           [A-Z]
lc_letter           [a-z]
letter              {lc_letter}|{uc_letter}
ascii_char          [^\"\n]
escaped_char        \\n|\\\"
digit               [0-9]
variable            {lc_letter}({lc_letter}|{digit})*
integer             {digit}+
text                \"({ascii_char}|{escaped_char})*\"
```

```
%{
/* Now follows the rule section. We wish to return the appropriate token in
   each case. We start with rules to ignore comments (everything from // to the
   end of line) and white space. Then come the three complex lexemes,
   "variable", "integer" and "text". In each case we call "mkxxx()" to build an
   appropriate symbol table entry from "yytext" and put the result in "yylval",
   as the attribute to go back with the token.

   We then include patterns to recognise the assign symbol, ":=", and the
   reserved words.

   Anything that has not been recognised will then be picked up by the last
   match, which is for single character tokens. This will only be used if
   nothing longer can be matched. Single character variables and integers will
   not be picked up by this, even though they are the same length, because
   their rule is specified earlier. An alternative approach would be to specify
   the individual single character tokens that are permissible and return an
   "ERROR" token for any other single character. The arrangement as it stands
   leaves detection of such errors to the parser. */
%}
```

```
%%

{comment}           {                           /* Ignore comments */ }
{whitespace}        {                           /* Ignore whitespace */ }
{variable}          { mkname( yytext ) ;        /* Save the variable name */
                      return VARIABLE ;         /* A variable name */ }
{integer}           { mkval() ;                 /* Save the integer value */
                      return INTEGER ;          /* A number */ }
{text}              { mktext() ;                /* Save the text string */
                      return TEXT ;             /* A string */ }
":="                { return ASSIGN_SYMBOL ;    /* ':=' */ }
FUNC                { return FUNC ;             /* 'FUNC' */ }
PRINT               { return PRINT ;            /* 'PRINT' */ }
RETURN              { return RETURN ;           /* 'RETURN' */ }
CONTINUE            { return CONTINUE ;         /* 'CONTINUE' */ }
IF                  { return IF ;               /* 'IF' */ }
THEN                { return THEN ;             /* 'THEN' */ }
ELSE                { return ELSE ;             /* 'ELSE' */ }
FI                  { return FI ;               /* 'FI' */ }
WHILE               { return WHILE ;            /* 'WHILE' */ }
DO                  { return DO ;               /* 'DO' */ }
DONE                { return DONE ;             /* 'DONE' */ }
VAR                 { return VAR ;              /* 'VAR' */ }
.                   { return yytext[0] ;        /* Single character operator */ }
```

%%

```
/* Support code */


void mkname( char *name)

/* Lookup a name in the symbol table. If not there set up a new one, returning
   the result in "yylval". Note that "yylval" is a union, defined in parser.h
   and so we must specify which member of the union (in this case "symb") we
   wish to use. We insert the name in the symbol table, but at this stage with
   type T_UNDEF, since we do not know what its type is. */

{
        struct symb *t ;                /* Pointer to looked up symbol */
        char        *s ;                /* Permanent text of string */
        int         len ;               /* Length of text */

        /* If the string exists return with it in yylval */

        if((t = lookup( name )) != NULL )
        {
                yylval.symb = t ;
                return ;
        }
        /* Unseen before, so make a permanent copy, set up a new symbol table
           node, insert it into the symbol table and assign it to yylval. */

        len = strlen( name ) ;
        s   = (char *)safe_malloc( len + 1 ) ; /* Space for perm copy */

        strncpy( s, name, len ) ;
        s[len] = EOS ;

        t        = get_symb() ;
        t->type  = T_UNDEF ;            /* Don't know which node type yet */
        t->TEXT1 = s ;                  /* Text argument */

        insert( t ) ;
        yylval.symb = t ;              /* Symbol type in union */

}       /* void  mkname( char *name) */


void  mkval( void)

/* Set up a node for an integer read by the scanner. We use the library routine
   "atoi()" to convert the text of "yytext" to an integer. */

{
        yylval.symb = mkconst( atoi( yytext )) ;

}       /* void  mkval( void ) */


void  mktext( void )

/* Text is treated very similarly to a variable name. "mktext()" uses
   "mkname()" to do most of the work, and then just changes the relevant
   fields. Strings will be put out as constant data at the end of the program
```

and we give it a label to mark its beginning. Note that there is no risk of
a piece of text being mistaken for a variable name during symbol lookup,
since the text field of a text node includes the surrounding quotes. */

```
{
        mkname( yytext ) ;
        yylval.symb->type = T_TEXT ;
        yylval.symb->VAL2 = next_label++ ;

}       /* mktext( void ) */
```

13.2.4 THE SYNTAX ANALYSER HEADER, parser.h

We run YACC with the -d option to generate a header file, y.tab.c; for clarity
we rename this parser.h when building the compiler. It includes a declaration
of the type to be used for YACC attributes, YYSTYPE. yylval will be declared
with this type. This is followed by definitions of the small integers used for each
token.

```
typedef union
{
        SYMB    *symb ;           /* For vars, consts and text */
        TAC     *tac ;            /* For most things */
        ENODE   *enode ;          /* For expressions */
} YYSTYPE;
#define FUNC    258
#define VARIABLE        259
#define ASSIGN_SYMBOL   260
#define INTEGER 261
#define PRINT   262
#define TEXT    263
#define RETURN  264
#define CONTINUE        265
#define IF      266
#define THEN    267
#define ELSE    268
#define FI      269
#define WHILE   270
#define DO      271
#define DONE    272
#define VAR     273
#define UMINUS  274


extern YYSTYPE yylval;
```

13.2.5 THE SYNTAX ANALYSER, parser.y

The syntax analyser is implemented using YACC. This is a very simple version,
with little attempt at syntax error recovery. In general, each YACC rule has a
semantic action which returns a list of the TAC to translate the non-terminal
being defined. Typically this is constructed in a corresponding routine in the
utilities section. These routines have names of the form do_xxx() to translate
the rule for xxx.

```
/***********************************************************************
 ***********************************************************************


        PPPPPPP    AAAA    RRRRRRR   SSSSSS   EEEEEEEE  RRRRRRR
        PPPPPPPP   AAAAAA  RRRRRRRR  SSSSSSSS EEEEEEE   RRRRRRRR
        PP    PP  AA    AA RR    RR  SS       EE        RR    RR
        PPPPPPP  AAAAAAAAA RRRRRRRR  SSSSSS   EEEEE     RRRRRRRR
        PP       AA    AA  RRRRRRR       SS   EE        RRRRRRR
        PP       AA    AA  RR  RR        SS   EE        RR   RR
        PP       AA    AA  RR   RR  SSSSSSSS  EEEEEEE   RR   RR
        PP       AA    AA  RR    RR  SSSSSS   EEEEEEEE  RR   RR


 ***********************************************************************
 ***********************************************************************


                        A Compiler for VSL
                        ==================

This is the YACC parser. It creates a tree representation of the program for
subsequent conversion to TAC.

Modifications:
==============

16 Nov 88 JPB:  First version
26 Apr 89 JPB:  Version for publication
27 Jul 89 JPB:  Final version for publication
15 Sep 92 JPB:  Bug, whereby do_bin overwrote the value of constants less
                than CONST_MAX when folding is now fixed.
23 Jan 96 JPB:  Various minor corrections for 2nd edition publication.

 ***********************************************************************
 ***********************************************************************/

%{

/* We include the standard headers, but not "parser.h", since that will be
   produced by YACC when the YACC program is translated. */

#include <stdio.h>
#include <ctype.h>
#include "vc.h"

/* These are the prototypes of routines defined and used in the parser */

TAC    *do_program( TAC *c ) ;
TAC    *do_func( SYMB *func,
                 TAC  *args,
                 TAC  *code ) ;
TAC    *declare_var( SYMB *var ) ;
TAC    *do_assign( SYMB  *var,
                   ENODE *expr ) ;
ENODE *do_bin( int    binop,
               ENODE *expr1,
               ENODE *expr2 ) ;
ENODE *do_un( int    unop,
              ENODE *expr ) ;
ENODE *do_fnap( SYMB  *func,
```

```
                ENODE *arglist ) ;
TAC   *do_lib( int    rtn,
               SYMB *arg ) ;
TAC   *do_if( ENODE *expr,
              TAC   *stmt ) ;
TAC   *do_test( ENODE *expr,
                TAC   *stmt1,
                TAC   *stmt2 ) ;
TAC   *do_while( ENODE *expr,
                 TAC   *stmt ) ;
ENODE *mkenode( ENODE *next,
                SYMB  *res,
                TAC   *code ) ;
void  yyerror( char *str ) ;


/* "program_tac" is the complete TAC recognised by the parser, and set up by
   yyparse, when the sentence symbol, <program>, is recognised. We can't make
   use of "yyval", since that is not exported by the parser if you make use of
   Bison rather than YACC. */


TAC  *program_tac ;                     /* The complete program TAC */
%}


/* %union defines the type of attribute to be synthesised by the semantic
   actions. The variables, constants and text produced by the lexical analyser
   will be symbol tables nodes. Most YACC rules will produce lists of TAC,
   however those involving expressions will need to use "enode's" to specify
   where the result of the TAC is put. */


%union
{
        SYMB  *symb ;        /* For vars, consts and text */
        TAC   *tac ;         /* For most things */
        ENODE *enode ;       /* For expressions */
}


/* Tokens. Most of these don't need types, since they have no associated
   attribute. However variables, integers and text have to have a more complex
   structure, since they return symbol table nodes as attributes. */


%token           FUNC                   /* 'FUNC' */
%token <symb>    VARIABLE               /* variable name */
%token           ASSIGN_SYMBOL          /* ':=' */
%token <symb>    INTEGER                /* integer number */
%token           PRINT                  /* 'PRINT' */
%token <symb>    TEXT                   /* quoted text */
%token           RETURN                 /* 'RETURN' */
%token           CONTINUE               /* 'CONTINUE' */
%token           IF                     /* 'IF' */
%token           THEN                   /* 'THEN' */
%token           ELSE                   /* 'ELSE' */
%token           FI                     /* 'FI' */
%token           WHILE                  /* 'WHILE' */
%token           DO                     /* 'DO' */
%token           DONE                   /* 'DONE' */
%token           VAR                    /* 'VAR' */
%token           UMINUS                 /* used for precedence */
```

```
/* Now type declarations for the non-terminals. Most non-terminals just return
   a list of TAC as result, however expressions also return a pointer to the
   symbol holding the result of the calculation. */

%type <tac>      program
%type <tac>      function_list
%type <tac>      function
%type <tac>      parameter_list
%type <tac>      variable_list
%type <enode>    argument_list
%type <enode>    expression_list
%type <tac>      statement
%type <tac>      assignment_statement
%type <enode>    expression
%type <tac>      print_statement
%type <tac>      print_list
%type <tac>      print_item
%type <tac>      return_statement
%type <tac>      null_statement
%type <tac>      if_statement
%type <tac>      while_statement
%type <tac>      block
%type <tac>      declaration_list
%type <tac>      declaration
%type <tac>      statement_list
%type <tac>      error
```

```
/* We define the precedence of the arithmetic operators, including a
   pseudo-token, "UMINUS" to be used for unary minus when it occurs in
   expressions. */

%left   '+' '-'
%left   '*' '/'
%right  UMINUS

%%
```

```
/* These are the grammar rules. "program" is the sentence symbol of the
   grammar. It can't just use the default rule to pass back a result, since
   with bison, the result is not put in a variable that is visible externally.
   The solution is to copy the result into the global variable "program_tac"
   for subsequent use. */

program             :        function_list
                             {
                                     program_tac = $1 ;
                             }
                    ;
```

```
/* "function_list" is typical of many rules with two parts. Where we have a
   "function_list" followed by a "function" we call "join_tac()" to combine the
   code for each into one. Note that this use of "join_tac()", involving a walk
   down one of the code lists is very inefficient if the code gets at all
   large. If we intend using VSL for major programs (admittedly unlikely), then
   we should wish to avoid this each time we join code. We should probably
   choose to use a non-linked TAC representation and place markers as discussed
   in chapter 6. */

function_list       :        function
                    |        function_list function
```

```
                                {
                                        $$ = join_tac( $1, $2 ) ;
                                }
                        ;
```

/* Note that when we start a new "function" we are able to set the temporary
   variable count back to zero, since temporary variable names need only be
   unique within the function where they are declared. Like most rules we call
   a subsidiary routine, "do_func()", to build the code.

   This is one of the places where we attempt rudimentary error recovery. We do
   not specify a synchronising set, but let the parser recover for itself. */

```
function                :       FUNC VARIABLE '(' parameter_list ')'
                                statement
                                {
                                        $$ = do_func( $2, $4, $6 ) ;
                                }
                        |       error
                                {
                                        error( "Bad function syntax " ) ;
                                        $$ = NULL ;
                                }
                        ;

parameter_list          :       variable_list
                        |
                                {
                                        $$ = NULL ;
                                }
                        ;

variable_list           :       VARIABLE
                                {
                                        $$ = declare_var( $1 ) ;
                                }
                        |       variable_list ',' VARIABLE
                                {
                                        /* If we get a duplicate declaration,
                                           t will be NULL. join_tac handles
                                           this correctly. */

                                        $$ = join_tac( declare_var( $3 ),
                                                        $1 ) ;
                                }
                        ;

statement               :       assignment_statement
                        |       return_statement
                        |       print_statement
                        |       null_statement
                        |       if_statement
                        |       while_statement
                        |       block
                        |       error
                                {
                                        error( "Bad statement syntax" );
                                        $$ = NULL ;
                                }
                        ;
```

```
assignment_statement     :        VARIABLE ASSIGN_SYMBOL expression
                                   {
                                           $$ = do_assign( $1, $3 ) ;
                                   }
                         ;
```

/* Rules for expressions. Note the use of "%prec UMINUS" to define the higher
   precedence of negation. */

```
expression               :        expression '+' expression
                                   {
                                           $$ = do_bin( TAC_ADD, $1, $3 ) ;
                                   }
                         |        expression '-' expression
                                   {
                                           $$ = do_bin( TAC_SUB, $1, $3 ) ;
                                   }
                         |        expression '*' expression
                                   {
                                           $$ = do_bin( TAC_MUL, $1, $3 ) ;
                                   }
                         |        expression '/' expression
                                   {
                                           $$ = do_bin( TAC_DIV, $1, $3 ) ;
                                   }
                         |        '-' expression  %prec UMINUS
                                   {
                                           $$ = do_un( TAC_NEG, $2 ) ;
                                   }
                         |        '(' expression ')'
                                   {
                                           $$ = $2 ;
                                   }
                         |        INTEGER
                                   {
                                           $$ = mkenode( NULL, $1, NULL ) ;
                                   }
                         |        VARIABLE
                                   {
                                           /* Check the variable is declared. If
                                              not we substitute constant zero, or
                                              we get all sorts of problems later
                                              on. */

                                           if( $1->type != T_VAR )
                                           {
                                                   error( "Undeclared variable in"
                                                       " expression" ) ;

                                                   $$ = mkenode( NULL,
                                                                 mkconst( 0 ),
                                                                 NULL ) ;
                                           }
                                           else
                                                   $$ = mkenode( NULL, $1,
                                                                 NULL ) ;
                                   }
                         |        VARIABLE '(' argument_list ')'
                                   {
                                           $$ = do_fnap( $1, $3 ) ;
                                   }
```

```
                    |       error
                            {
                                    error( "Bad expression syntax" ) ;
                                    $$ = mkenode( NULL, NULL, NULL ) ;
                            }
                    ;

argument_list       :
                            {
                                    $$ = NULL ;
                            }
                    |       expression_list
                    ;

expression_list     :       expression
                    |       expression ',' expression_list
                            {

                                    /* Construct a list of expr nodes */

                                    $1->next = $3 ;
                                    $$        = $1 ;
                            }
                    ;

print_statement     :       PRINT print_list
                            {
                                    $$ = $2 ;
                            }
                    ;

print_list          :       print_item
                    |       print_list ',' print_item
                            {
                                    $$ = join_tac( $1, $3 ) ;
                            }
                    ;

/* PRINT items are handled by calls to library routines. These take as their
   argument the library routine to call and the symbol to pass as argument. */

print_item          :       expression
                            {
                                    /* Call printn library routine */

                                    $$ = join_tac( $1->tac,
                                                   do_lib( LIB_PRINTN,
                                                   $1->res )) ;
                            }
                    |       TEXT
                            {

                                    */ Call prints, passing the address of
                                       the string */

                                    $$ = do_lib( LIB_PRINTS, $1 ) ;
                            }
                    ;
```

```
return_statement          :         RETURN expression
                                    {
                                            TAC *t = mktac( TAC_RETURN, $2->res,
                                                            NULL, NULL ) ;
                                            t->prev = $2->tac ;
                                            free_enode( $2 ) ;
                                            $$      = t ;
                                    }
                          ;


null_statement            :         CONTINUE
                                    {
                                            $$ = NULL ;
                                    }
                          ;


/* Note the use of two different routines to handle the different types of IF
   statement. We could have shared this code for conciseness. */

if_statement              :         IF expression THEN statement FI
                                    {
                                            $$ = do_if( $2, $4 ) ;
                                    }
                          |         IF expression THEN statement
                                    ELSE statement FI
                                    {
                                            $$ = do_test( $2, $4, $6 ) ;
                                    }
                          ;


while_statement           :         WHILE expression DO statement DONE
                                    {
                                            $$ = do_while( $2, $4 ) ;
                                    }
                          ;


block                     :         '{' declaration_list statement_list '}'
                                    {
                                            $$ = join_tac( $2, $3 ) ;
                                    }
                          ;


declaration_list          :
                                    {
                                            $$ = NULL ;
                                    }
                          |         declaration_list declaration
                                    {
                                            $$ = join_tac( $1, $2 ) ;
                                    }
                          ;


declaration               :         VAR variable_list
                                    {
                                            $$ = $2 ;
                                    }
                          ;


statement_list            :         statement
```

```
    |         statement_list statement
              {
                       $$ = join_tac( $1, $2 ) ;
              }
        ;

%%

/* These are the routines to support the various YACC rules. It is invariably
   clearer to put anything but the simplest semantic action in a routine,
   because the layout of YACC bunches code to the right so much. */

TAC *do_func( SYMB *func,                      /* Function */
              TAC  *args,                      /* Its args */
              TAC  *code )                     /* Its code */

/* For a function we must add TAC_BEGINFUNC and TAC_ENDFUNC quadruples
   around it, and a new label at the start. We then enter the name of the
   function in the symbol table. It should not have been declared as a variable
   or function elsewhere, and so should still have type T_UNDEF.

   The function may already be the subject of function calls. The address of
   the quadruples for these calls are held in the LABEL2 field of its symbol
   table entry, ready for backpatching. We run down this list backpatching in
   the address of the starting label, and then replace the field with the
   address of the starting label, also updating the type to T_FUNC.

   Note that there is a fault in the compiler at this point. If we never
   declare a function that is used, then its address will never be backpatched.
   This is a semantic check that needs to be added at the end of parsing. */

{       TAC *tlist ;                     /* The backpatch list */

        TAC *tlab ;                      /* Label at start of function */
        TAC *tbegin ;                    /* BEGINFUNC marker */
        TAC *tend ;                      /* ENDFUNC marker */

        /* Add this function to the symbol table. If it's already there its been
           used before, so backpatch the address into the call opcodes. If
           declared already we have a semantic error and give up. Otherwise
           patch in the addresses and declare as a function */

        if( func->type != T_UNDEF )
        {
                error( "function already declared" ) ;
                return NULL ;
        }

        tlab   = mktac( TAC_LABEL,    mklabel( next_label++ ), NULL, NULL ) ;
        tbegin = mktac( TAC_BEGINFUNC, NULL, NULL, NULL ) ;
        tend   = mktac( TAC_ENDFUNC,   NULL, NULL, NULL ) ;

        tbegin->prev = tlab ;
        code         = join_tac( args, code ) ;
        tend->prev   = join_tac( tbegin, code ) ;

        tlist = func->LABEL2 ;                          /* List of addresses if any */

        while( tlist != NULL )
        {
                TAC *tnext = tlist->LB ;        /* Next on list */
```

```
                    tlist->LB  = tlab ;
                    tlist      = tnext ;
        }

        func->type  = T_FUNC ;              /* And declare as func */
        func->LABEL2 = tlab ;

        return tend ;

}       /* TAC *do_func( SYMB *func,
                         TAC  *args,
                         TAC  *code ) */


TAC *declare_var( SYMB *var )

/* All variable names may be used only once throughout a program. We check here
   that they have not yet been declared and if so declare them, setting their
   stack offset to -1 (an invalid offset) and marking their address descriptor
   empty. Note that this is a fault in the compiler. We really do need to mark
   the beginning and end of blocks in which variables are declared, so that
   scope can be checked. */

{
        if( var->type != T_UNDEF )
        {
                error( "variable already declared" ) ;
                return NULL ;
        }

        var->type  = T_VAR ;
        var->ADDR2 = -1 ;                     */ Unset address */

        /* TAC for a declaration */

        return  mktac( TAC_VAR, var, NULL, NULL ) ;
}       /* TAC *declare_var( SYMB *var ) */


TAC *do_assign( SYMB  *var,       /* Variable to be assigned */
                ENODE *expr )     /* Expression to assign */

/* An assignment statement shows the use of expression nodes. We construct a
   copy node to take the result of the expression and copy it into the
   variable, having performed suitable semantic checks. Note that if we
   discover that the variable has not been declared, we declare it, to prevent
   further non-declaration errors each time it is referenced. */

{
        TAC  *code ;

        /* Warn if variable not declared, then build code */

        if( var->type != T_VAR )
                error( "assignment to non-variable" ) ;

        code       = mktac( TAC_COPY, var, expr->res, NULL ) ;
        code->prev = expr->tac ;
        free_enode( expr ) ;                 /* Expression now finished with */
```

```
            return code ;

}        /* TAC *do_assign( SYMB  *var,
                              ENODE *expr )  */


ENODE *do_bin(   int     binop,        /* TAC binary operator */
                 ENODE *expr1,         /* Expressions to operate on */
                 ENODE *expr2 )

/* We then have the first of the arithmetic routines to handle binary
   operators. We carry out one of the few optimisations in the compiler here,
   constant folding. We might think of reusing one of the expression nodes for
   efficiency. However because constants up to CONST_MAX are held in shared
   symbols, we risk altering the value of such constants in future use. For
   simplicity we just create a new constant node for the result, rather than
   sorting out if we can reuse the node. If we can't do folding we generate the
   result into a temporary variable, which we first declare, returning an
   expression node for the TAC with the temporary in the result field. */

{
        TAC  *temp ;                   /* TAC code for temp symbol */
        TAC  *res ;                    /* TAC code for result */

        /* Do constant folding if possible. Calculate the constant into newval
           and make a new constant node for the result. Free up expr2. */

        if(( expr1->ETYPE == T_INT ) && ( expr2->ETYPE == T_INT ))
        {
                int    newval ;        /* The result of constant folding */

                switch( binop )        /* Choose the operator */
                {
                case TAC_ADD:

                        newval = expr1->EVAL1 + expr2->EVAL1 ;
                        break ;

                case TAC_SUB:

                        newval = expr1->EVAL1 - expr2->EVAL1 ;
                        break ;

                case TAC_MUL:

                        newval = expr1->EVAL1 * expr2->EVAL1 ;
                        break ;

                case TAC_DIV:

                        newval = expr1->EVAL1 / expr2->EVAL1 ;
                        break ;
                }

                expr1->res = mkconst(newval);  /* New space for result */
                free-enode( expr2 ) ;          /* Release space in expr2 */

                return expr1 ;                 /* The new expression */
        }
```

```
        /* Not constant, so create a TAC node for a binary operator, putting
           the result in a temporary. Bolt the code together, reusing expr1 and
           freeing expr2. */

        temp      = mktac( TAC_VAR, mktmp(), NULL, NULL ) ;
        temp->prev = join_tac( expr1->tac, expr2->tac ) ;
        res       = mktac( binop, temp->VA, expr1->res, expr2->res ) ;
        res->prev = temp ;

        expr1->res = temp->VA ;
        expr1->tac = res ;
        free_enode( expr2 ) ;

        return expr1 ;

}       /* ENODE *do_bin( int     binop,
                          ENODE *expr1,
                          ENODE *expr2 ) */


ENODE *do_un( int     unop,             /* TAC unary operator */
              ENODE *expr )             /* Expression to operate on */

/* This is an analagous routine to deal with unary operators. In the interest
   of generality it has been written to permit easy addition of new unary
   operators, although there is only one at present. */


{
        TAC   *temp ;                   /* TAC code for temp symbol */
        TAC   *res ;                    /* TAC code for result */

        /* Do constant folding if possible. Calculate the constant into expr */

        if( expr->ETYPE == T_INT )
        {
                switch( unop )          /* Choose the operator */
                {
                case TAC_NEG:

                        expr->EVAL1 = - expr->EVAL1 ;
                        break ;
                }

                return expr ;           /* The new expression */
        }

        /* Not constant, so create a TAC node for a unary operator, putting
           the result in a temporary. Bolt the code together, reusing expr. */

        temp      = mktac( TAC_VAR, mktmp(), NULL, NULL ) ;
        temp->prev = expr->tac ;
        res       = mktac( unop, temp->VA, NULL, expr->res ) ;
        res->prev = temp ;

        expr->res = temp->VA ;
        expr->tac = res ;

        return expr ;

}       /* ENODE *do_un( int     unop,
                         ENODE *expr ) */
```

```
ENODE *do_fnap( SYMB   *func,            /* Function to call */
                ENODE *arglist )          /* Its argument list */
```

/* Construct a function call to the given function. If the function is not yet
   defined, then we must add this call to the backpatching list. Return the
   result of the function in a temporary. Note the qualification about
   backpatching above in the definition of "do_func()"

   When constructing a function call we put the result in a temporary. We join
   all the TAC for the expressions first, then join the code for the TAC_ARG
   instructions, since arg instructions must appear consecutively. */

```
{
        ENODE  *alt ;                    /* For counting args */
        SYMB   *res ;                    /* Where function result will go */
        TAC    *code ;                   /* Resulting code */
        TAC    *temp ;                   /* Temporary for building code */

        /* Check that this is a valid function. In this case it must either be
           T_UNDEF or Y_FUNC. If it is declare the result, run down the
           argument list, joining up the code for each argument, then generate
           a sequence of arg instructions and finally a call instruction */

        if(( func->type != T_UNDEF ) && ( func->type != T_FUNC ))
        {
                error( "function declared other than function" );
                return NULL ;
        }

        res  = mktmp() ;                        /* For the result */
        code = mktac( TAC_VAR, res, NULL, NULL ) ;

        for( alt = arglist ; alt != NULL ; alt = alt->next )  /* Join args */
                code = join_tac( code, alt->tac ) ;

        while( arglist != NULL )         /* Generate ARG instructions */
        {
                temp      = mktac( TAC_ARG, arglist->res, NULL, NULL ) ;
                temp->prev = code ;
                code      = temp ;

                alt = arglist->next ;
                free_enode( arglist ) ;   /* Free the space */
                arglist = alt ;
        } ;

        temp      = mktac( TAC_CALL, res, (SYMB *)func->LABEL2, NULL ) ;
        temp->prev = code ;
        code      = temp ;

        /* If the function is undefined update its backpatching list with the
           address of this instruction and then return an expression node for
           the result */

        if( func->type == T_UNDEF )
                func->LABEL2 = code ;

        return mkenode( NULL, res, code ) ;

}       /* ENODE *do_fnap( SYMB   *func,
                           ENODE *arglist ) */
```

```
TAC *do_lib( int    rtn,              /* Routine to call */
             SYMB *arg )              /* Argument to pass */

/* PRINT items are handled by calls to library routines. These take as their
   argument the library routine to call and the symbol to pass as argument.
   This routine constructs a call to a library routine with a single argument.
*/

{
        TAC *a = mktac( TAC_ARG, arg, NULL, NULL ) ;
        TAC *c = mktac( TAC_CALL, NULL, (SYMB *)library[rtn], NULL ) ;

        c->prev = a ;

        return c ;

}       /* TAC *do_lib( int    rtn,
                        SYMB *arg ) */


TAC *do_if( ENODE *expr,              /* Condition */
            TAC    *stmt )            /* Statement  to execute */

/* For convenience we have two routines to handle IF statements, "do_if()"
   where there is no ELSE part and "do_test()" where there is. We always
   allocate TAC_LABEL instructions, so that the destinations of all branches
   will appear as labels in the resulting TAC code. */

{
        TAC *label = mktac( TAC_LABEL, mklabel( next_label++ ), NULL, NULL ) ;
        TAC *code  = mktac( TAC_IFZ, (SYMB *)label, expr->res, NULL ) ;

        code->prev = expr->tac ;
        code       = join_tac( code, stmt ) ;
        label->prev = code ;

        free_enode( expr ) ;          /* Expression finished with */

        return label ;

}       /* TAC *do_if( ENODE *expr,
                       TAC    *stmt ) */


TAC *do_test( ENODE *expr,            /* Condition */
              TAC    *stmt1,          /* THEN part */
              TAC    *stmt2 )         /* ELSE part */

/* Construct code for an if statement with else part */

{
        TAC *label1 = mktac( TAC_LABEL, mklabel( next_label++ ), NULL, NULL ) ;
        TAC *label2 = mktac( TAC_LABEL, mklabel( next_label++ ), NULL, NULL ) ;
        TAC *code1  = mktac( TAC_IFZ, (SYMB *)label1, expr->res, NULL ) ;
        TAC *code2  = mktac( TAC_GOTO, (SYMB *)label2, NULL, NULL ) ;

        code1->prev  = expr->tac ;                    /* Join the code */
        code1        = join_tac( code1, stmt1 ) ;
        label1->prev = code2 ;
        code2->prev  = code1 ;
```

```
        label1      = join tac( label1, stmt2 ) ;
        label2->prev = label1 ;

        free_enode( expr ) ;           /* Free the expression */

        return label2 ;
}       /* TAC *do_test( ENODE *expr,
                         TAC   *stmt1,
                         TAC   *stmt2 ) */


TAC *do_while( ENODE *expr,            /* Condition */
               TAC   *stmt )           /* Body of loop */

/* Do a WHILE loop. This is the same as an IF statement with a jump back at the
   end. We bolt a goto on the end of the statement, call do_if to construct the
   code and join the start label right at the beginning */

{
        TAC *label = mktac( TAC_LABEL, mklabel( next_label++ ), NULL, NULL ) ;
        TAC *code  = mktac( TAC_GOTO, (SYMB *)label, NULL, NULL ) ;

        code->prev = stmt ;            /* Bolt on the goto */

        return join_tac( label, do_if(expr, code )) ;

}       /* TAC *do_while( ENODE *expr,
                          TAC   *stmt ) */


ENODE *mkenode( ENODE *next,
                SYMB  *res,
                TAC   *code )

/* The routine to make an expression node. We put this here rather than with
   the other utilities in "main.c", since it is only used in the parser. */

{
        ENODE *expr = get_enode() ;

        expr->next = next ;
        expr->res  = res ;
        expr->tac  = code ;

        return expr ;

}       /* ENODE *mkenode( ENODE *next,
                           SYMB  *res,
                           TAC   *code ) */


void yyerror( char *str )

/* The Yacc default error handler. This just calls our error handler */

{
        error( str ) ;

}       /* void yyerror( char *str ) */
```

13.2.6 THE CODE GENERATOR, cg.c

The code generator of any compiler is never small. This is not because of any inherent complexity, but because of the large number of cases to be considered.

The approach used here is to take each instruction in turn and translate it into VAM assembler. We use a register descriptor to minimize loading and storing of variables. Registers are spilled prior to any branch or label. The registers' descriptors are cleared at any label. There is no address descriptor; instead we locate names in registers by searching the register descriptor.

```
/******************************************************************************
 ******************************************************************************


                         CCCCC     GGGGGG
                        CCCCCCC   GGGGGGGG
                        CC        GG
                        CC        GG   GGGG
                        CC        GG     GG
                        CC        GG     GG
                        CCCCCCC   GGGGGGGG
                         CCCCC     GGGGGG



 ******************************************************************************
 ******************************************************************************

                         A Compiler for VSL
                         ==================

This is the code generator section

Modifications:
==============

22 Nov 88 JPB:  First version
26 Apr 89 JPB:  Version for publication
 1 Aug 89 JPB:  Final version for publication
13 Jun 90 JPB:  Now refers to library directory (noted by R C Shaw, Praxis).
 9 May 91 JPB:  load_reg call in cg_cond removed to avoid conflict (J
                Johnson)
23 Jan 96 JPB:  Various minor corrections for 2nd edition publication.

 ******************************************************************************
 ******************************************************************************/


#include <stdio.h>
#include <ctype.h>
#include "vc.h"

/* Constants used here. First we define some of the registers. We reserve
   register R1 as the stack pointer and use registers R2 - R4 in the calling
   and return sequences. */
```

```
#define R_ZERO        0                    /* Constant zero */
#define R_P           1                    /* Stack pointer */
#define R_CALL        2                    /* Address of called routine */
#define R_RET         3                    /* Return address */
#define R_RES         4                    /* Result reg and last reserved */
#define R_GEN         5                    /* First general purpose register */
#define R_MAX         16                   /* 16 regs */
```

/* The stack frame holds the dynamic link at offset zero and the return address
   at offset 4. */

```
#define P_OFF         0                    /* Offset of stack pointer on frame */
#define PC_OFF        4                    /* Offset of ret address on frame */
#define VAR_OFF       8                    /* Offset of variables on frame */
```

/* To make the code clearer we define flags MODIFIED and UNMODIFIED as TRUE and
   FALSE respectively for setting the mod field of the register descriptor. */

```
#define MODIFIED      TRUE                 /* Entries for descriptors */
#define UNMODIFIED    FALSE
```

/* These are static variables used throughout this section. The register
   descriptor is an array of anonymous structures with a field to hold the most
   recent item slaved in the register and a field to mark whether the register
   has been modified since last written to memory.

   "tos" is the top of stack in the current function and "next_arg" is the
   number of the next argument to load on the stack. */

```
struct                                     /* Reg descriptor */
{
        struct symb *name ;                /* Thing in reg */
        int         modified ;             /* If needs spilling */
}    rdesc[R_MAX] ;
int  tos ;                                 /* Top of stack */
int  next_arg ;                            /* Next argument to load */
```

/* These are the prototypes of routines defined here. Routines to translate TAC
   instructions generally have the form "cg_xxx()" where xxx is the name of a TAC
   instruction of group of TAC instructions. */

```
void  cg( TAC *tl ) ;
TAC   *init_cg( TAC *tl ) ;
void  cg_instr( TAC *c ) ;
void  cg_bin( char *op,
              SYMB *a,
              SYMB *b,
              SYMB *c ) ;
void  cg_copy( SYMB *a,
               SYMB *b ) ;
void  cg_cond( char *op,
               SYMB *a,
               int  l ) ;
void  cg_arg( SYMB *a ) ;
void  cg_call( int  f,
               SYMB *res ) ;
void  cg_return( SYMB *a ) ;
void  cg_sys( char *fn ) ;
void  cg_strings( void ) ;
void  cg_str( SYMB *s ) ;
```

```
void   flush_all( void ) ;
void   spill_all( void ) ;
void   spill_one( int   r ) ;
void   load_reg( int    r,
                 SYMB *n ) ;
void   clear_desc( int    r ) ;
void   insert_desc( int    r,
                    SYMB *n,
                    int    mod ) ;
int    get_rreg( SYMB *c ) ;
int    get_areg( SYMB *b,
                 int   cr ) ;


void   cg( TAC *tl )

/* The code generator is initialised by "cg_init()", finding the start of the
   TAC list in the process (since the syntax analysis phase has given us the
   end of the list, and the code generator works from the start of the list).

   We first copy a header file to the output containing initialisation code and
   then loop generating code for each TAC instruction. The code is preceded by
   a comment line in the assembler giving the TAC instruction being translated.
   After generating code for the TAC, we copy the library file and then
   generate code for all the text strings used in the program.

   Note that in the book the header and lib files are just referred to as
   "header" and "lib", thus assuming that they will be in the same directory
   that the compiler is run in. We have included a #defined library path here
   for greater flexibility. */

{
        TAC *tls = init_cg( tl ) ;              /* Start of TAC */

        cg_sys( LIB_DIR "header" ) ;            /* Standard header */

        for( ; tls != NULL ; tls = tls->next )  /* Instructions in turn */
        {
                printf( "\\" ) ;
                print_instr( tls ) ;
                cg_instr( tls ) ;
        }

        cg_sys( LIB_DIR "lib" ) ;               /* Library */
        cg_strings() ;                          /* String data */

}       /* void  cg( TAC *tl ) */

TAC *init_cg( TAC *tl )

/* Initialisation involves clearing the register descriptors (apart from zero
   in R0), setting the top of stack and next_arg indices and clearing the free
   lists for address and register descriptors. We finally find the end of the
   TAC list, setting .cb next fields in the TAC as we do so. */

{
        int  r ;
        TAC *c ;                        /* Current TAC instruction */
        TAC *p ;                        /* Previous TAC instruction */
```

```
            for( r = 0 ; r < R_MAX ; r++ )
                    rdesc[r].name = NULL ;

            insert_desc( 0, mkconst( 0 ), UNMODIFIED ) ;      /* R0 holds 0 */

            tos      = VAR_OFF ;               /* TOS allows space for link info */
            next_arg = 0 ;                     /* Next arg to load */

            /* Tidy up and reverse the code list */

            c = NULL ;                         /* No current */
            p = tl ;                           /* Preceding to do */

            while( p != NULL )
            {
                    p->next = c ;              /* Set the next field */
                    c       = p ;              /* Step on */
                    p       = p->prev ;
            }

            return c ;

}       /* TAC *init_cg( TAC *tl ) */


void  cg_instr( TAC *c )

/* Generate code for a single TAC instruction. This is just a switch on all
   possible TAC instructions. Hopefully if we have written the front end
   correctly the default case will never be encountered. For most cases we just
   call a subsidiary routine "cg_xxx()" to do the code generation. */

{
        switch( c->op )
        {
        case TAC_UNDEF:

                error( "cannot translate TAC_UNDEF" ) ;
                return ;

        case TAC_ADD:

                cg_bin( "ADD", c->VA, c->VB, c->VC ) ;
                return ;

        case TAC_SUB:

                cg_bin( "SUB", c->VA, c->VB, c->VC ) ;
                return ;

        case TAC_MUL:

                cg_bin( "MUL", c->VA, c->VB, c->VC ) ;
                return ;

        case TAC_DIV:

                cg_bin( "DIV", c->VA, c->VB, c->VC ) ;
                return ;
```

```
    case TAC_NEG:

            cg_bin( "SUB", c->VA, mkconst( 0 ), C->VB ) ;
            return ;

    case TAC_COPY:

            cg_copy( c->VA, c->VB ) ;
            return ;

    case TAC_GOTO:

            cg_cond( "BRA", NULL, c->LA->VA->VAL1 ) ;
            return ;

    case TAC_IFZ:

            cg_cond( "BZE", c->VB, c->LA->VA->VAL1 ) ;
            return ;

    case TAC_IFNZ:

            cg_cond( "BNZ", c->VB, c->LA->VA->VAL1 ) ;
            return ;

    case TAC_ARG:

            cg_arg( c->VA ) ;
            return ;

    case TAC_CALL:

            cg_call( c->LB->VA->VAL1, c->VA ) ;
            return ;

    case TAC_RETURN:

            cg_return( c->VA ) ;
            return ;

    case TAC_LABEL:

            /* We generate an appropriate label. Note that we must flush
               the register descriptor, since control may arrive at this
               label from other points in the code. */

            flush_all() ;
            printf( "L%u:\n", c->VA->VAL1 ) ;
            return ;

    case TAC_VAR:

            /* Allocate 4 bytes for this variable to hold an integer on the
               current top of stack */

            c->VA->ADDR2 = tos ;
            tos += 4 ;
            return ;
```

```
        case TAC_BEGINFUNC:

                /* At the start of a function we must copy the return address
                   which will be in R_RET onto the stack. We reset the top of
                   stack, since it is currently empty apart from the link
                   information. */

                tos = VAR_OFF ;
                printf( "        STI  R%u,%u(R%u)\n", R_RET, PC_OFF, R_P ) ;
                return ;

        case TAC_ENDFUNC:

                /* At the end of the function we put in an implicit return
                   instruction. */

                cg_return( NULL ) ;
                return ;

        default:

                /* Don't know what this one is */

                error( "unknown TAC opcode to translate" ) ;
                return ;
        }

}       /* void  cg_instr( TAC *c ) */


void  cg_bin( char *op,            /* Opcode to use */
              SYMB *a,             /* Result */
              SYMB *b,             /* Operands */
              SYMB *c )

/* Generate code for a binary operator

    a := b op c

  VAM has 2 address opcodes with the result going into the second operand

  This is a typical code generation function. We find and load a separate
  register for each argument, the second argument also being used for the
  result. We then generate the code for binary operator, updating the register
  descriptor appropriately. */

{
        int  cr = get_rreg( c ) ;       /* Result register */
        int  br = get_areg( b, cr ) ;   /* Second argument register */

        printf( "        %s  R%u,R%u\n", op, br, cr ) ;

        /* Delete c from the descriptors and insert a */

        clear_desc( cr ) ;
        insert_desc( cr, a, MODIFIED ) ;
}       /* void  cg_bin( char *op,
                         SYMB *a,
                         SYMB *b,
                         SYMB *c ) */
```

```
void  cg_copy( SYMB *a,
               SYMB *b )

/* Generate code for a copy instruction

       a := b

   We load b into a register, then update the descriptors to indicate that a
   is also in that register. We need not do the store until the register is
   spilled or flushed. */

{
        int  br = get_rreg( b ) ;          /* Load b into a register */

        insert_desc( br, a, MODIFIED ) ; /* Indicate a is there */

}       /* void  cg_copy( SYMB *a,
                           SYMB *b ) */


void  cg_cond( char *op,
               SYMB *a,                    /* Condition */
               int  l )                    /* Branch destination */

/* Generate for "goto", "ifz" or "ifnz". We must spill registers before the
   branch. In the case of unconditional goto we have no condition, and so "b"
   is NULL. We set the condition flags if necessary by explicitly loading "a"
   into a register to ensure the zero flag is set. A better approach would be
   to keep track of what is in the status register, so saving this load. */

{
        spill_all() ;

        if( a != NULL )
        {
                int  r ;

                for( r = R_GEN; r < R_MAX ; r++ )   /* Is it in reg? */
                        if( rdesc[r].name == a )
                                break ;

                /* Bug fix 3/5/91 to reload into the existing register
                   correctly. */

                if( r < R_MAX )

                        /* Reload into existing reg. Don't use load_reg, since
                           it updates rdesc */

                        printf( "        LDR  R%u,R%u\n", r, r ) ;
                else
                        (void)get_rreg( a ) ;  /* Load into new register */
        }
        printf( "        %s L%u\n", op, l ) ;  /* Branch */

}       /* void  cg_cond( char *op,
                           SYMB *a,
                           int  l ) */
```

```
void  cg_arg( SYMB *a )
```

/* Generate for an ARG instruction. We load the argument into a register, and
   then write it onto the new stack frame, which is 2 words past the current
   top of stack. We keep track of which arg this is in the global variable
   "next_arg". We assume that ARG instructions are always followed by other ARG
   instructions or CALL instructions. */

```
{
        int  r = get_rreg( a ) ;

        printf( "        STI  R%u,%u(R%u)\n", r, tos + VAR_OFF + next_arg,
                R_P ) ;
        next_arg += 4 ;

}       /* void  cg_arg( SYMB *a ) */


void  cg_call( int    f,
               SYMB *res )
```

/* The standard call sequence is

```
        LDA  f(R0),R2
        STI  R1,tos(R1)
        LDA  tos(R1),R1
        BAL  R2,R3
      ( STI  R4,res )
```

   We flush out the registers prior to a call and then execute the standard
   CALL sequence. Flushing involves spilling modified registers, and then
   clearing the register descriptors. We use BAL to the call, which means
   R_RET will hold the return address on entry to the function which must be
   saved on the stack. After the call if there is a result it will be in R_RES
   so enter this in the descriptors. We reset "next_arg" before the call,
   since we know we have finished all the arguments now. */

```
{
        flush_all() ;
        next_arg = 0 ;
        printf( "        LDA  L%u,R%u\n", f, R_CALL ) ;
        printf( "        STI  R%u,%u(R%u)\n", R_p, tos, R_P ) ;
        printf( "        LDA  %u(R%u), R%u\n", tos, R_P, R_P ) ;
        printf( "        BAL  R%u,R%u\n", R_CALL, R_RET ) ;

        if( res != NULL )                       /* Do a result if there is one */
                insert_desc( R_RES, res, MODIFIED ) ;

}       /* void  cg_call( int    f,
                          SYMB *res ) */


void  cg_return( SYMB *a )
```

/* The standard return sequence is

```
      ( LDI  a,R4 )
        LDI  4(R1),R2      return program counter
```

```
        LDI  0(R1), R1    return stack pointer
        BAL  R2,R3

   If "a" is NULL we don't load anything into the result register.
*/

{
        if( a != NULL )
        {
                spill_one( R_RES ) ;
                load_reg( R_RES, a ) ;
        }

        printf( "       LDI  %u(R%u),R%u\n", PC_OFF, R_P, R_CALL ) ;
        printf( "       LDI  %u(R%u),R%u\n", P_OFF, R_P, R_P ) ;
        printf( "       BAL  R%u,R%u\n", R_CALL, R_RET ) ;

}       /* void cg_return( SYMB *a ) */


void  cg_sys( char *fn )                    /* File name */

/* This routine is used to copy standard header and library files into the
   generated code. */

{
        FILE *fd = fopen( fn, "r" ) ; /* The library file */
        int c ;

        if( fd == NULL )
        {
                error( "cannot open system file" ) ;
                exit( 0 ) ;
        }

        while((c = getc( fd )) != EOF )
                putchar( c ) ;

        fclose( fd ) ;

}       /* void  cg_sys( char *fn ) */


void cg_strings( void )

/* This routine runs through the symbol table at the end of code generation to
   find all the strings, calling "cg_str()" to generate each string as a series
   of bytes declarations. It finally generates label zero to mark the end of
   code. */

{
        int  i ;

        for( i = 0 ; i < HASHSIZE ; i++)    /* Find all symbol table chains */
        {
                SYMB *sl ;
```

```
                   for( sl = symbtab[i] ; sl != NULL ; sl = sl->next )
                       if( sl->type == T_TEXT )
                           cg_str( sl ) ;
        }

        printf( "LO:\n" ) ;

}       /* void  cg_strings( void ) */


void  cg_str( SYMB *s )

/* Generate bytes for this string. Ignore the quotes and translate escapes */

{
        char *t = s->TEXT1 ;                /* The text */
        int   i ;

        printf( "L%u:\n", s->VAL2 ) ;       /* Label for the string */

        for( i = 1 ; t[i + 1] != EOS ; i++ )
            if( t[i] == '\\' )
                switch( t[++i] )
                {
                        case 'n':

                                printf( "       DB   %u\n", '\n' ) ;
                                break ;

                        case '\"':

                                printf( "       DB   %u\n", '\"' ) ;
                                break
                }
            else
                printf( "       DB   %u\n", t[i] ) ;

        printf( "       DB   0\n" ) ;        /* End of string */

}       /* void  cg_str( SYMB *s ) */


/* These are the support routines for the code generation. "flush_all()" is
   used to write all modified registers and clear the registers at points where
   their validity can not be guaranteed (after labels and function calls).
   "spill_all()" is used to write all modified registers at points where we
   wish memory to be consistent (prior to a branch). "spill_one()" is used to
   write a specific register out if it is modified. */


void  flush_all( void )

/* Spill all registers, and clear their descriptors. Although we don't spill
   the result register (it is only set on a return, and therefore never needs
   saving for future use), we do clear its descriptor! */

{
        int r ;

        spill_all() ;
        for( r = R_GEN ; r < R_MAX ; r++)   /* Clear the descriptors */
```

```
                      clear_desc( r ) ;

          clear_desc( R_RES ) ;                /* Clear result register */

}        /* void  flush_all( void ) */


void  spill_all( void )

/* Spill all the registers */

{
          int r ;

          for( r = R_GEN ; r < R_MAX ; r++ )
                  spill_one( r ) ;

}        /* spill_all( void ) */


void  spill_one( int r )

/* Spill the value in register r if there is one and it's modified */

{
          if( (rdesc[r].name != NULL) && redesc[r].modified )
          {
                  printf( "        STI  R%u,%u(R%u)\n", r, rdesc[r].name->ADDR2,
                          R_P ) ;
                  rdesc[r].modified = UNMODIFIED ;
          }

}        /* void  spill_one( int  r ) */


void  load_reg( int   r,              /* Register to be loaded */
                SYMB *n )             /* Name to load */

/* "load_reg()" loads a value into a register. If the value is in a different
   register it uses LDR. If it is a constant it uses LDA indexed off R0 and if
   a piece of text, the address of the text is loaded with LDA. Variables are
   loaded from the stack with LDI.

   We update the register descriptor accordingly */

{
          int  s ;

          /* Look for a register */

          for( s = 0 ; s < R_MAX ; s++ )
                  if( rdesc[s].name == n )
                  {
                          printf("        LDR  R%u,R%u\n", s, r ) ;
                          insert_desc( r, n, rdesc[s].modified ) ;
                          return ;
                  }
```

```
        /* Not in a reg. Load appropriately */

        switch( n->type )
        {
        case T_INT:

                printf( "        LDA    %u(R0),R%u\n", n->VAL1, r ) ;
                break ;

        case T_VAR:

                printf("         LDI    %u(R%u),R%u\n", n->ADDR2, R_P, r ) ;
                break ;

        case T_TEXT:

                printf( "        LDA    L%u,R%u\n", n->VAL2, r ) ;
                break ;
        }

        insert-desc( r, n, UNMODIFIED ) ;
}       /* void  load_reg( int   r,
                           SYMB *n ) */
```

/* We have three routines to handle the register descriptor. "clear_desc()"
   removes any slave information in a register, "insert_desc()" inserts slave
   information. */

```
void  clear_desc( int  r )               /* Register to delete */

/* Clear the descriptor for register r */

{
        rdesc[r].name = NULL ;

}       /* void  clear_desc( int  r ) */

void  insert_desc( int    r,
                   SYMB  *n,
                   int    mod )
```

/* Insert a descriptor entry for the given name. First as a precaution delete
   it from any existing descriptor. */

```
{
        int  or ;                        /* Old register counter */

        /* Search through each register in turn looking for "n". There should
           be at most one of these. */

        for( or = R_GEN ; or < R_MAX ; or++ )
        {
                if( rdesc[or].name == n )
                {
                        /* Found it, clear it and break out of the loop. */

                        clear_desc( or ) ;
                        break ;
                }
        }
```

```
        /* We should not find any duplicates, but check, just in case. */

        for( or++ ; or < R_MAX ; or++ )

                if( rdesc[or].name == n )
                {
                        error( "Duplicate slave found" ) ;
                        clear_desc( or ) ;

        /* Finally insert the name in the new descriptor */

        rdesc[r].name     = n ;
        rdesc[r].modified = mod ;

}       /* void  insert_desc( int   r,
                              SYMB *n,
                              int   mod ) */
```

```
/* These two routines implement the simple register allocation algorithm
   described in chapter 10. "get_rreg()" gets a register that will hold an
   operand and be overwritten by a result. "get_areg()" gets a register that
   will hold an operand that will not be overwritten. */


int  get_rreg( SYMB *c )

/* Get a register to hold the result of the computation

       a := b op c

   This must initially hold c and will be overwritten with a. If c is already
   in a register we use that, spilling it first if necessary, otherwise we
   choose in order of preference from

       An empty register
       An unmodified register
       A modified register

   In the last case we spill the contents of the register before it is used. If
   c is not in the given result register we load it. Clearly we cannot use R0
   for this purpose, even if c is constant zero. We also avoid using the
   reserved registers. Note that since c may be the same as b we must update
   the address and register descriptors. */

{
        int      r ;                    /* Register for counting */

        for( r = R_GEN ; r < R_MAX ; r++ )    /* Already in a register */
                if( rdesc[r].name == c )
                {
                        spill_one( r ) ;
                        return r ;
                }

        for( r = R_GEN ; r < R_MAX ; r++ )
                if( rdesc[r].name == NULL )  /* Empty register */
                {
                        load_reg( r, c ) ;
                        return r ;
                }
```

```
            for( r = R_GEN ; r < R_MAX ; r++ )
                    if( !rdesc[r].modified )      /* Unmodified register */
                    {
                            clear_desc( r ) ;
                            load_reg( r, c ) ;
                            return r ;
                    }

            spill_one( R_GEN ) ;                  /* Modified register */
            clear_desc( R_GEN ) ;
            load_reg( R_GEN, c ) ;
            return R_GEN ;

    }       /* int get_rreg( SYMB *c ) */

int  get_areg( SYMB *b,
               int   cr )                       /* Register already holding b */

/* Get a register to hold the second argument of the computation

        a := b op c

    This must hold b and will not be overwritten. If b is already in a register
    we use that, otherwise we choose in order of preference from

        An empty register
        An unmodified register
        A modified register

    In the last case we spill the contents of the register before it is used. If
    b is not in the given argument register we load it. We can use R0 for this
    purpose, even if b is constant zero, but we avoid using the reserved
    registers. We may not use cr unless it already contains b. */

{
        int      r ;                    /* Register for counting */

        for( r = R_ZERO ; r < R_MAX ; r++ )
                if( rdesc[r].name == b )              /* Already in register */
                        return r ;

        for( r = R_GEN ; r < R_MAX ; r++ )
                if( rdesc[r].name == NULL )           /* Empty register */
                {
                        load_reg( r, b ) ;
                        return r ;
                }

        for( r = R_GEN ; r < R_MAX ; r++ )
                if( !rdesc[r].modified && (r != cr))  /* Unmodified register */
                {
                        clear_desc( r ) ;
                        load_reg( r, b ) ;
                        return r ;
                }
```

```
        for( r = R_GEN ; r < R_MAX ; r++ )
            if( r != cr )                          /* Modified register */
            {
                    spill_one( r ) ;
                    clear_desc( r ) ;
                    load_reg( r, b );
                    return r ;
            }

}       /* int  get_areg( SYMB *b,
                          int   cr ) */
```

13.2.7 THE HEADER FILE, header

This is the code inserted at the start of compiled code. We set the stack pointer to the first location after the end of code, conveniently defined by L0. We then set a self-referential dynamic link at the bottom of the stack and load a return address that in fact points to some halt code in the library in R3. This will be saved as return address by the first routine to run.

```
\
\       Standard prolog
\
\       Modifications:
\       ==============
\
\       26 Jan 96: Jeremy Bennett. Version for 2nd edition publication (unchanged
\                  from first edition).
\
        LDA   L0,R1                      \ Set stack pointer
        STI   R1,0(R1)                   \ Save on stack
        LDA   L1,R3                      \ Return address for main routine
\
```

13.2.8 THE LIBRARY FILE, lib

The library is appended to the code generated by the compiler. In addition to the code to print out numbers and strings, it contains a standard termination code at L1.

```
\       Library routines
\
\       Modifications:
\       ==============
\
\       26 Jan 96: Jeremy Bennett. Version for 2nd edition publication (unchanged
\                  from first edition).
\
\
\       End of run routine
\
L1:
        HALT
\
\       Print a number recursively
\
L2:
        STI   R3,4(R1)                   \ Save the return address
```

```
        LDI   8(R1),R15        \ Copy arg to R15
        LDA   10(R0),R5        \ Constant 10
        DIV   R15,R5           \ Non-zero if more than one digit
        BZE   L3               \ Branch if only 1 digit
\
        STI   R5,12(R1)        \ Save on stack for later
        STI   R5,24(R1)        \ Copy to new stack frame
        LDA   L2,R2            \ Address to call
        STI   R1,16(R1)        \ Save stack pointer
        LDA   16(R1),R1        \ Increment stack pointer
        BAL   R2,R3            \ Call recursively
        LDA   10(R0),R15       \ Constant 10 in R15
        LDI   8(R1),R5         \ Original number
        LDI   12(R1),R6        \ Divided number
        MUL   R6,R15           \ Multiply back by 10 in R15
        SUB   R5,R15           \ Subtract from original for digit
L3:
        LDA   48(R0),R5        \ ASCII '0' in R5
        ADD   R5,R15           \ Add to get desired digit in R15
        TRAP                   \ Print the digit
        LDI   4(R1),R2         \ Return address in R2
        LDI   0(R1),R1         \ Restore stack pointer
        BAL   R2,R3            \ Return
\
\       Print a string
\
L4:
        STI   R3,4(R1)         \ Save the return address
        LDI   8(R1), R5        \ String pointer in R5
        LDA   16777216(R0),R7  \ 256 cubed for shifting 24 bits right
L5:
        LDI   0(R5),R6         \ Next char in top byte  of R6
        LDR   R7,R15           \ Constant 256 cubed
        DIV   R6,R15           \ Char in R15
        BZE   L6               \ EOS branch to exit
        TRAP                   \ Print the char
        LDA   1(R5),R5         \ Step to next char
        BRA   L5               \ Round again
L6:
        LDI   4(R1),R2         \ Return address in R2
        LDI   0(R1),R1         \ Restore stack pointer
        BAL   R2,R3            \ Return
\
```

13.3   Building the compiler

YACC is used first to generate an LALR(1) parser in C from parser.y. We run this with the -d option to obtain a header file. We rename these parser.c and parser.h, respectively. LEX is then used to obtain a lexical analyser in C from scanner.1 which we rename scanner.c. Finally, we compile main.c, scanner.c, parser.c, and cg.c to give a complete compiler.

The current version of the compiler runs under both DOS and Unix. The compilation of the whole system is best controlled through the Unix utility, *make*, which is now available under DOS. Using Bison, Flex and D. J. Delorie's version of GCC for DOS a suitable make mile might be:

```
#
# A combined Makefile to build the VC compiler, VAS assembler and VAM
# simulator
#
#     make <component>
#
# where component is vc, vas or vam as appropriate.
#
#
# Modifications:
# =============
#
# 23 Jan 96: DOS version of the combined makefile for 2nd edition publication


# Specify the compiler, scanner and parser generators and the flags

CC    = gcc
YACC  = bison
LEX   = flex
CP    = copy /b
RM    = del

# Some associated file names

YACCOUT = y_tab.c
YACCHDR = y_tab.h
LEXOUT  = lexyy.c

# Specify some flags

CFLAGS    = -g -ansi -pedantic -DDJGPP
YACCFLAGS = -d -y
LEXFLAGS  =
LDFLAGS   = -lbison -lflex


# Now the rules for generating one from the other

.y.c:
.y.h:
        $(YACC) $(YACCFLAGS) $*.y
        $(CP) $(YACCOUT) $*.c
        $(CP) $(YACCHDR) $*.h
        $(RM) $(YACCOUT)
        $(RM) $(YACCHDR)

.l.c:
        $(LEX) $(LEXFLAGS) $*.l
        $(CP) $(LEXOUT) $*.c
        $(RM) $(LEXOUT)

.c.o:
        $(CC) -c $(CFLAGS) $*.c


# The compiler files involved

HDRS = vc.h \
       parser.h
```

```
CSRCS = main.c \
       cg.c

SRCS = $(CSRCS) \
       scanner.c \
       parser.c

OBJS = main.o \
       parser.o \
       scanner.o \
       cg.o


# Create everything for dos

all: vc.exe vas.exe vam.exe

vc.exe: vc
        copy /b c:\djgpp\bin\stub.exe+vc vc.exe

vas.exe: vas

        copy /b c:\djgpp\bin\stub.exe+vas vas.exe

vam.exe: vam
        copy /b c:\djgpp\bin\stub.exe+vam vam.exe


# Create a new compiler

vc: $(OBJS)
        $(CC) $(CFLAGS) $(OBJS) $(LDFLAGS) -o vc


# Create a new VAS assembler

vas: vas.o
        $(CC) $(CFLAGS) vas.o -o vas


# Create a new VAM simulator

vam: vam.o
        $(CC) $(CFLAGS) vam.o -o vam


# Compiler source file dependencies

parser.c: parser.y
parser.h: parser.y
scanner.c: scanner.l
main.o: main.c vc.h parser.h
scanner.o: scanner.c vc.h parser.h
parser.o: parser.c vc.h parser.h
cg.o: cg.c vc.h

# Assembler source file dependencies

vas.c vas.h: vas.y
vas.o: vas.h
```

This file also builds the support utilities `vas` and `vam`, described in Appendix A if required.

Note the copying of `y_tab.c` and `y_tab.h` to `parser.c` and `parser.h` respectively. Although Bison could do this directly (by use of the `-o` and not the `-y` flag), this version will also work with YACC. The same approach is used with Flex to create `scanner.c`. The use of the flag `-DDJGPP` ensures code appropriate to use on DOS will be compiled when necessary.

It is a simple matter to modify this file for use with *make* under Unix.

13.4 Running the compiler

The following is a small test program to print out factorial numbers:

```
FUNC main()
{
        VAR   i

        i := 0

        WHILE 11 - i
        DO
        {
            PRINT "f( ", i, " ) = ", f( i ), "\n"
            i := i + 1
        }
        DONE
}


FUNC f( n )
        IF n
        THEN
            RETURN n * f( n - 1 )
        ELSE
            RETURN 1
        FI
```

If compiled, assembled, and run on the standard VAM simulator it will print out factorials of the integers from 0 to 10 in a total of 7852 clock cycles.

Note the relatively small effect of register slaving. Basic blocks tend to be small, and without global register allocation (which implies a need for dataflow analysis) it is not easy to get particularly effective use of a lot of registers. The following is the result of running the compiler on the VSL program above:

```
\
\       Standard prolog
\
\       Modifications:
\       ==============
\
\       26 Jan 96: Jeremy Bennett. Version for 2nd edition publication (unchanged
\                  from first edition).
\
```

```
        LDA   L0,R1              \ Set stack pointer
        STI   R1,0(R1)           \ Save on stack
        LDA   L1,R3              \ Return address for main routine
\
\       label L15
L15:
\       beginfunc
        STI   R3,4(R1)
\       var i
\       i  := 0
        LDR   R0,R5
\       label L13
        STI   R5,8(R1)
L13:
\       var T0
\       T0    := 11 - i
        LDI   8(R1),R5
        LDA   11(R0),R6
        SUB   R6,R5
\       ifz T0 goto L14
        STI   R5,12(R1)
        LDR   R5,R5
        BZE   L14
\       arg L10
        LDA   L10,R7
        STI   R7,24(R1)
\       call L4
        LDA   L4,R2
        STI   R1,16(R1)
        LDA   16(R1),R1
        BAL   R2,R3
\       arg i
        LDI   8(R1),R5
        STI   R5,24(R1)
\       call L2
        LDA   L2,R2
        STI   R1,16(R1)
        LDA   16(R1),R1
        BAL   R2,R3
\       arg L11
        LDA   L11,R5
        STI   R5,24(R1)
\       call L4
        LDA   L4,R2
        STI   R1,16(R1)
        LDA   16(R1),R1
        BAL   R2,R3
\       var T1
\       arg i
        LDI   8(R1),R5
        STI   R5,28(R1)
\       T1 = call L18
        LDA   L18,R2
        STI   R1,20(R1)
        LDA   20(R1), R1
        BAL   R2,R3
\       arg T1
        LDR   R4,R5
        STI   R5,28(R1)
\       call L2
```

```
        STI  R5,16(R1)
        LDA  L2,R2
        STI  R1,20(R1)
        LDA  20(R1),R1
        BAL  R2,R3
\       arg L12
        LDA  L12,R5
        STI  R5,28(R1)
\       call L4
        LDA  L4,R2
        STI  R1,20(R1)
        LDA  20(R1),R1
        BAL  R2,R3
\       var T2
\       T2 := i + 1
        LDA  1(R0),R5
        LDI  8(R1),R6
        ADD  R6,R5
\       i := T2
        STI  R5,20(R1)
\       goto L13
        STI  R5,8(R1)
        BRA  L13
\       label L14
L14:
\       endfunc
        LDI  4(R1),R2
        LDI  0(R1),R1
        BAL  R2,R3
\       label L18
L18:
\       beginfunc
        STI  R3,4(R1)
\       var n
\       ifz n goto L16
        LDI  8(R1),R5
        BZE  L16
\       var T4
\       var T3
\       T3 := n - 1
        LDA  1(R0),R6
        SUB  R5,R6
\       arg T3
        STI  R6,16(R1)
        STI  R6,28(R1)
\       T4 = call L18
        LDA  L18,R2
        STI  R1,20(R1)
        LDA  20(R1),R1
        BAL  R2,R3
\       var T5
\       T5 := n * T4
        LDR  R4,R5
        LDI  8(R1),R6
        MUL  R6,R5
\       return T5
        STI  R4,12(R1)
        LDR  R5,R4
        LDI  4(R1),R2
        LDI  0(R1),R1
```

```
         BAL   R2,R3
\        goto L17
         BRA   L17
\        label L16
L16:
\        return 1
         LDA   1(R0),R4
         LDI   4(R1),R2
         LDI   0(R1),R1
         BAL   R2,R3
\        label L17
L17:
\        endfunc
         LDI   4(R1),R2
         LDI   0(R1),R1
         BAL   R2,R3
\        Library routines
\
\        Modifications:
\        ==============
\
         26 Jan 96: Jeremy Bennett. Version for 2nd edition publication (unchanged
                    from first edition).
\
\
\        End of run routine
\
L1:
         HALT
\
\        Print a number recursively
\
L2:
         STI   R3,4(R1)              \ Save the return address
         LDI   8(R1),R15             \ Copy arg to R15
         LDA   10(R0),R5             \ Constant 10
         DIV   R15,R5                \ Non-zero if more than one digit
         BZE   L3                    \ Branch if only 1 digit
\
         STI   R5,12(R1)             \ Save on stack for later
         STI   R5,24(R1)             \ Copy to new stack frame
         LDA   L2,R2                 \ Address to call
         STI   R1,16(R1)             \ Save stack pointer
         LDA   16(R1),R1             \ Increment stack pointer
         BAL   R2,R3                 \ Call recursively
         LDA   10(R0),R15            \ Constant 10 in R15
         LDI   8(R1),R5              \ Original number
         LDI   12(R1),R6             \ Divided number
         MUL   R6,R15                \ Multiply back by 10 in R15
         SUB   R5,R15                \ Subtract from original for digit
L3:
         LDA   48(R0),R5             \ ASCII '0' in R5
         ADD   R5,R15                \ Add to get desired digit in R15
         TRAP                        \ Print the digit
         LDI   4(R1),R2              \ Return address in R2
         LDI   0(R1),R1              \ Restore stack pointer
         BAL   R2,R3                 \ Return
\
\        Print a string
\
```

```
L4:
        STI   R3,4(R1)                \ Save the return address
        LDI   8(R1),R5                \ String pointer in R5
        LDA   16777216(R0),R7         \ 256 cubed for shifting 24 bits right
L5:
        LDI   0(R5),R6                \ Next char in top byte of R6
        LDR   R7,R15                  \ Constant 256 cubed
        DIV   R6,R15                  \ Char in R15
        BZE   L6                      \ EOS branch to exit
        TRAP                          \ Print the char
        LDA   1(R5),R5                \ Step to next char
        BRA   L5                      \ Round again
L6:
        LDI   4(R1),R2                \ Return address in R2
        LDI   0(R1),R1                \ Restore stack pointer
        BAL   R2,R3                   \ Return
\
L10:
        DB    102
        DB    40
        DB    32
        DB    0
L11:
        DB    32
        DB    41
        DB    32
        DB    61
        DB    32
        DB    0
L12:
        DB    10
        DB    0
L0:
```

Exercises

In this chapter we suggest only some practical problems. There is no doubt that
the only way really to understand compilers is to write or modify one. In that
sense these exercises are perhaps the most useful of the book.

PRACTICAL PROBLEMS

The first five of these exercises were used for a number of years at Bath
University as part of a ten lecture introductory course on compiler techniques.
The last few exercises are major projects, and I should be interested in hearing of
students' experience in tackling them.

13.1. Get the VSL compiler, vc, running, together with the VAS assembler and
      VAM simulator. Prove it works by giving a listing of the output from the
      following program (to compute the first nine factorials), and determining
      how many clock cycles it takes to run:

```
FUNC main()
{
      VAR   i

      i := 0

      WHILE 10 - i
      DO
      {
            PRINT "f( ", i, " ) = ", f( i ), "\n"
            i := i + 1
      }
      DONE
}


FUNC f( n )
      IF n
      THEN
            RETURN n * f( n - 1 )
      ELSE
            RETURN 1
      FI
```

13.2. Add an exponentiation operator, ^, to VSL. It should have higher priority than the other arithmetic operators, and bind to the right. Check that it works by parsing the following test program:

```
FUNC main()
{
      VAR   i

      i := 0

      WHILE 11 - i
      DO
      {
            PRINT "2 ^ ", i, " = ", 2^i, "\n"
            i := i + 1
      }
      DONE
}
```

13.3. Design a new TAC for the exponentiation operator. Extend the compiler front-end to output this. Supply suitable output to prove that you have done this successfully.

13.4. Write a VAM library routine to perform integer exponentiation by repeated multiplication. Supply output from the VAM simulator to prove it works. How many cycles does it take to compute five cubed?

13.5. Modify the code generator to call your library routine for exponentiation. Run the demo program above, and convince yourself it works. Give an output listing of the code generated, and determine how many clock cycles it takes to execute.

13.6. Extend the parser to use synchronizing sets when recovering from errors.

13.7. At present the library routine, PRINTN, does not deal with negative numbers. Extend it to do so.

13.8. Add a general register slave that can remember more than one item held in a register. Add address descriptors to symbol table entries.

13.9. Add a peephole optimizer either before or after the code generator.

13.10. Write a more general run-time system that allows you to build libraries of VAM routines and link them. This involves thinking about relocation of absolute addresses in VAM code.

13.11. Add a middle end, which takes a tree representation from the parser, applies appropriate optimizations, and passes a TAC representation on to the code generator.

13.12. As preparation for an optimizer, add a module to break TAC generated by the front end into basic blocks.

13.13. Provide a simple basic block optimizer for the compiler.

13.14. Build a global optimizer for the compiler.

Appendix A
VSL, VAM, and VAS

This appendix contains the formal grammar of VSL, the definition of the VSL Abstract Machine, and details of an assembler for mnemonic VAM code.

A.1 The grammar of VSL

This is the formal grammar of VSL. Note that in one or two places, shorthand notations have been used to save space (in the definition of *letter*, *digit*, and *printable_character*). Their meaning should be obvious.

In addition to the specified syntax, VSL programs may have comments inserted. These are introduced by // and last until the end of the line.

program	→ *function_list*
function_list	→ *function* | *function_list function*
function	→ **FUNC** *variable* **(** *parameter_list* **)** *statement*
parameter_list	→ *variable_list* | ε
variable_list	→ *variable* | *variable_list* **,** *variable*
variable	→ *letter* | *variable alphanumeric*
alphanumeric	→ *letter* | *digit*
letter	→ **a** | **b** | ... | **y** | **z**
digit	→ **0** | **1** | ... | **8** | **9**
statement	→ *assignment_statement* | *return_statement* | *print_statement* | *null_statement* | *if_statement* | *while_statement* | *block*
assignment_statement	→ *variable* **:=** *expression*
expression	→ *expression binary_operator expression* | *unary_operator expression* | **(** *expression* **)** | *integer* | *variable* | *variable* **(** *argument_list* **)**
binary_operator	→ **+** | **−** | ***** | **/**
unary_operator	→ **−**
integer	→ *digit* | *integer digit*
argument_list	→ ε | *expression_list*
expression_list	→ *expression* | *expression* **,** *expression_list*

print_statement	→ **PRINT** *print_list*
print_list	→ *print_item* | *print_list* , *print_item*
print_item	→ *expression* | " *text* "
text	→ *text_character* | *text_character text*
text_character	→ *printable_character* | *escaped_character*
printable_character	→ any printable ASCII character
escaped_character	→ \n
return_statement	→ **RETURN** *expression*
null_statement	→ **CONTINUE**
if_statement	→ **IF** *expression* **THEN** *statement* **FI** |
	IF *expression* **THEN** *statement* **ELSE** *statement* **FI** |
while_statement	→ **WHILE** *expression* **DO** *statement* **DONE**
block	→ { *declaration_list statement_list* }
declaration_list	→ ε | *declaration_list declaration*
declaration	→ **VAR** *variable_list*
statement_list	→ *statement* | *statement_list statement*

A.1.1 SEMANTICS OF VSL

A VSL program commences by executing the fist function defined. All variables are local to the function and have scope over the block in which they are declared. Arguments to functions are effectively local variables declared at the level of the body of the function. It should be noted that the compiler of Chapter 12 does not implement variable declarations with these semantics. The statements of the function are executed in turn until a return statement or the end of the function is encountered.

Expressions are evaluated with their conventional arithmetic meaning using unsigned arithmetic. When used as conditions for IF statements and WHILE statements, zero means false and non-zero means true. The null statement does nothing.

A.2 The VSL Abstract Machine

The VSL Abstract Machine (VAM) is a simple load-store register machine with a byte-stream instruction set. Memory is byte addressed (a maximum of 4 Gbytes), registers operate on words, which are 4 bytes long (stored with most significant byte at the lowest address). A block diagram of VAM is shown in Fig. A.1. Each instruction consists of a byte opcode, a byte containing two register arguments (if there are any), and 4 bytes containing an offset (if there is one). Offsets wrap round the 4 Gbyte address space, and so effectively can be considered as 2's complement signed integers. There are 16 registers, each holding 32 bits of which register 0 is permanently zero. A single status bit records whether the result of load, store, or arithmetic operations was zero. The instruction set is as follows.

All arithmetic is unsigned. Branch offsets are from the address at the start of the branch instruction.

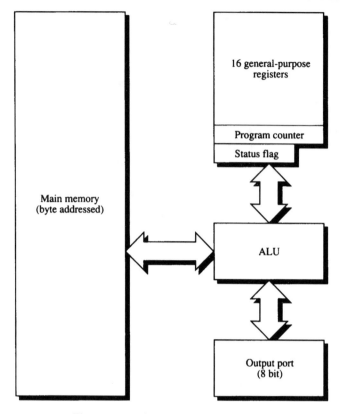

Figure A.1   The VSL Abstract Machine

Opcode	*Timing*	*Action*
HALT	1	Halt the machine
NOP	1	Does nothing
TRAP	10	Output the least significant byte of R15 as an ASCII character
ADD Rx, Ry	1	Add Rx and Ry, putting the result in Ry
SUB Rx, Ry	1	Subtract Ry from Rx, putting the result in Ry
MUL Rx,Ry	5	Multiply Rx by Ry, putting the result in Ry
DIV Rx,Ry	10	Divide Rx by Ry, putting the result in Ry
STI Rx,offset(Ry)	2	Store Rx at the address given by offset added to the contents of Ry. All offsets are treated as 32 bit 2's complement signed integers
LDI offset(Rx),Ry	2	Load Ry with the value at the address given by offset added to the contents of Rx

LDA offset(Rx),Ry	2	Load Ry with offset added to the contents of Rx
LDR Rx,Ry	1	Copy Rx into Ry
BZE offset	2/1	Branch to offset from the current instruction if the zero flag is set. The zero flag is set if a zero value is loaded or stored or is the result of an arithmetic instruction. Other opcodes do not affect it. The timing is 2 ticks if the branch is taken, 1 otherwise
BNZ offset	2/1	Branch to offset from the current instruction if the zero flag is unset. The timing is 2 ticks if the branch is taken, 1 otherwise
BRA offset	2	Branch to offset from the current instruction
BAL Rx,Ry	2	Branch to the address in Rx, putting the address of the instruction following this one in Ry

A.2.1 A SIMULATOR FOR VAM

VAM does not exist as hardware (yet!). However, it is a simple matter to implement the machine as a simulator. A simulator written in C and its documentation is available as described in Appendix B.

A.3 A mnemonic assembler for VAM

It is often clearer to generate a mnemonic form of the assembler in a compiler. This is the approach used in the VSL compiler of Chapter 12. A simple assembler is available for VAM. Opcodes are preceded by white space on a line in their mnemonic form and separated by more white space from the arguments. Arguments are separated by commas. The 16 registers appear as R0 to R15. Memory references are written as nnn(Ry) to mean the address given by the (decimal) offset nnn added to the contents of Ry. Labels of the form Lnnn are defined at the start of the line, preceded by no white space and followed by a colon. They may be used as the targets of branch instructions or arguments to load instructions. The assembler will translate these into branch offsets and absolute addresses indexed off R0 as appropriate. In addition a pseudo-opcode, DB, with a single constant argument is added to define a byte of storage (useful for initialized data such as strings). Comments may be introduced either at the end of an instruction or on a line of their own starting with a backslash (\).

The assembler is available in machine-readable form as described in Appendix B.

Appendix B
Software availability

The software described in Chapter 13, together with a number of support utilities is available via the Internet using anonymous FTP or electronic mail. All the compilers and other tools used can be similarly obtained, while there is a great deal of further information available through Usenet user groups and the World-Wide Web.

B.1   The VC compiler system

All the files described in Chapter 13 are available by anonymous FTP from `ftp.mcgraw-hill.co.uk` in the directory `pub/j.p.bennett/vc`. Two versions of the makefile are provided, `makefile.dos`, for use with GNU *make* under DOS and `makefile.unx` for *make* under Unix.

Source is also provided for a simple assembler, `vas`, and an emulator for VAM, `vam`. These programs assume that the original VSL program is in a file ending in `.vsl`. The `vc` compiler will produce the corresponding file ending in `.vas`, which can be used as input to the VAS assembler, producing VAM code in the corresponding file ending in `.vam`. This can then be used as input to the VAM simulator.

The factorial program of Chapter 13 is supplied as the source file `fact.vsl`. It can be compiled and run by the sequence of commands:

```
vc test.vsl
vas test.vas
vam test.vam
```

The VAM simulator can also be run with the `-t` flag, to trace execution of the program. This gives a dump of all registers, the memory around the current program counter and the stack as each instruction is executed. For example:

```
vam -t test.vam
```

In addition to the code covered in this book, the standard distribution includes various enhancements and extensions which others have made to the system.

The authors in each case have kindly made their code available to the wider computing community.

As bug reports are received (and corrections or improvements suggested), they are noted in the file BUGS, and where possible corrections are made to the source code of the distribution. Similarly, corrections or suggested improvements to the text of the book are noted in the file CORRECT. I am very grateful to all those who take the trouble to contact me with such bugs and corrections.

B.2 Supporting utilities

The code in this book has been tested on DOS and Unix, using the GNU C compiler from the Free Software Foundation (FSF), and on DOS GNU make, Bison and Flex.

The FSF has produced a wide range of highly useful software over the years. The general conditions for using it are that you make it freely available to others, and don't sell any software that incorporates their free software. A full legal specification of what this means is supplied as part of all their distributions.

While this is no problem for most teaching and even commercial environments, there is a slight problem if you wish to use Bison to produce software to sell. Any parser produced by Bison includes the Bison parse engine, which is FSF code. Thus you cannot sell the code on. The only solutions are:

- Don't sell the software, but give it away freely (much to be encouraged); or
- Use a commercial parser generator, such as YACC, and pay a licence fee for selling on their parse engine; or
- Find a freely available parser generator with looser restrictions on its use. BYACC is reputed to be an appropriate tool.

FSF software is available from many sites around the world by anonymous FTP. Users in the UK in particular will find the Imperial College archive at src.doc.ic.ac.uk in the directory computing/gnu a good starting point.

The Flex lexical analyser generator is not made available under the FSF general licence. However, it is freely available, and usually appears with other FSF software. It is certainly in the computing/gnu directory at Imperial College described above.

For PC users, D. J. Delorie's version of the GNU C compiler, djgpp, is recommended. This is available from grape.ecs.clarkson.edu by anonymous FTP in directory ~ftp/pub/msdos/djgpp as well as many archive sites around the world.

B.3 Other software and information available on the Internet

A great many compiler systems exist around the world, a number of which have been mentioned in the 'Further reading' sections of each chapter. The Internet locations of these systems is for ever changing, but the best source of information is the Usenet discussion group `comp.compilers`. Their regular Frequently Asked Questions (FAQ) posting gives pointers to up-to-date archives of software systems in use around the world.

INDEX